Metro Detroit's High School Basketball Rivalries

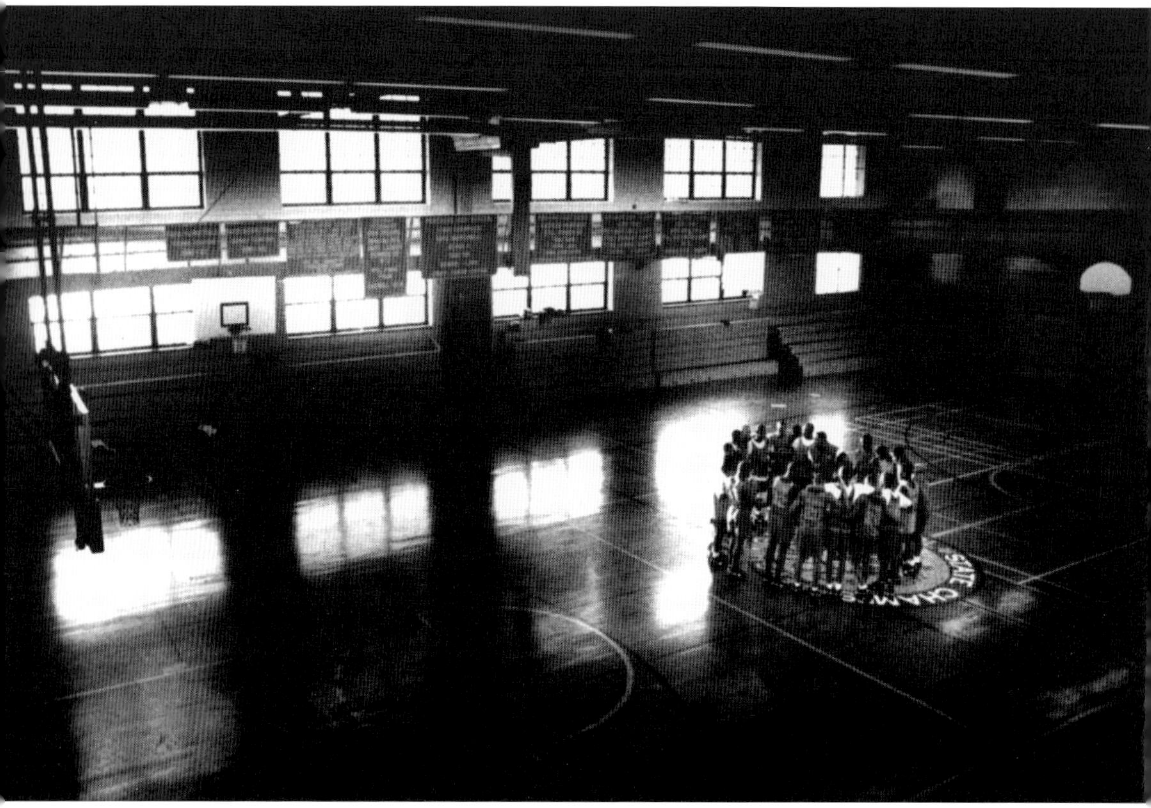

Detroit Pershing's Doughboys play in an outdated, worn-down gym without any of the modern amenities of newer, state-of-the-art facilities, but perhaps no gym better represents metro Detroit's past, present, and future. Save for the floor's painting, this is the same gym that Will Robinson coached in, Spencer Haywood dunked in, Ralph Simpson blocked shots in, and Steve Smith scored 30 in. It is a room filled with dreams-turned-reality that begs the question asked in all of Detroit's hardwood palaces, new and old, city or suburban alike: where will tomorrow's basketball showstoppers, heartbreakers, and buzzer-beaters emerge from in the Motor City? (The Detroit News/Joe DeVera.)

FRONT COVER: Please see page 114. (MHSAA archives.)

BACK COVER: River Rouge commences the first of four-straight titles with this 83-50 win over Kalamazoo Hackett in the 1969 Class B finals at Michigan State University's Jenison Field House. (River Rouge High School.)

COVER BACKGROUND: The 1958 Class B championship game for Class B at Michigan State University's historic Jenison Field House produced one of just five losses in 38 games for River Rouge in semifinal or finals play for a 50-year period from 1949 to 1999. The Panthers dropped a 62-51 decision to East Lansing High School. (River Rouge High School.)

Metro Detroit's High School Basketball Rivalries

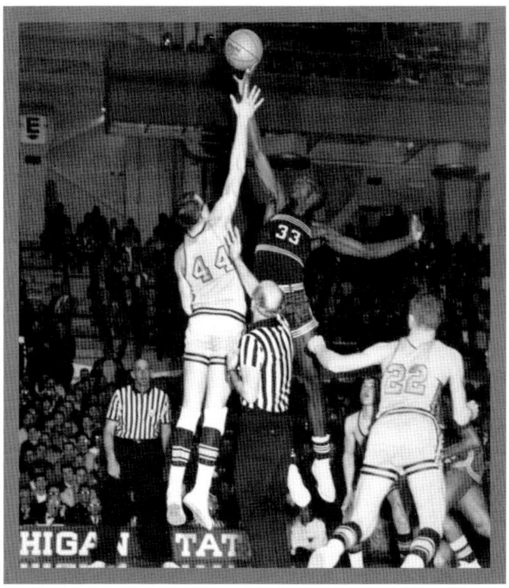

T. C. Cameron

ARCADIA PUBLISHING

ISBN 978-0-7385-6014-4

Published by Arcadia Publishing
Charleston SC, Chicago IL, Portsmouth NH, San Francisco CA

Printed in the United States of America

Library of Congress Control Number: 2009925462

For all general information contact Arcadia Publishing at:
Telephone 843-853-2070
Fax 843-853-0044
E-mail sales@arcadiapublishing.com
For customer service and orders:
Toll-Free 1-888-313-2665

Visit us on the Internet at www.arcadiapublishing.com

I dedicate this book to my two sets of parents, the ones I have been without and the in-laws I have been gifted by marriage. My mother and father, Scott and Nancy, were taken before they could have realized this dream becoming a reality for me, and I miss them both dearly. At the same time, Janie and Kim have become the parents I have missed for what seems like a lifetime.

CONTENTS

ACKNOWLEDGMENTS

I acknowledge the thousands of coaches, athletic directors, officials, student-athletes, cheerleaders, parents, and volunteers who make prep basketball possible every year. From the public address to popcorn, scorekeepers and ticket takers too, none of this happens without all of you.

Thanks to John Johnson, Tom Minter, Tom Rashid, Mark Uyl, and the rest of the dedicated staff of the Michigan High School Athletic Association (MHSAA). The MHSAA provides opportunity to all of Michigan's student-athletes, and involvement in youth athletics makes servants of us all in this important mission. Where would so many of us be in this life—myself included—without educational athletics?

To Glen Gilbert, Jeff Khuen, Jim Evans, Keith Dunlap, the all-knowing "Kozmo," and the editorial staff at the *Oakland Press* for sharing the paper's considerable archive. As Oakland County's original beacon of journalism, the county is a better place because of this paper's daily presence.

Sincere thanks to Bob Houlihan, Tom Markowski and the *Detroit News* for archives, pictures, and insight. Your paper's dedication to metro Detroit's youth for over 100 years remains a palpable asset to the entire region. The outstanding archivists at the *News*, specifically Linda Culpepper and Danielle Kaltz, made my research visits to 615 Lafayette Boulevard in "the D" the highlight of writing this book.

Thanks to P. J. Grabowski and Meyke Phelps from the University of Detroit–Mercy Sports Information Department; Jim Streeter, Greg Steiner, and Sarah Van Metre from Eastern Michigan University's Sports Information Department; Scott Rex from the same office at Central Michigan University; Michael Carrier and Orrin J. Tibbits from Detroit Catholic Central High. Brother Rice, coach Bill Norton, Royal Oak Kimball's Chuck Jones, Rob Goddard from Orchard Lake St. Mary's, and Detroit Mackenzie's Dick Honig: a healthy share of this region's prep and collegiate history has passed through your capable hands.

Thanks to the archivists and curators at the Berkley, Ferndale, and River Rouge Historical Museums, as well as the staff librarians and archivists at the public libraries in Detroit, Royal Oak, Birmingham, and Farmington Hills.

To Rick Massa, Mike Smith, Mike Hesson, Stephanie Caruso and Vic Michaels, thanks for allowing me to pose an endless stream of questions and photograph identifications. To the athletic directors, coaches, and historians that space does not allow me to list individually, please accept my sincere thanks.

INTRODUCTION

If you grew up in Detroit or its surrounding suburbs in the 1950s, 1960s, or 1970s, before cable television infiltrated your life followed closely by the internet, there were more tangible outlets grabbing for your attention during the summer, like playing baseball at local parks, riding your bicycle to a beach or neighborhood swimming pools, or begging your parents for a quarter so you could take in a matinee at the local theater. During the fall, football dominated. The winters signaled the end to bike rides and the beginning of basketball season. Basketball was played in the local gyms or outside in parks or, if you were fortunate enough, in your backyard, where your father or uncle was kind enough to nail a backboard to the side or on top of the family garage.

More than a sport, pickup basketball games were a social event. It is where you hung out with friends and made new ones. And as you grew older, it was the high school teams that captured your interest. If you were good enough to make the cut, you were part of the team. If not, a seat on the bleachers is where you found yourself twice a week cheering as loud as your friends standing next to you. Basketball games were as much a part of high school as the dances were on Saturday nights, sometimes more so, depending on how good your team was. If you did not go, you were often ostracized—even ridiculed—for not showing support.

In towns like River Rouge, Dearborn, Grosse Pointe, and Ferndale it was regional and state titles that were talked about, and sometimes won. Heroes played, and legends were born. Before stars like Madonna and Sting made the one-word name fashionable, names like Haywood, DeBusschere, Betts, Flowers, and "the Judge" in southwest Detroit took on a star-status all their own.

For players and fans in the Detroit Public School League and the Detroit Catholic High School League, the road to the "Big House," the memorial building on the campus of the University of Detroit, was often the first destination. In 1977, the name of the building was changed to Calihan Hall in honor of the former Titan coach Bob Calihan. In the Detroit Public School League in the late 1940s, Miller High was the dominant team, winning league titles in 1947, 1949, and 1950. Sammy Gee was Miller's top player and one of the first All-America players selected from Detroit. Miller would remain a strong team over the next five years or so, but it would never win another Detroit Public School League title. Just five schools—Cass Tech, Eastern, Northwestern, Pershing, and Southeastern—would win titles over the next 17 seasons.

Eastern's four-title run from 1959 to 1962 was matched by Northwestern from 1964 to 1967. The infamous Reggie Harding led those Eastern teams. At seven feet tall, Harding was believed to be both the first seven-footer to play in the Detroit Public School League and among the first to go straight from high school to the NBA. Harding was named to *Parade* magazine's All-America team in 1961 and played with the Pistons during the 1963–1964 season. In one of its enclaves, Hamtramck, there was Rudy Tomjanovich of Hamtramck High causing a stir. Although his teams never won a district title, he was a folk hero and was named All-America by the *Basketball News* in 1966.

Northwestern's Curtis Jones was at the top of his game in the late 1960s. Many thought Jones was one of the best players ever to come out of Detroit. The team's leading scorer and a playground legend in later years, Jones, backed by future Kansas City Royal John Mayberry, led Northwestern to a 63-61 victory over Detroit Pershing in the 1967 Detroit Public School League final. Jones made the winning shot from the top of the key. Pershing gained revenge in the Class A tournament as Spencer Haywood and Ralph Simpson each scored 29 points in a 77-71 victory in a regional semifinal. In the state semifinals, Haywood scored 35 points and Simpson added 23 in an 84-78 win over Detroit Catholic Central. Against Flint Central, Simpson took over, scoring a state-final record 43 points in Pershing's 90-66 victory. Hayward, double-teamed throughout that game, still scored 24 points that included 14 of 18 from the free throw line.

Haywood would later say the loss to Northwestern in the Detroit Public School League refocused the Doughboys toward another goal. It was a hallmark victory for Pershing and the city. For 31 years, beginning in 1931, Detroit Public School League did not partake in the Michigan High School Athletic Association (MHSAA) tournament. Pershing was the league's first state champion since Detroit Northern won the Class A title in 1930.

The summer following Pershing's triumph, the city would experience the unforgettable riots of 1967. So many urban areas in the United States suffered through the violence the late 1960s brought, and Detroit was among the worst of them. Busing students from one area of town to another became a heated debate. The white flight, as it became known then, took place as thousands left the city for the suburbs. A number of athletic contests were marred by violence. Still the games went on, and often they would be the one haven where differences between blacks and whites would be forgotten, even if for just a couple of hours or so.

The Detroit Catholic League had its years of greatness too. Detroit Austin's teams of the late 1950s were as good as any the league has seen, thanks to Dave DeBusschere, one of the greatest players in state history and one of the best athletes of his time. DeBusschere, who would be voted one of the top 50 players in NBA history, starred in one of the most memorable state finals. After losing to Muskegon Heights in the Class A final in 1957, Austin made a return trip and this time the Friars outlasted the Chet Walker–led Benton Harbor team 71-68. At six feet, five and a half inches, DeBusschere was a tremendous shooter and an outstanding rebounder.

Austin won the 1958 Detroit Catholic League title, 72-49, over Grosse Pointe St. Paul. DeBusschere scored 37 points in that game, and he had 32 in the 63-40 victory over Detroit Northeastern for the Motor City championship. Class A schools would play at the district level for the first time in that 1958 campaign. In prior years, due to the limited number of schools in this class, the Class A tournament began with regional play. Austin defeated Grosse Pointe High in a 1958 regional final before disposing of Highland Park in the Class A quarters, 65-48, as DeBusschere led the way with 31 points. Against state semifinalist Dearborn Fordson, the 1953 state champion, DeBusschere had 24 points and Paul Miller added 16 in the Friars' 58-42 victory.

In that historic final, Austin led 39-33 at halftime and DeBusschere scored 20. He picked up his third foul early in the third quarter and scored but two points and Austin trailed 49-48 with eight minutes to play. DeBusschere returned to score 10 in the fourth but fouled out with 3 minutes and 10 seconds left. Two more Friars fouled out but they held on as Gary Ruprich made two free throws to give Austin a 70-64 lead with less than 30 seconds remaining. Austin would close its doors 20 years later, following the 1977–1978 season. The Friars won their last league title in 1970, upsetting Frank Tanana and Detroit Catholic Central in the final.

Detroit Catholic Central had its moments too. Bill Foley coached the Shamrocks to the Class A title in 1961, and Bernie Holowicki, who previously mentored Detroit De La Salle, came to Catholic Central and guided the Shamrocks to the Class A title in 1976. That Shamrock team was the last nonpublic school team to win the Class A title.

The Roy Burkhart–coached Ferndale teams won Class A titles in 1963 and 1966, but the story of basketball in the Detroit area could not be complete without telling the story of one legendary school: the Rouge.

River Rouge High won 12 Class B titles between 1954 and 1972, all with the greatest coach in state history, Lofton Greene, coaching the Panthers. Greene won five straight from 1961 to 1965 and then a strong of four from 1969 to 1972. And many of the championship games were not close. Willie Betts was a *Detroit News* Dream Team selection in 1964 and also made the *Detroit Free Press* Class B All-State first team the previous season. Betts is the only player to start four consecutive state championship games. Greene stayed for 41 years at River Rouge High and had the greatest dynasty of all time. A teacher of fundamentals, Greene used a fast-breaking offense and pressure defense. It was simply known as "Loftonball."

Other great players to play for Greene were Bill Kilgore, Lou Hyatt, and Malcolm Moulton. The Rouge would win two more Class B titles in the late 1990s, but the ones we remember best are those coached by Greene, who was also known as the "Old Kentuckian."

This was certainly the heyday for Detroit basketball. Times have changed, as have the names and faces. School closings in the Detroit Public School League and Catholic League have left but a shell of what they once were. Teams from Detroit Country Day, a private school located in Beverly Hills, often dominated the Class B tournament with players like Chris Webber and Shane Battier. Beginning in 1987, teams from the Detroit Public School League won eight consecutive Class A titles; the league has had just one Class A champion since.

Yes, the game has changed, but it is still metro Detroit's game, a game we love to watch—especially when that month of March arrives.

Tom Markowski
The *Detroit News*

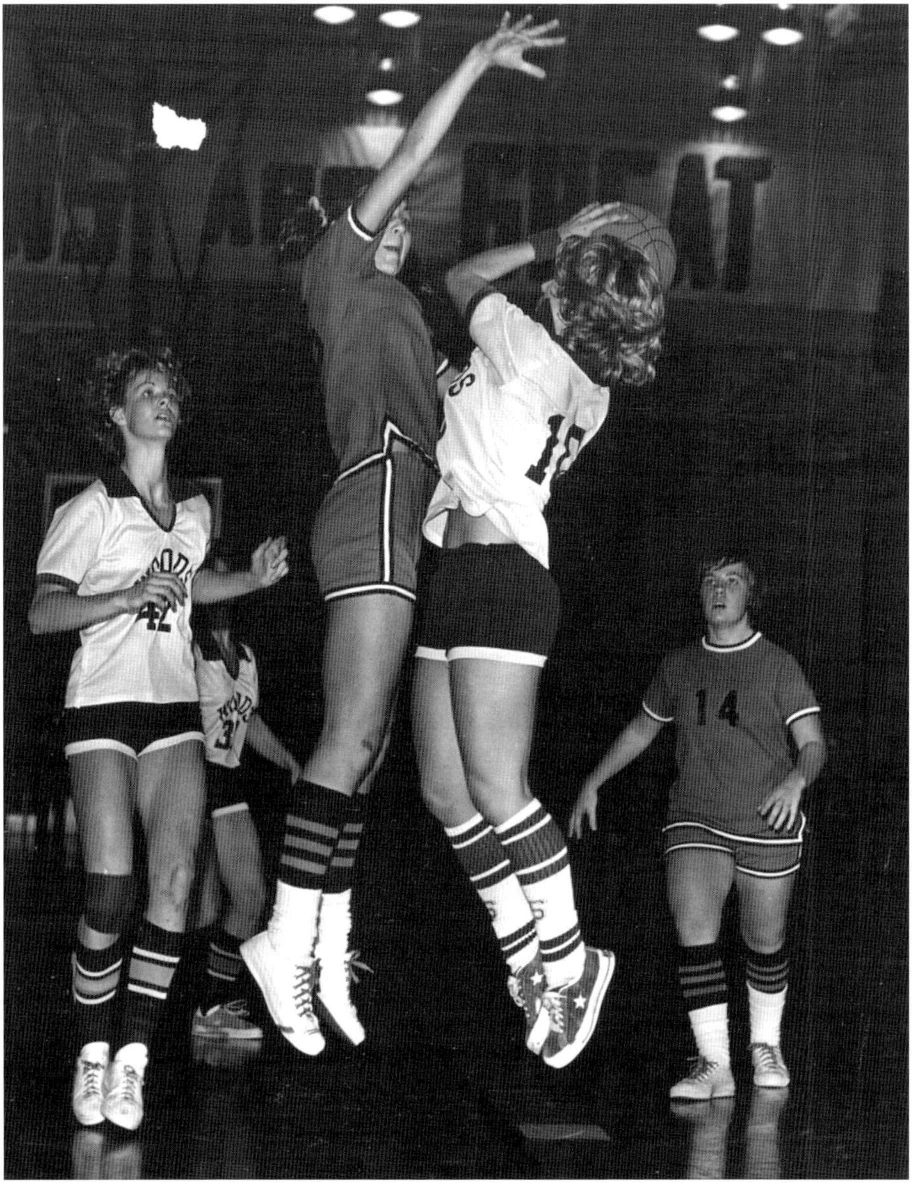

The year 1972 was not any more notable in state, national, or world history than any other year, but ask the players and coaches associated with girls' basketball in the state of Michigan and one is likely to receive a different answer. With the passing of the federal law that became better known as Title IX, girls' basketball became a required varsity sport at all coed schools that offered boys' basketball. Metro Detroit's first public school state champions came in 1975. Warren Woods High, which later combined in 1983 with Warren Tower's Vikings, earned the Class B title with a 46-43 triumph over Tecumseh's Indians, while Detroit Northeastern won the 1975 Class A title. Coach Carol Susalla guided her Warren Warriors (seen here in white) to this championship. Notice the knee-high socks and low-cut Converse All-Star shoes, staples of the 1950s and 1960s, as the shoe of choice for most players in the 1970s. (MHSAA archive/Robert Moore.)

1

THE CITY GAME

New York City's Forty-second Street and Park Avenue—Grand Central Station's intersection—is named Pershing Square. New Yorkers associate the World War I general and his soldiers with their famed train station; Detroiters associate Pershing's Doughboys with a different but equally contested battle: Detroit public school prep basketball.

Nestled among blighted streets and desolate neighborhoods in a once-proud city are the member schools of the Detroit Public School League (PSL). No other league—locally or nationally—has produced so much collegiate and professional basketball talent from as small a population as the PSL. Teeming cities like New York, Chicago, and Los Angeles dwarf Detroit's population, but Detroit's high schools preen proudly among the tallest trees of accomplished hardwood history.

"The PSL was the place to be, and still is, because of the competition," said Detroit Martin Luther King High grad George Gervin, known as Twiggy in high school. "When I was at King, guys used to sit around all the time and talk about which big city had the best basketball. We used to say the brothers in New York City, all they could do was dribble. The brothers in Chicago, all they could do was talk. The brothers in Detroit? All we did was score—score at will."

Gervin became one of professional basketball's most prolific scorers, named to the NBA's Greatest 50 Players list in 1998. Other standouts include Willie "Stick" Iverson, Spencer Haywood, Derrick Coleman, Jalen Rose, Ralph Simpson, and Robert "Tractor" Traylor among a seemingly endless list of accomplished players from the city. City schools earned the respect of the entire state for their team game too. An amazing 43 PSL teams have competed in the Michigan High School Athletic Association (MHSAA) championship game, and from 1979 to 2000, a Detroit proper school played for the Class A title in 20 of 22 years.

The PSL is a badge of honor for players, coaches, and referees alike. For players, it is not just about being a Southwestern Prospector, Redford Huskie, Northwestern Colt, or Cooley Cardinal. They play for their school, but they played in the PSL. State championships are nice, but like New York City, the city championship defines the player, the season, and the school. For officials, regular-season games convey ability; PSL playoff assignments are crowning achievements and resume builders.

Detroit's public schools own a basketball legacy built upon talent and tradition even legends dream about.

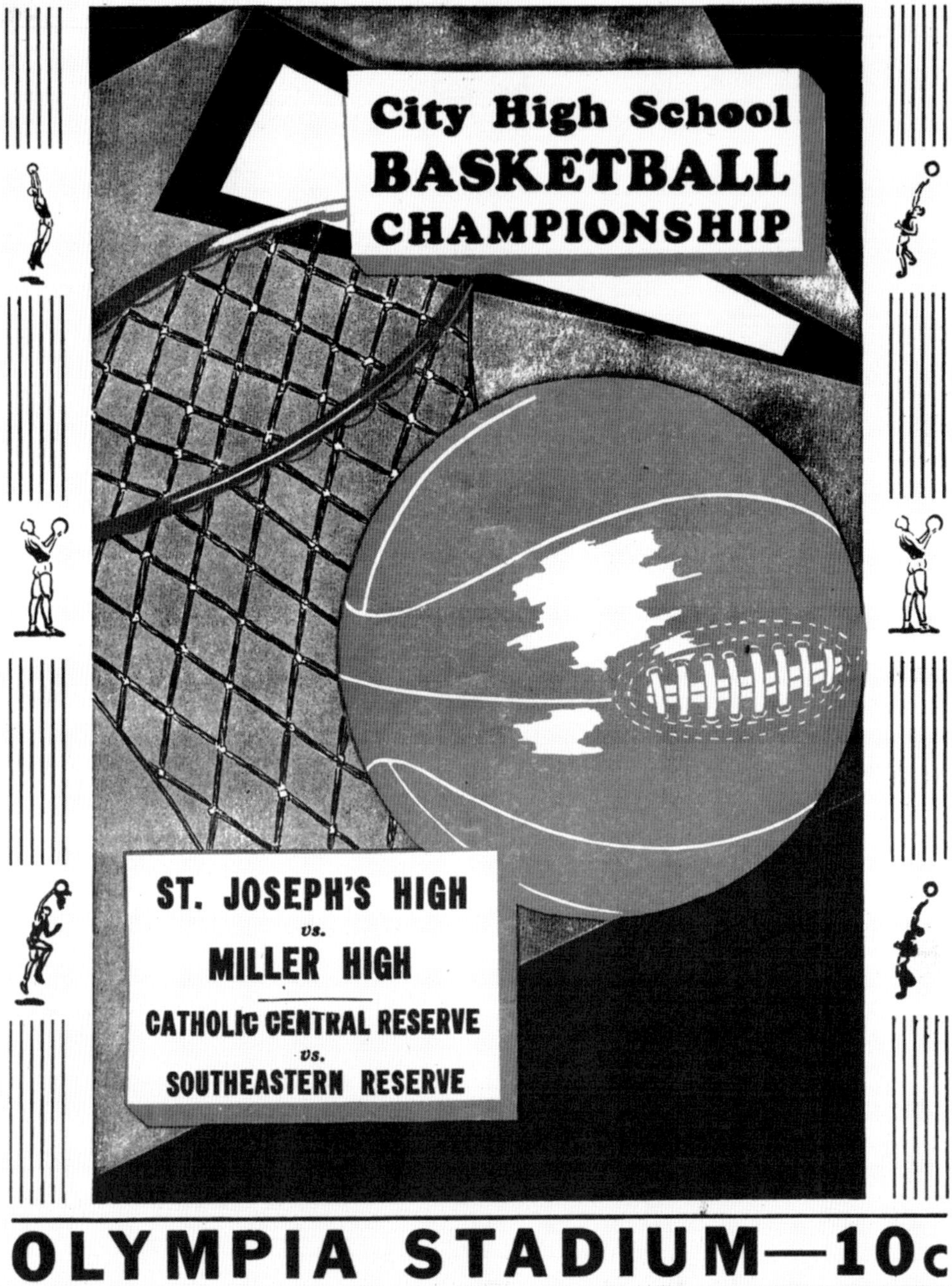

The most famous city championship in metro Detroit history was played at Olympia Stadium in 1947. A total of 16,041 fans poured into the now-demolished stadium—another 1,500 were turned away—to watch Detroit Miller High defeat Detroit St. Joesph's Blue Jays 47-34. No single varsity basketball game since has come close to this game's attendance. Catholic Central's Shamrocks defeated Southeastern's Jungaleers 46-38 in the junior varsity contest. (CHSL archive.)

Detroit St. Joseph head coach Joe Huerth (left) is gracious in defeat at Olympia Stadium after Will Robinson's Miller Trojans won the 1947 inaugural city title game. After Miller closed, Robinson led Detroit Pershing to league titles in 1963 and 1972, state titles in 1967 and 1970. Since the game's inception, Detroit's public schools have won 39 of 51 games versus Detroit Catholic League champions, since renamed the Operation Friendship Game. (The Detroit News archive.)

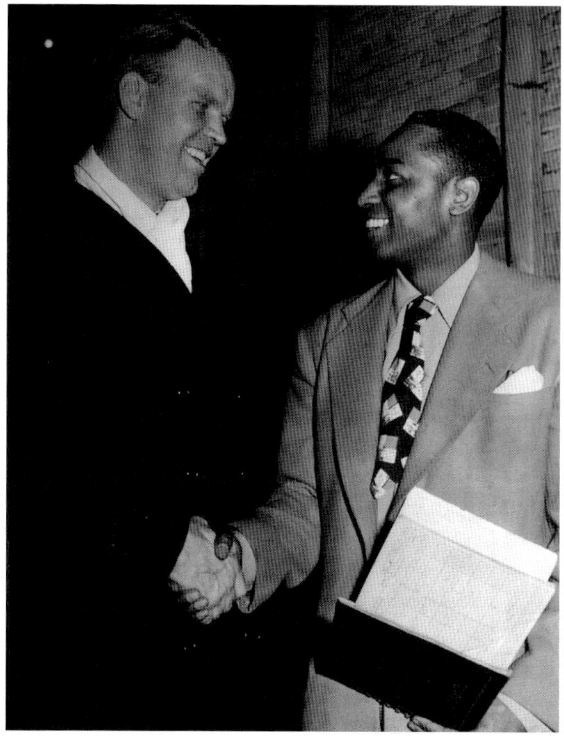

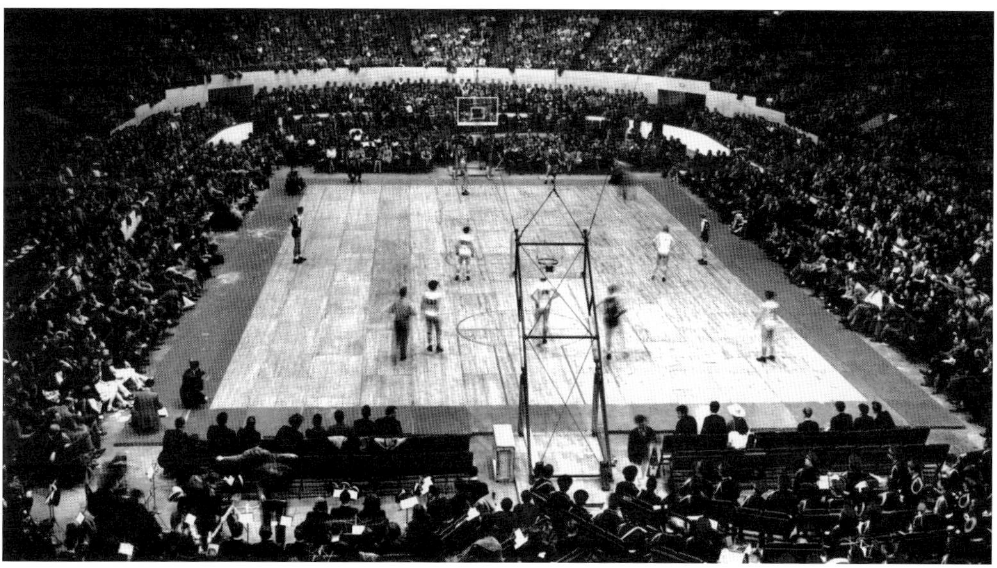

Affectionately called the "Ole Red Barn," Detroit's Olympia Stadium hosted 13 PSL title tilts from 1928 to 1952 and was the first building to ever host all four class championship games of the MHSAA's boys' basketball tournament (1928–1930). The Detroit Red Wings' home until December 1979, Olympia also hosted boxing, wrestling, union and religious rallies, Elvis, the Beatles, Led Zeppelin—arguably rock 'n' roll's greatest band—and the occasional traveling circus before being razed in the summer of 1986. (The Detroit News archives.)

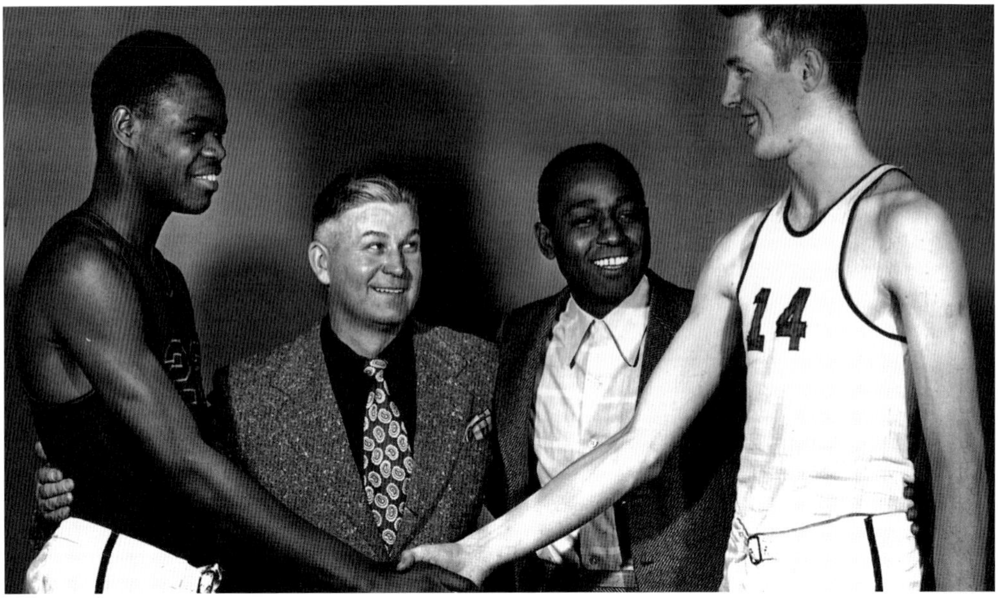

Will Robinson, in the wake of the 1943 race riots, provided a steady hand when he came to Motown in 1944 to coach Miller High. Miller captain Albert Bolton, seen to the left of Cooley coach Walt Wegerly, shakes hands with Cooley captain James Mongeau to the right of Robinson before the 1948 Metropolitan League title game played on March 3 at Olympia Stadium. Miller defeated Cooley 44-29 but forfeited months later due to the use of an ineligible player. (The Detroit News/Wood.)

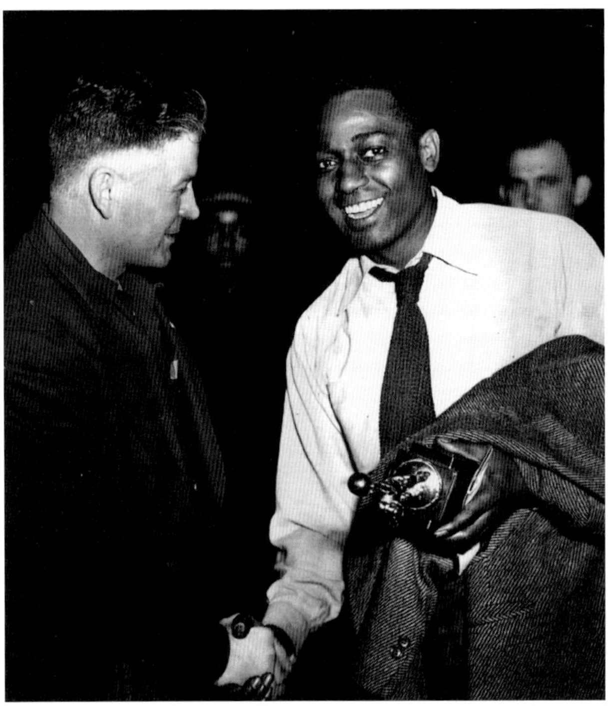

Walt Wegerly and Will Robinson meet after the 1948 Metropolitan League title game. Racial segregation was a staple of Detroit's city schools during the post–World War II era. Whereas Miller was mostly black, Cooley was mostly white. The backdrop fueled rivalries as much as any championship at stake. While busing became a near-riotous issue in the 1960s and 1970s, school sports usually provided a respectful respite from the tumultuous change. (The Detroit News/Erik Strylander.)

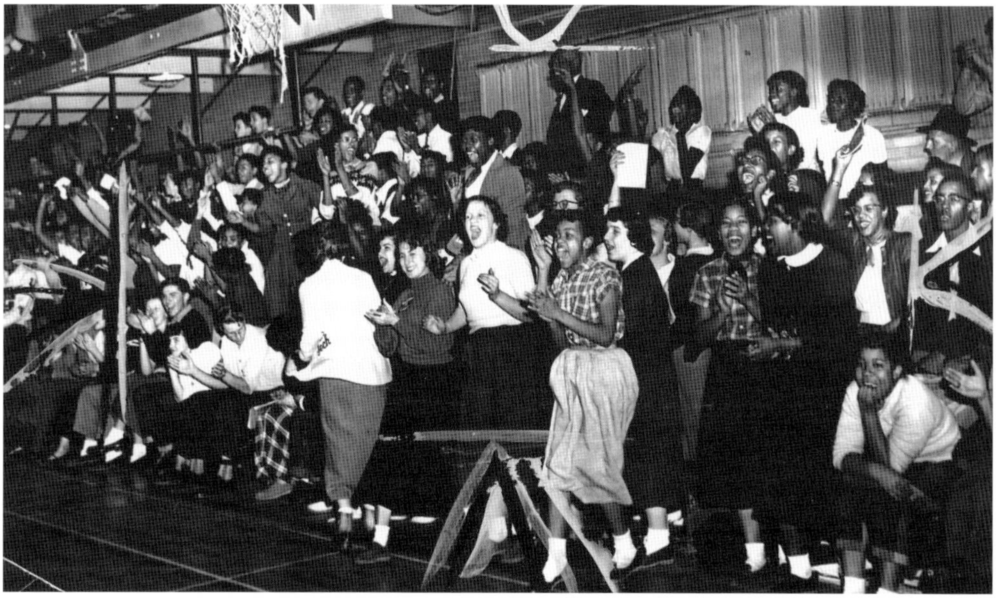

Cass Tech welcomed rival Detroit Northeastern to Bagley Avenue for this 1952 Metropolitan League game. Notice the diversity of black and white students sitting together, cheering for their Technicians. Detroit was a national model for racial harmony in the 1950s but several racially charged decisions by Detroit's political leadership later polarized the city. Regardless, school sports remain a safe haven much as they were nearly 60 years ago. (The Detroit News/ Erik Strylander.)

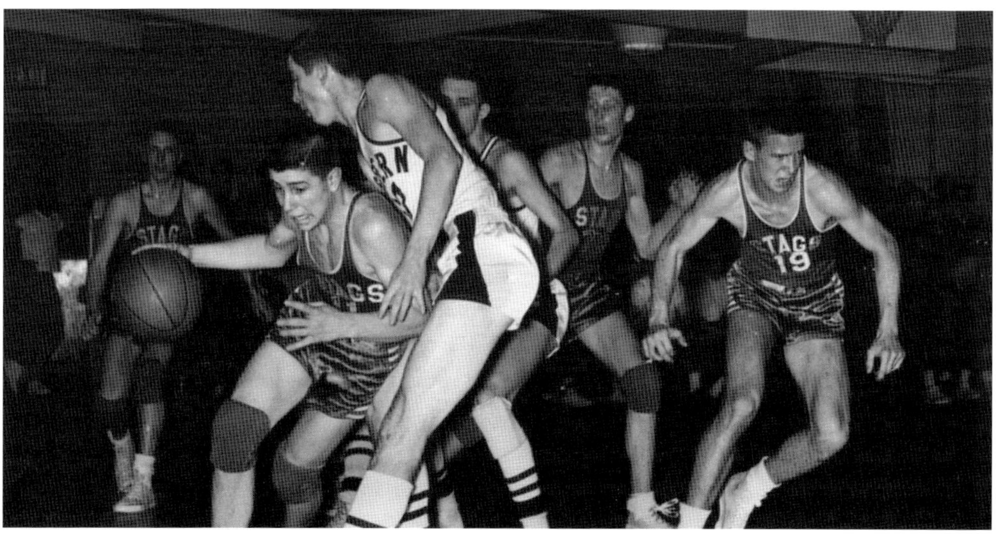

Dick Honig and his Detroit Mackenzie Stags had plenty of drive but they could not lasso down Ed Jenkins and Detroit Western's Cowboys in a 67-63 loss on February 14, 1958. Mackenzie track star Jim Oliphant (19) and Jim Fitzgerald (22) are also pictured. Honig, described as diminutive in the *Detroit Times*, scored 18 on five field goals and eight free throws. John Kastl netted an outstanding 28 points for Western. (Dick Honig collection.)

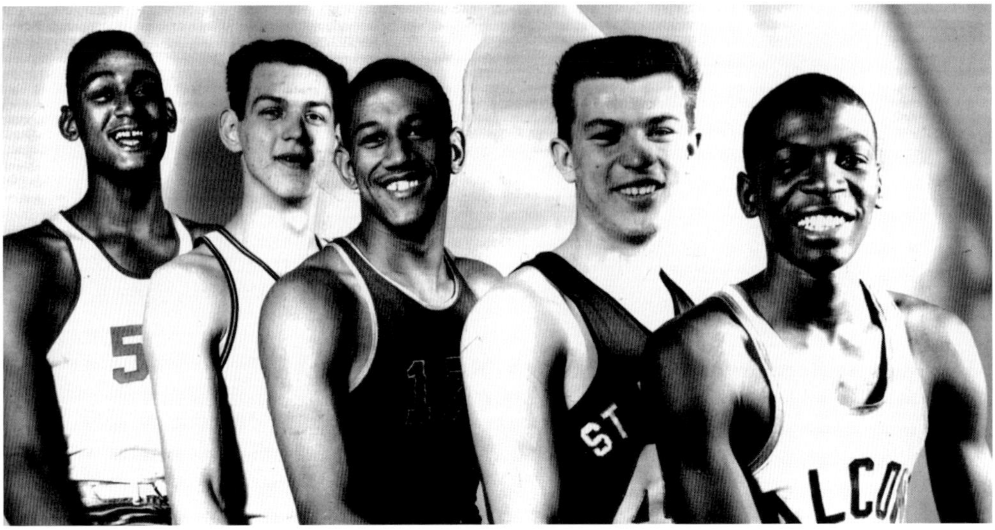

The *Detroit News*'s All-City team of 1959 includes (from left to right) Eastern's Reggie Harding (the PSL's first seven-footer), Holy Redeemer's Bill Chmielewski, Pershing's Lonnie Sanders, Hamtramck St. Florian's Syl Jankowski, and Northeastern's David "Smokey" Gaines. The 6 foot, 10 inch Chmielewski played at the University of Dayton and was MVP of the National Invitation Tournament in 1962. Clarkston's Tim McCormick (1984), Southwestern's Voshon Leonard (1993), and Murray-Wright's Robert Traylor (1997) also earned the tournament's MVP award. (The Detroit News/John Jolokai.)

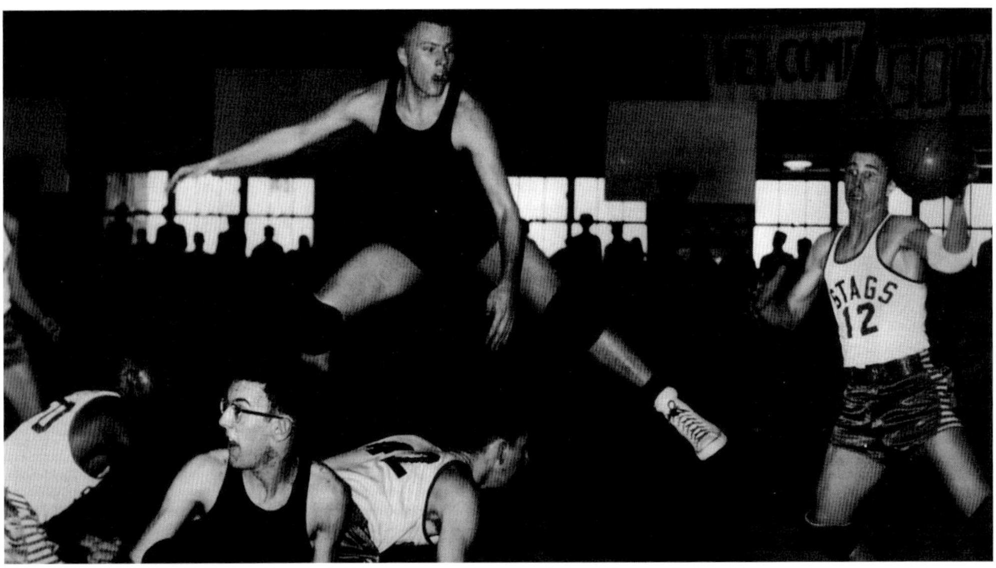

This scrum for possession occurred in Detroit Cooley's 56-48 win at Detroit Mackenzie on January 16, 1959. Larry Kaluzny (25) goes airborne over Mackenzie's Don Bell (42), who is opposite Cooley's Ken MacKay on the floor. With the ball is Dick Honig, who scored 19 on this day. Honig parlayed baseball success into a spot on the 1965 NCAA champion University of Michigan diamond team. (Dick Honig collection.)

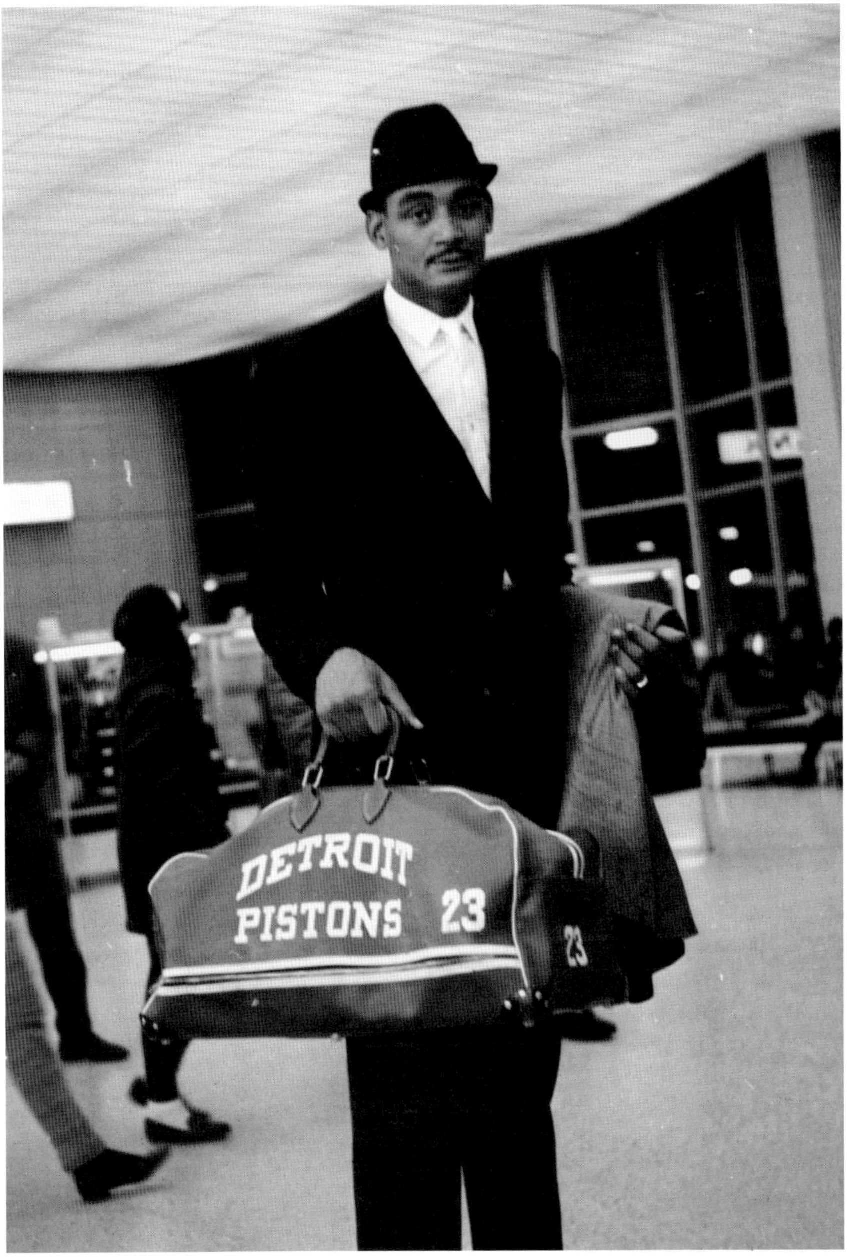

Reggie Harding's promising future was lost to crime and drugs. Harding, the PSL's first seven-footer and a *Parade* All-American at Eastern High in 1961, became the first NBA player drafted without playing collegiately. Famed for carrying a pistol in his gym bag, Harding is still remembered for attempting an armed robbery at a Detroit liquor store whose owner identified Harding—wearing a ski mask—by name. Harding replied, "Man, I told you it wasn't me." Peter Benjaminson's *The Lost Supreme* biography of Florence Ballard recants Harding allegedly raping Ballard at knifepoint in 1960. Harding was shot to death at a Detroit intersection in 1972; he was just 30 years old. (DetroitPSLBasketball.com.)

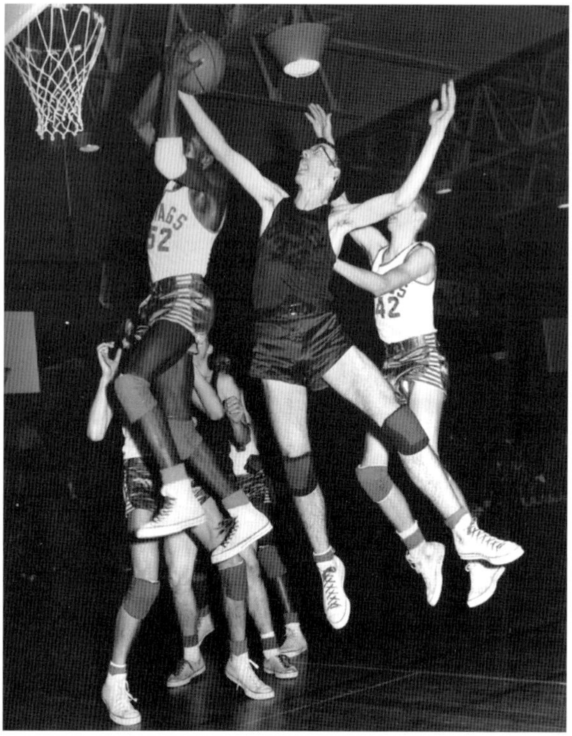

Detroit Cooley's Ken MacKay pulls a rebound away from Detroit Mackenzie forward Gordon Bonaparte during the Cardinals' 56-48 win in the 1958–1959 PSL season. The game was a third-place battle in the Metropolitan's West Side Division. (Dick Honig collection.)

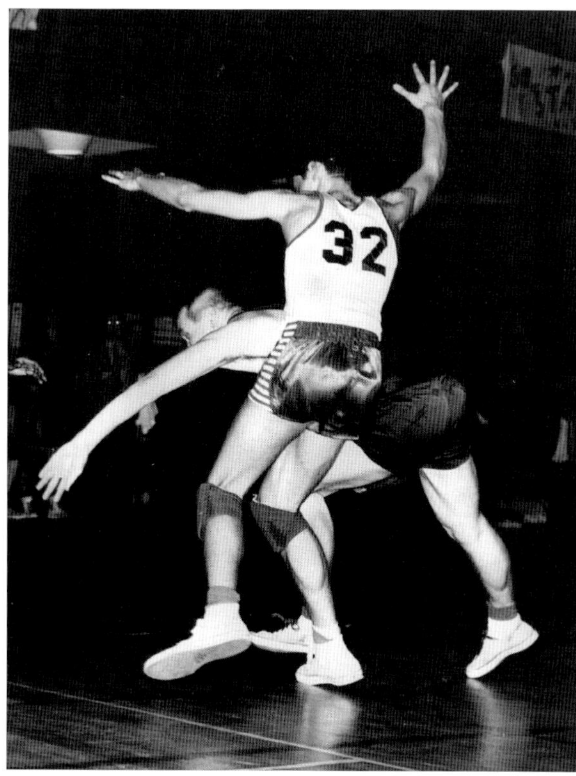

Detroit Cooley's Larry Cutright, who scored 14 fourth-quarter points, takes out Detroit Mackenzie's Jim Fitzgerald (32) in Cooley's 56-48 win in the January 16, 1959, Metropolitan League game. Cutright, also a football and baseball star at Cooley, scored nine field goals and six of nine free throws for a game-high 24 points. (Dick Honig collection.)

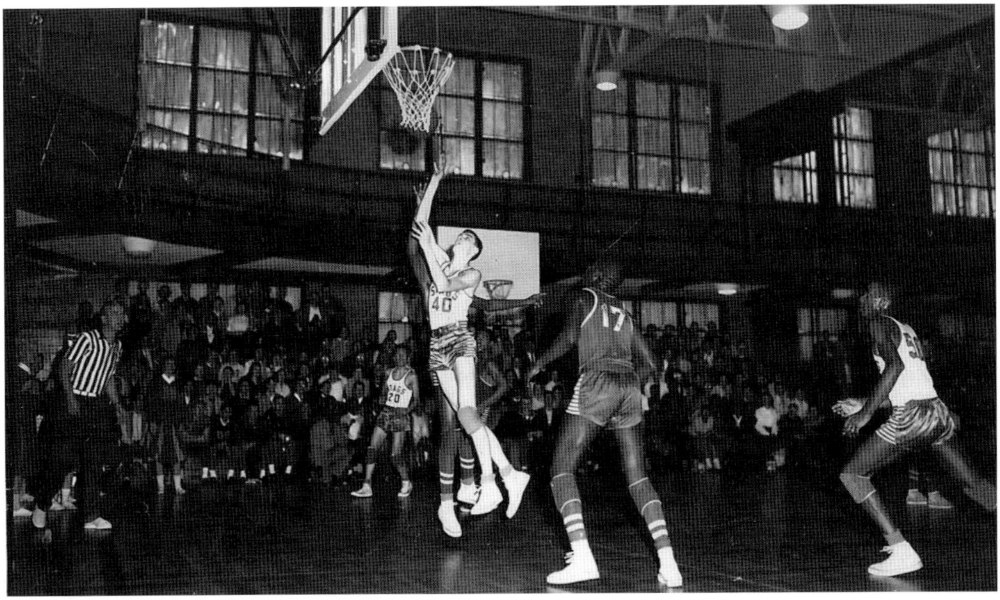

Detroit Northwestern dominated among Detroit public schools from 1950 to 1969. The Colts made 13 PSL Final Fours, 11 title games, and won six PSL crowns. This 1959 game was played on February 13 at Detroit Mackenzie in front of a full house for the 4:00 p.m. tip-off. Northwestern escaped the Stags with a 56-53 decision despite this layin by Mackenzie forward John Markiewicz (40). Northwestern's Willie Thomas (17) watches as Mackenzie's Roy Clinkscales (50) enters the fray. (Dick Honig collection.)

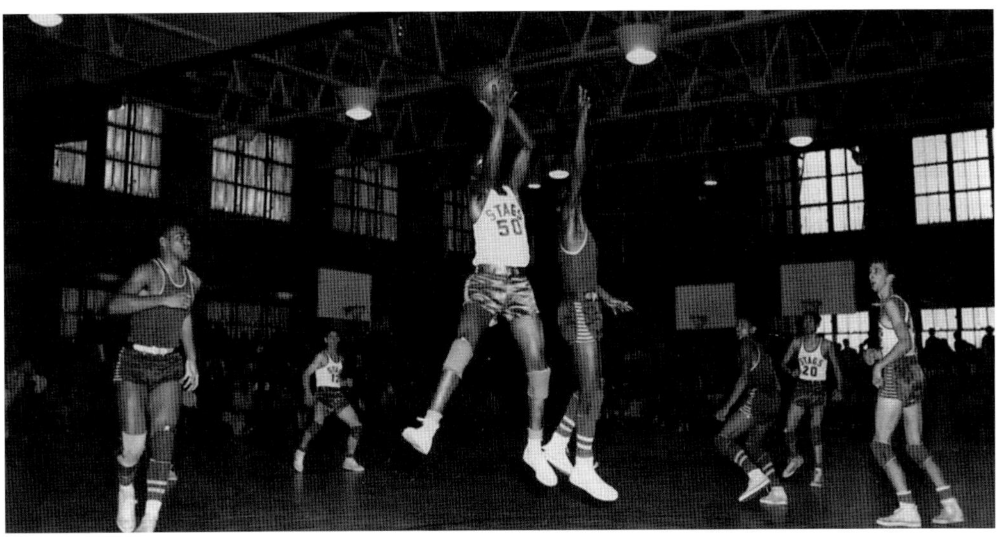

Mackenzie's Roy Clinkscales secures the rebound among several Northwestern Colts and teammates Dick Honig (12) and Jerry Takesue (20). Note the many practice baskets adorning the floor at Detroit Mackenzie. Many of Detroit's public school games are played in exact replicas of this gym today, with the same cast-iron running tracks, large-scale windows, and erector set–like trusses. (Dick Honig collection.)

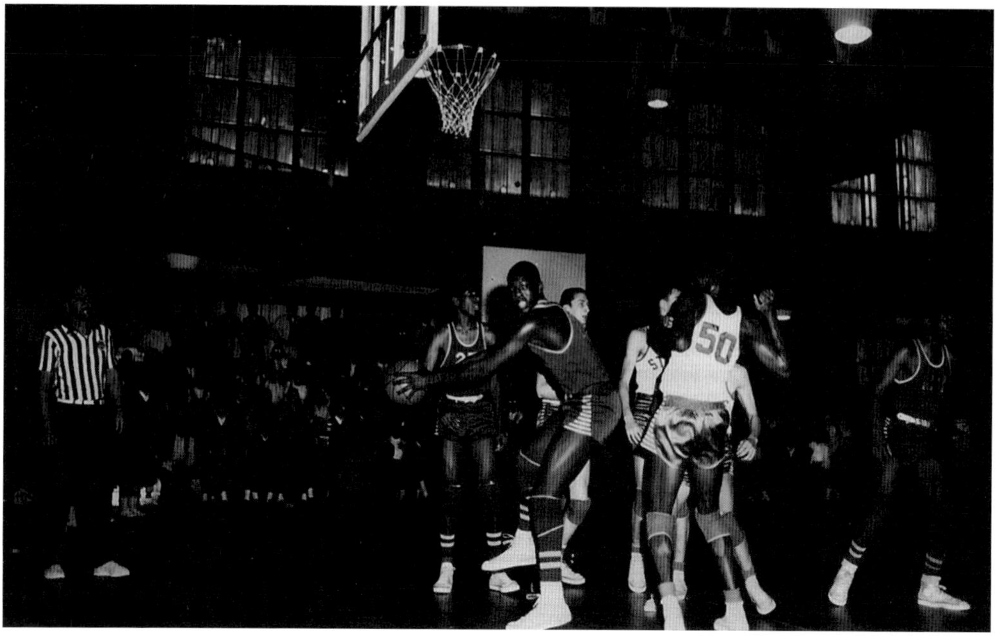

Detroit Northwestern's Willie Thomas secures the rebound as Northwestern's Bill Street (25) watches. Street averaged 17 points per game and earned a spot on the *Detroit Times*'s All-Metro team of 1959. (Dick Honig collection.)

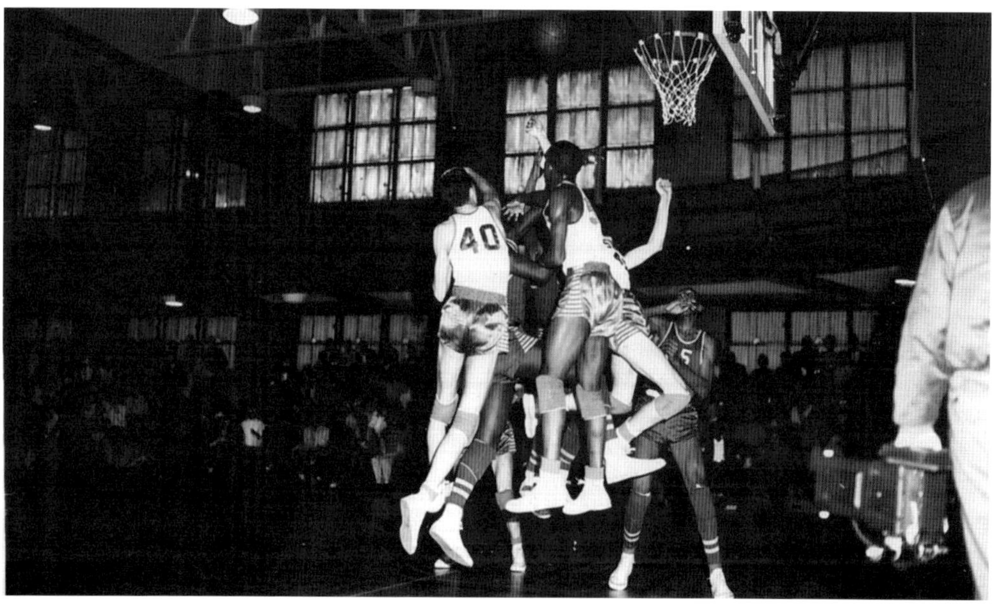

For 31 years, Detroit public schools played a regular-season tournament, put on a city tournament, and hosted a post-season tournament because Detroit public schools did not participate in the MHSAA's statewide brackets from 1931 to 1961. Eastern, coached by Bob Samaras, ultimately defeated Northwestern, shown here battling Mackenzie in the regular season, by a 70-52 count in the PSL tournament title game. (Dick Honig collection.)

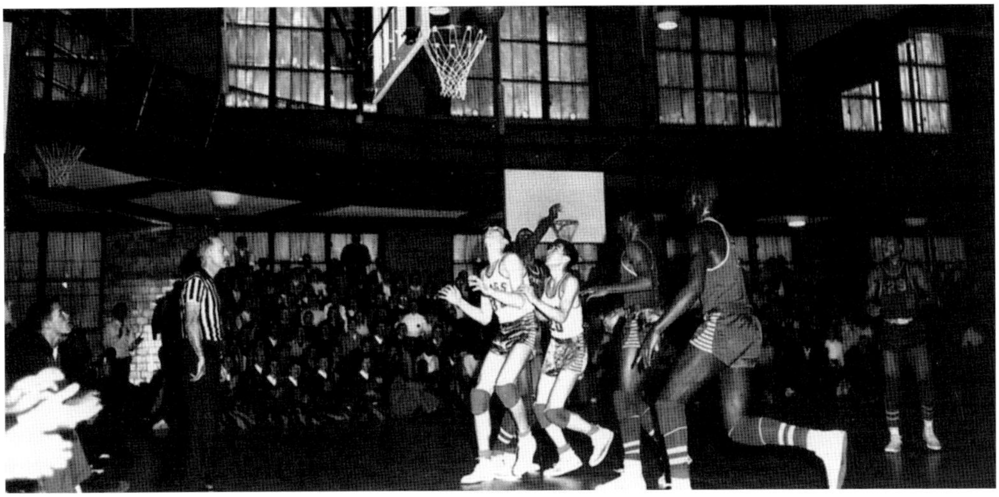

As the 1959 PSL post-season tournament began, Mackenzie (shown above) eliminated archrival Redford while Cody, Northwestern, Northeastern, Western, Wilber Wright, and Pershing advanced. Northeastern eliminated Mackenzie, blew out Northwestern in the semifinal, and bested Detroit Central in the championship, 72-68, to win the city's inclusive, post-season championship. Eastern, Mackenzie, Northeastern, and Wilber Wright are all closed today. (Dick Honig collection.)

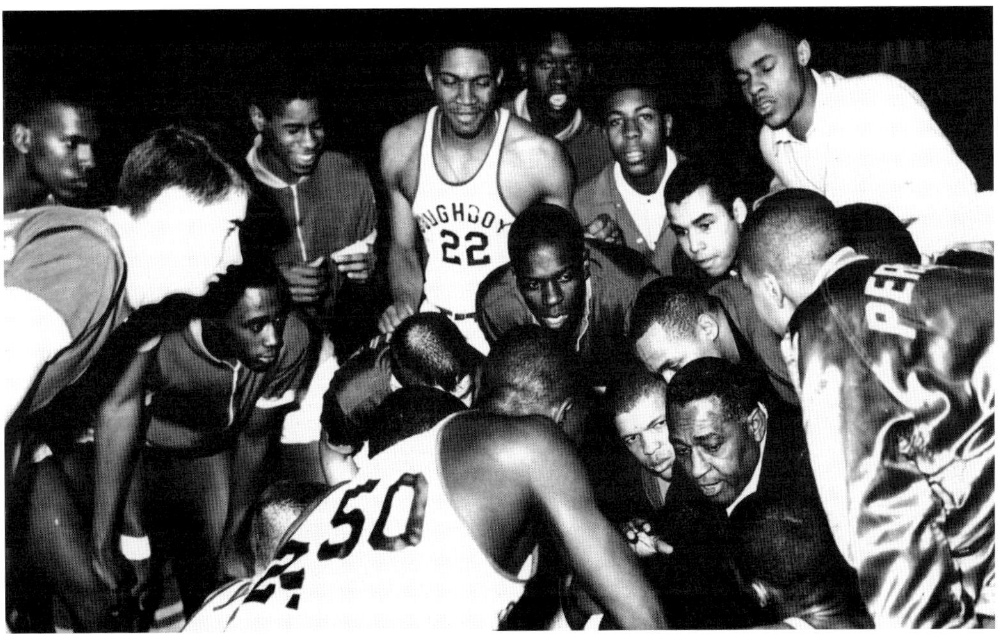

Ferndale's 1963 Class A title became possible when Royal Oak Kimball stunned coach Will Robinson's Pershing Doughboys 39-32 in this first-round game of the district playoffs. Pershing played 13 Class A quarterfinals, eight finals, and won four state titles since the PSL returned to the MHSAA tournament in 1962. The Doughboys also played four consecutive Class A title games from 1992 to 1995. (The Detroit News/James R. Kilpatrick.)

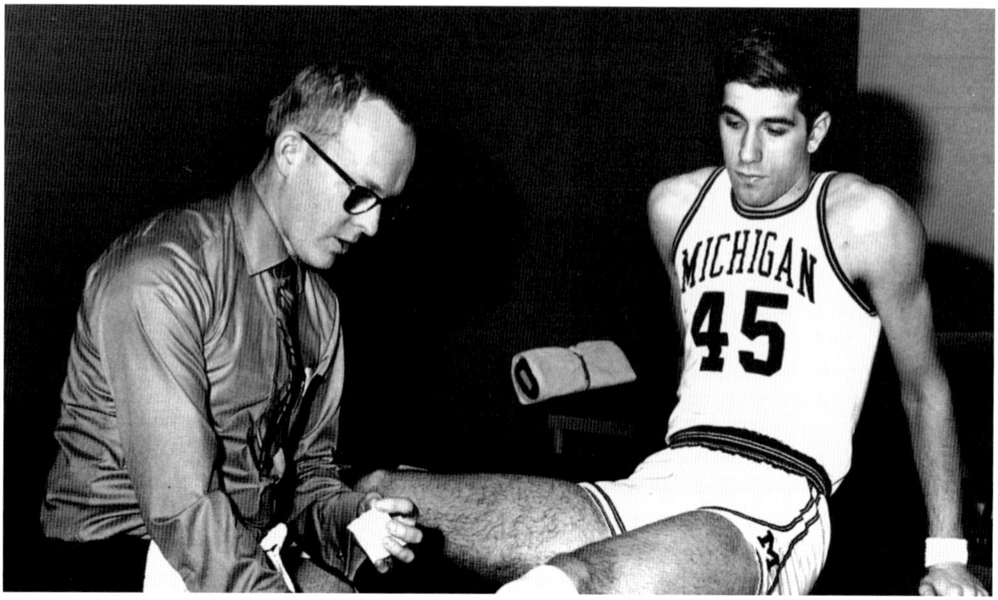

Hamtramck High's Rudy Tomjanovich was a legend at the University of Michigan, earning 1970 All-America honors and three All-Big Ten selections. His 11-year professional career ended as Houston's third all-time scorer with five All-Star games. The name Rudy T adorned his NBA uniforms because his last name was too long. As coach he won back-to-back NBA titles with Houston in 1994 and 1995. His "never underestimate the heart of a champion" speech is still regaled. Rudy T's No. 45 is retired at both Michigan and Houston. (The Detroit News/Drayton "Doc" Holcomb.)

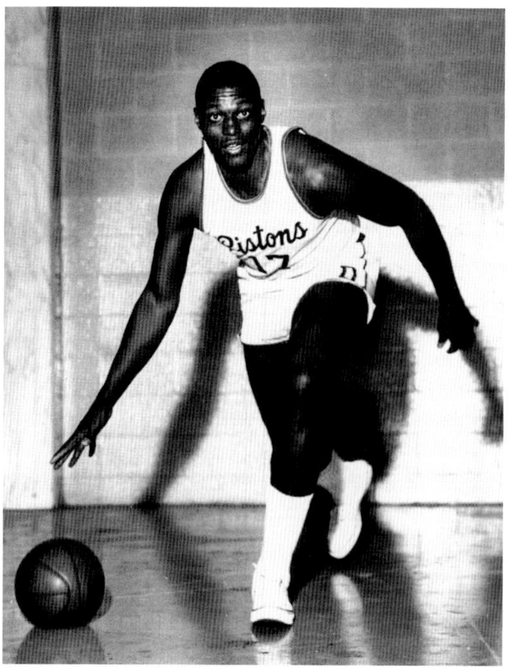

The Detroit Pistons drafted Detroit Cass Tech grad Bill Buntin in the 1965 NBA draft. All-America twice at the University of Michigan (1964–1965), Buntin earned three All-Big Ten selections and led Michigan to the 1965 Big Ten title. On May 9, 1968, Buntin suffered a fatal heart attack during a pickup basketball game. (The Detroit News/James R. Kilpatrick.)

Spencer Haywood made Detroit's Pershing Doughboys a force to be reckoned with as the Technicians discovered on January 6, 1967, at Detroit Cass Tech. Haywood lettered for the University of Detroit, won Olympic gold in Mexico City with Team USA in 1968, played 14 seasons of professional basketball, and authored a book with Scott Ostler titled *Spencer Haywood: The Rise, the Fall, the Recovery*. Haywood successfully challenged the NBA's player draft rules as a violation of antitrust laws in 1971. (The Detroit News/James R. Kilpatrick.)

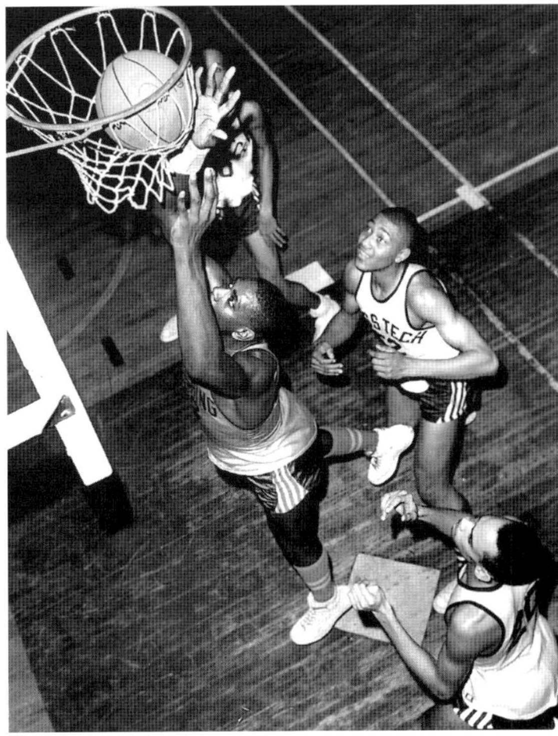

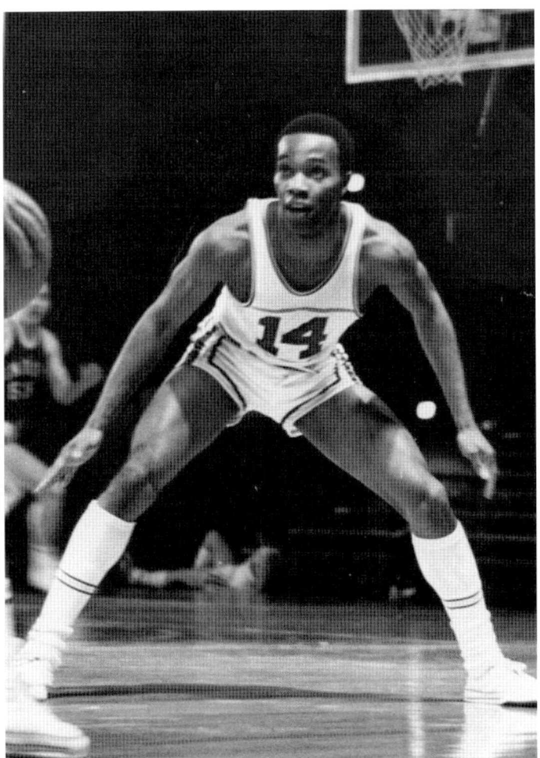

Willie "Stick" Iverson led the PSL's return to the MHSAA tournaments after a 31-year hiatus by helping Detroit Pershing past Ferndale, Royal Oak Dondero, Warren Fitzgerald, Royal Oak Kimball, and Detroit Martin Luther King before bowing to Saginaw in the 1962 Class A semifinals. Iverson, who played with Bill Hardy and Mel "Baby" Daniels at Pershing, had a short-lived professional career but became an All-American (second team) at Central Michigan University in 1967. (Central Michigan University Sports Information.)

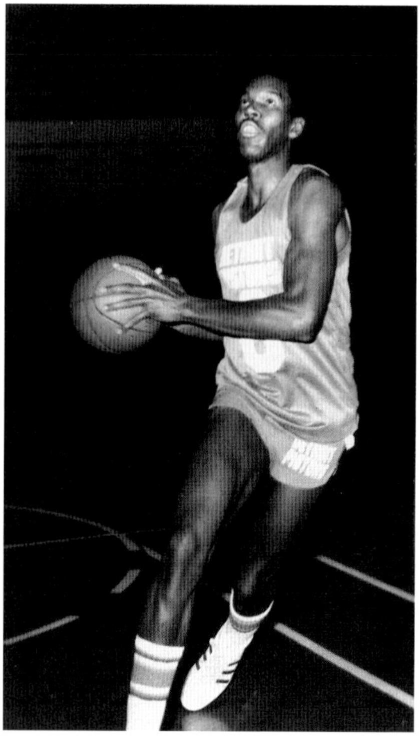

Because coaches focused so much on stopping Pershing's Spencer Haywood, teammate Ralph Simpson emerged as an equally dangerous all-PSL talent. Simpson is best remembered for his 29 points in a regional final versus Detroit Northwestern, 23 points in the semifinals, and a then state record 43 in the 1967 Class A championship game versus Flint Central. His 21 field goals in the 1967 finals remains the state record. (The Detroit News/Anderson.)

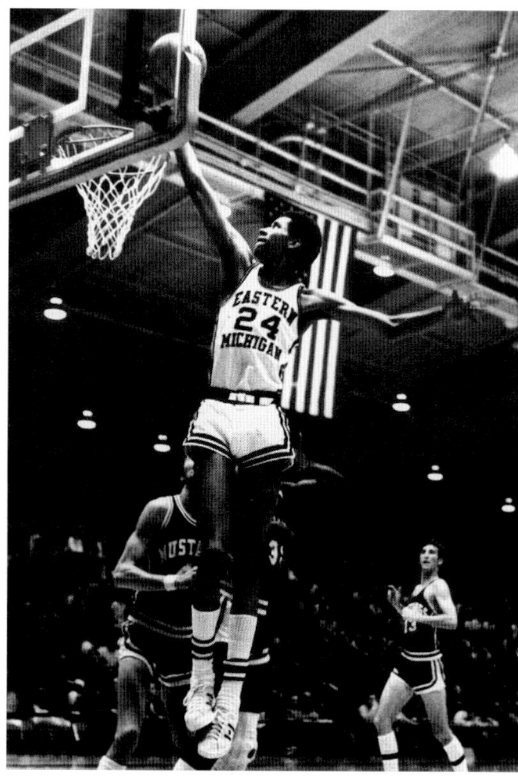

George Gervin's best efforts in the mid-1960s at Detroit's Martin Luther King High were not good enough to get the Crusaders into the PSL's Final Four, much less the PSL title game, and Gervin never made an all-PSL team. The "Iceman" led Eastern Michigan University to the National Association of Intercollegiate Athletics (NAIA) championship game of 1971 and was named one of the NBA's 50 Greatest Players in 1997, boasting four seasons as the NBA's scoring leader. (Eastern Michigan University Sports Information.)

Detroit Northwestern's Lamont King (24) is helpless to defend as Detroit Mumford's Billy Berris scores two of his 24 points in Mumford's near upset of the Colts on December 16, 1967. Berris, nicknamed "SuperJew" by his Northwestern teammates, went 12 of 12 from the charity stripe but King's 40-point effort ensured a 75-74 victory for Northwestern. Mumford's only PSL title was in 1969, prompting the chant, "We lost Billy Berris, but we got Steve Harris" when the Mustangs took the PSL's 1969 title game. (Berris family archive.)

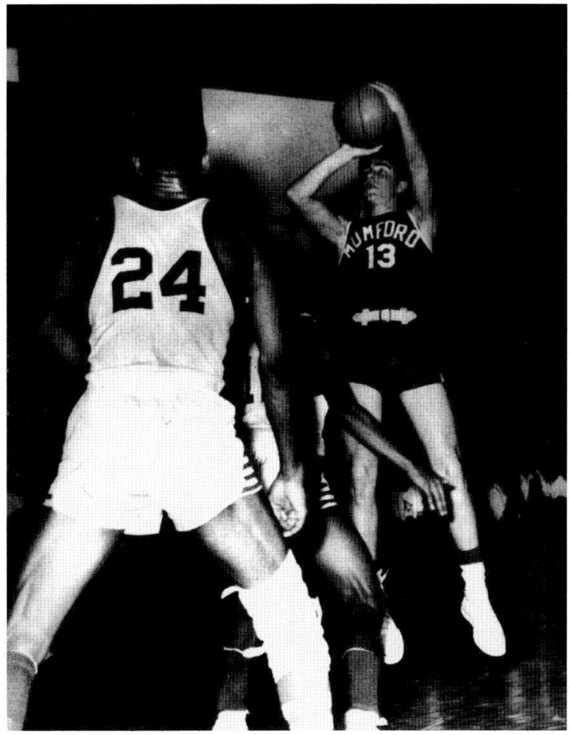

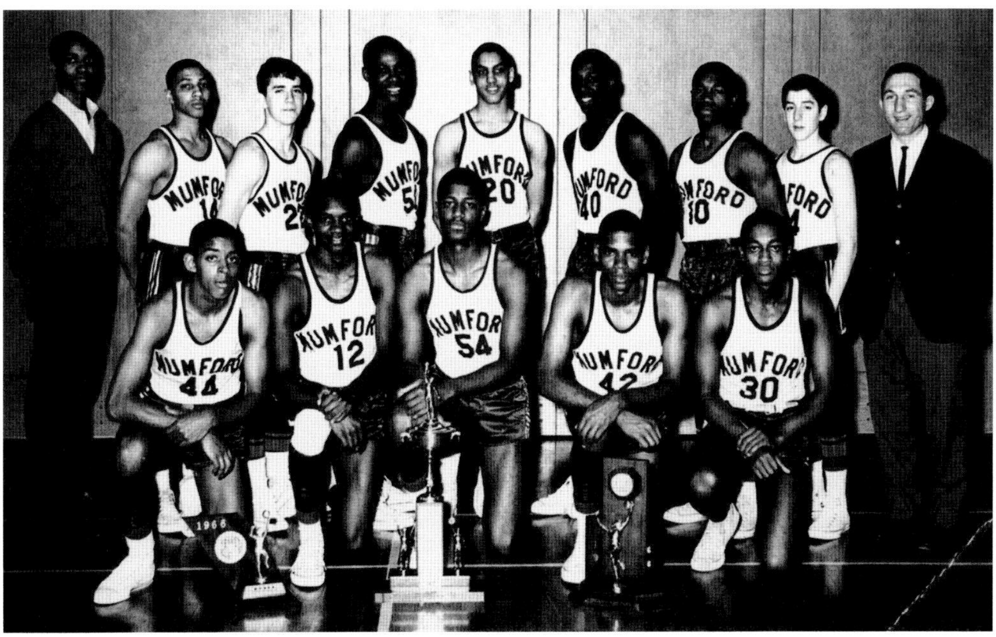

Mumford High's Sam Taub (second row, far right) coached in the 1960s and won Mumford's only PSL title in 1969. This is the 1965–1966 Mustangs, who battled fellow city powers at the time from Eastern, Northwestern, and Pershing. Larry Moore (54) coached city and suburban varsity basketball in the 1990s and the first decade of the 21st century. (Berris family collection.)

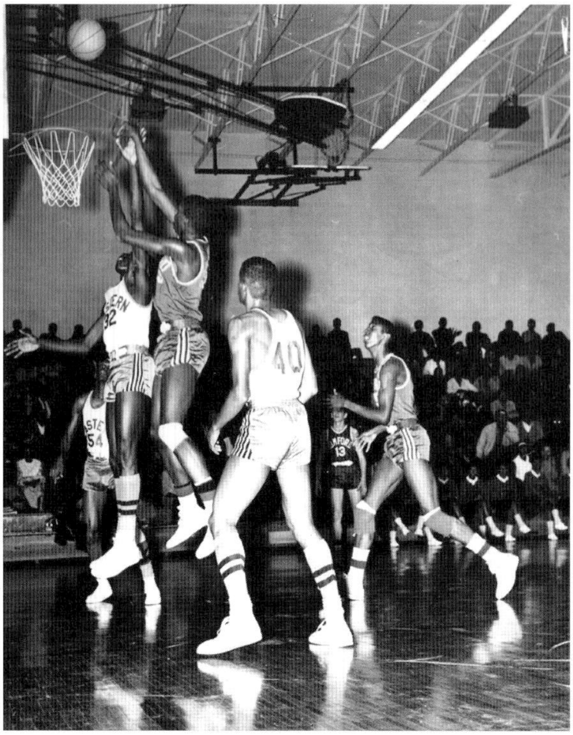

Mustang Arthur "Spider" Webb and a leaping Mike Murdock (32) help Detroit Mumford attack east side rival Detroit Eastern in this 1968 game, the winner and date are unknown. Many prep basketball stars missed their proverbial 15 minutes of fame in 1968 because Detroit's newspaper strike meant little or no prep coverage. Coach Gene Bolden's Murray-Wright Pilots defeated defending Class A state champion Detroit Pershing for the PSL title by a 69-66 score. Eastern closed in 1969. (Billy Berris collection.)

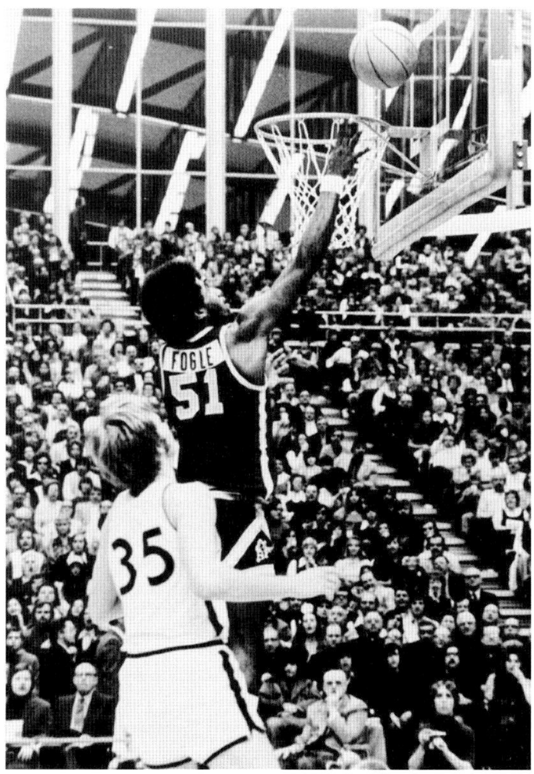

Larry Fogle remains legendary almost 40 years after his final game for Detroit Cooley. His PSL-record 73 points versus Detroit Cody on February 4, 1972, remain fifth highest in MHSAA history. Fogle scored 1,309 points in 44 games at Canisius College and led the nation in scoring in 1973–1974 at 33.4 points per game. (Canisius College Sports Information Department.)

Earvin "Magic" Johnson and Lansing Everett visited Detroit's Northwestern High for a scrimmage on February 8, 1977. Johnson's team locked horns with another metro team in 1977, needing overtime to elude Birmingham Brother Rice, 62-56, in the 1977 MHSAA final after Brother Rice's Kevin Smith banked a heroic half-court heave to force overtime. Johnson and Detroit Henry Ford High's Greg Kelser attended Michigan State University and helped the Spartans win the 1979 NCAA title. Both Kelser and Johnson had their numbers retired at Michigan State University. (The Detroit News/Donald Batten.)

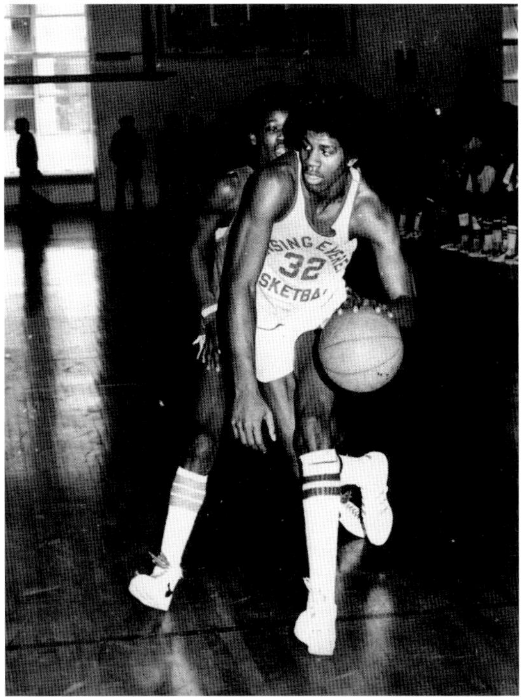

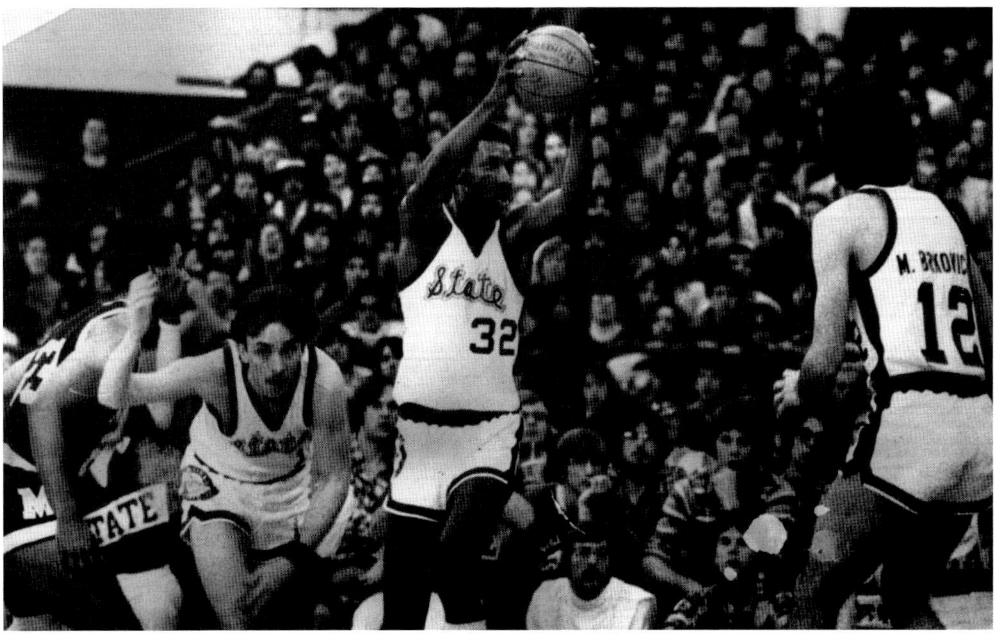

Henry Ford High's Greg "Special K" Kelser illustrated how rugged the PSL was in the 1970s. His Ford High Trojans never appeared in a PSL Final Four. Kelser was a senior All-American at Michigan State University and headlined with Magic Johnson, including this February 17, 1979, game Michigan State University won against archrival Michigan at Jenison Field House, 80-57. (The Detroit News/Drayton "Doc" Holcomb.)

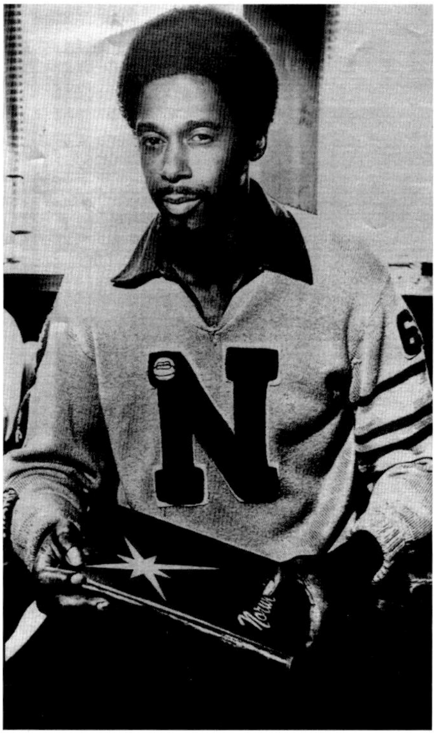

George Gervin called Detroit Northwestern's Curtis Jones the best player he ever saw. Jones made national news from his Detroit ghetto in 1982 by filing a lawsuit against his prep and collegiate coaches, claiming to be pushed through school despite being unqualified for higher learning. Jones, 50, whose drug use was well documented, died in 1999. (The Oakland Press.)

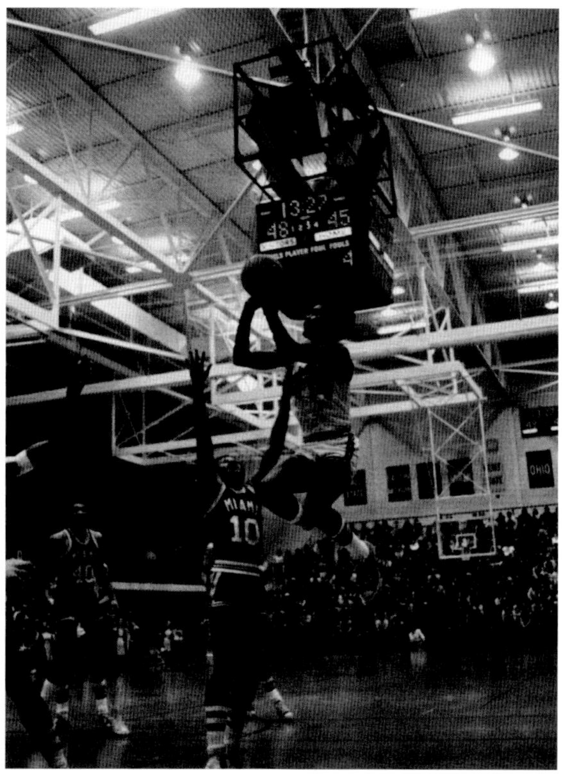

James McElroy from Detroit Murray-Wright shows his incredible leaping ability during a Mid-American Conference game versus Ohio's Miami University at Central Michigan University in the 1970s. McElroy played briefly for the Detroit Pistons during his seven-year NBA career. The Pilots, who played in three PSL Final Fours and two title games in the 1970s, were a consolidation of the name Wilber Wright into Philip J. Murray–Wright High School. The school closed in 2007. (Central Michigan University.)

Antoine "the Judge" Joubert scores two of 44 points against Southfield in Detroit Southwestern's 81-57 Class A semifinal win of 1983. Joubert set the Class A finals scoring record (122 points in the 1983 quarterfinal, semifinal, and final) in addition to the individual Class A final and semifinal game scoring records (47, 44). Joubert's finals game record was broken in 2009. Scoring 2,208 career points, the Judge became Michigan's first Class A player to pass the 2,000-point mark and earned the 1983 Mr. Basketball award as the state's best player. (The Detroit News/Harold Robinson.)

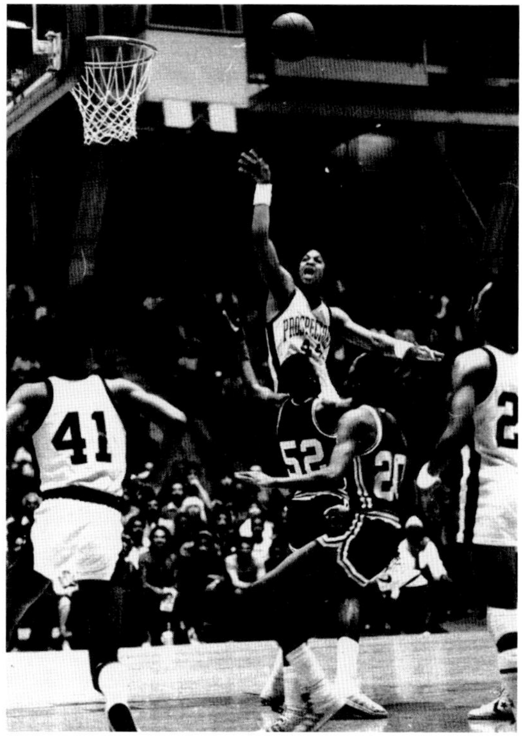

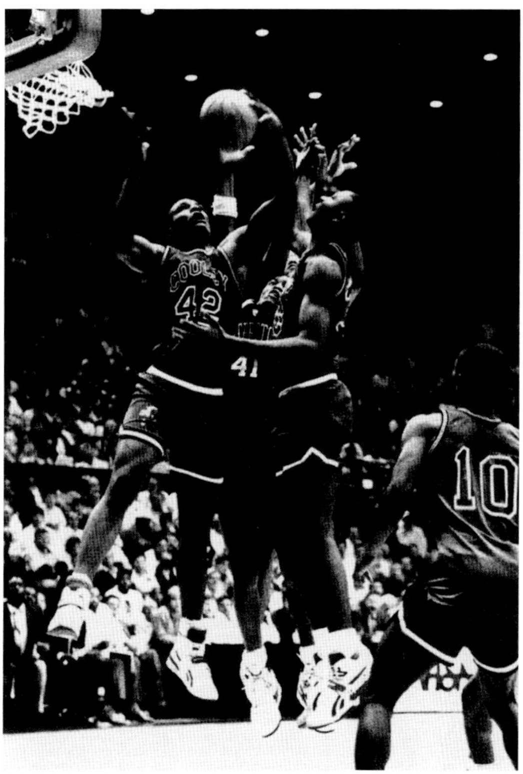

No two schools waged a fiercer rivalry in metro Detroit than Detroit Cooley and Detroit Southwestern did in the mid-1980s through the early 1990s. Southwestern won the PSL from 1981 to 1983, 1985, and 1987 to 1991, but coach Ben Kelso's Cooley teams won three consecutive MHSAA titles in the Class A bracket from 1987 to 1989, eliminating Southwestern in all three seasons. This is Cooley's 85-73 conquest over Southwestern in the 1989 Class A final at the University of Michigan's Crisler Arena. (MHSAA archives.)

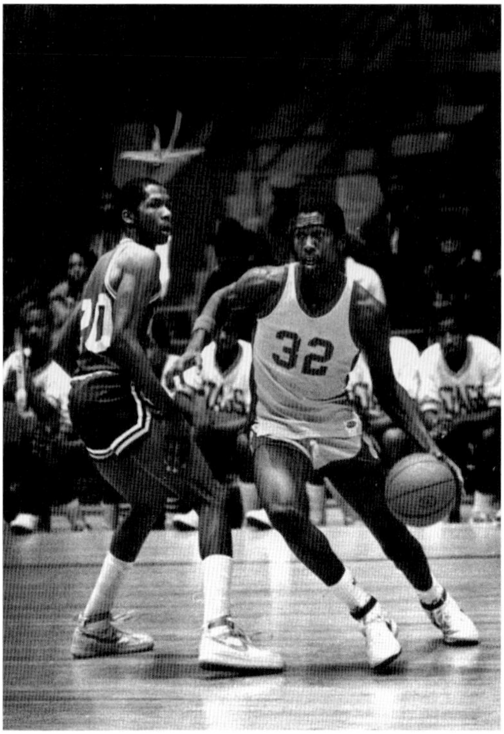

Detroit Chadsey star Demetrius Gore drives past Mackenzie's Duane Macells in this 1983 PSL game. Gore, a PSL legend from the 1980s, attended the University of Pittsburgh. Chadsey was scheduled to close in 2007 with Detroit's Mackenzie, Northern, and Redford, three longtime Detroit prep school institutions, but was spared and remained open through 2009. (The Detroit News/David Kryszak.)

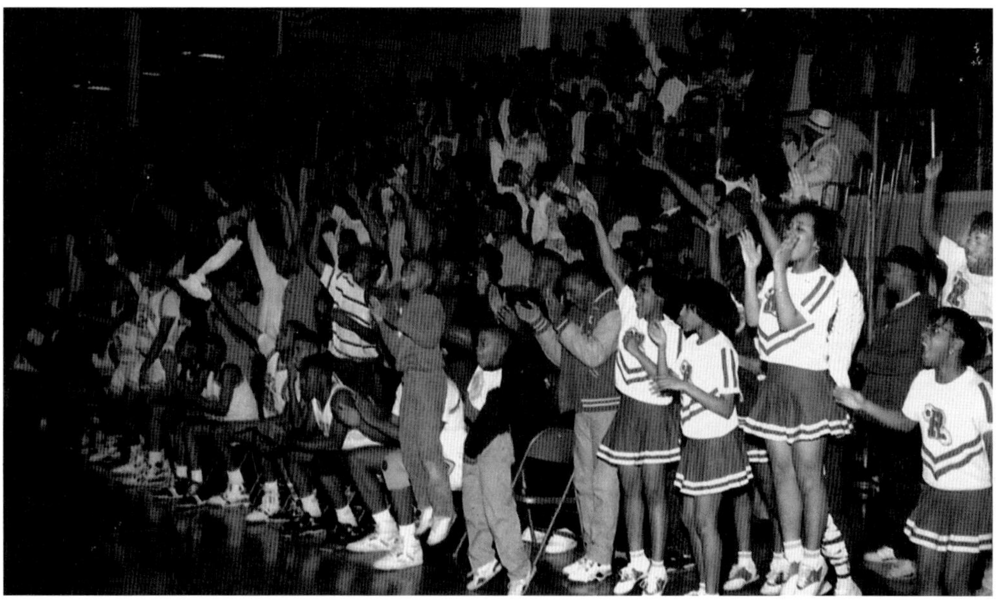

Faithful followers of Detroit's Redford High were rewarded in 1985 when the Huskies advanced to their first regional final in school history. Redford, not known for basketball prowess until the school's final 12 years, had advanced past a district bracket just twice before this 84-55 loss to fellow PSL member Detroit Mackenzie. Both Redford and Mackenzie closed in 2007. (Nancy Jewitt collection.)

Detroit Cooley became the first and only PSL team to win three consecutive Class A MHSAA championships after the Cardinals defeated Detroit Southwestern, Flint Northwestern (seen here), and Southwestern again from 1987 to 1989. Teammates Daniel Lyton and Michael Talley also became the only Class A players in MHSAA history to win three straight Class A titles. (MHSAA archives/Gary Shook.)

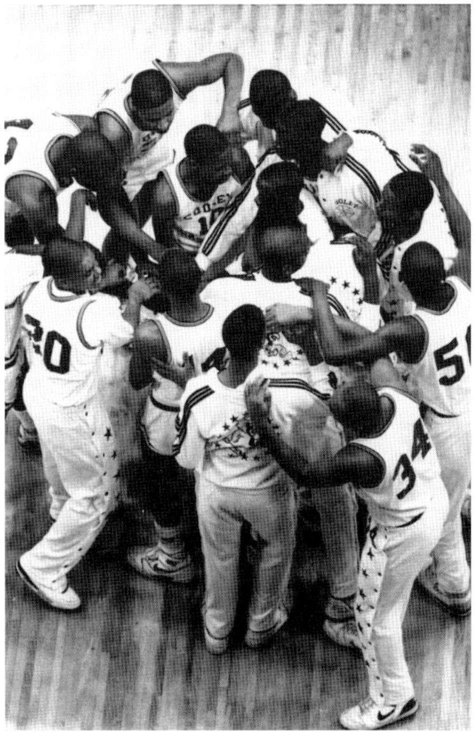

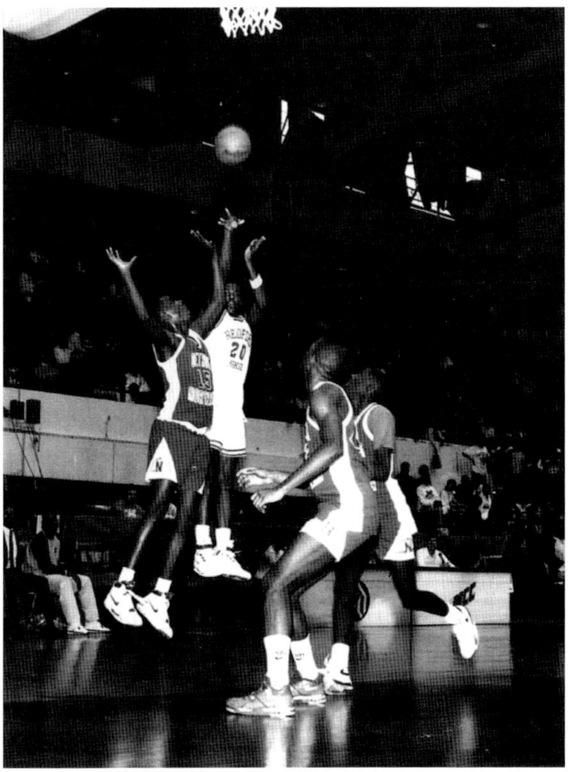

Detroit Northern, where Syracuse and NBA star Derrick Coleman attended, went to an amazing five MHSAA Final Fours in seven seasons from 1986 to 1992, including this 1990 quarterfinal victory over Detroit Redford by a 77-51 count. Northern advanced to three consecutive Class A semifinals in 1990–1992, won the PSL title in 1986, and closed in 2007. (Nancy Jewitt collection.)

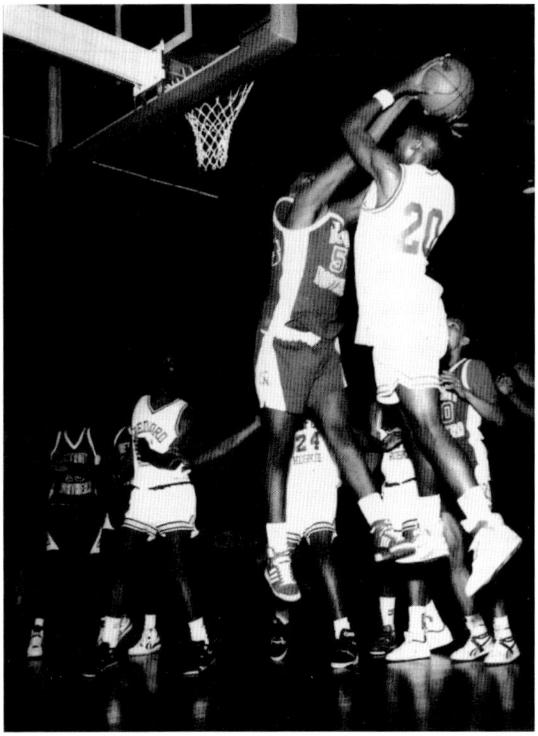

The road to the 1990 Class A quarterfinal at the University of Detroit's Calihan Hall for Detroit Redford included a triumph over perennial powers from four different leagues. They eluded Detroit Catholic Central's Shamrocks, 74-59, and the Blue Jays of Southfield, 68-47, Dearborn Edsel Ford, 63-47, and three-time defending Class A champion Detroit Cooley, 69-62, in the regional final, before this 77-51 loss to Detroit Northern. (Nancy Jewitt collection.)

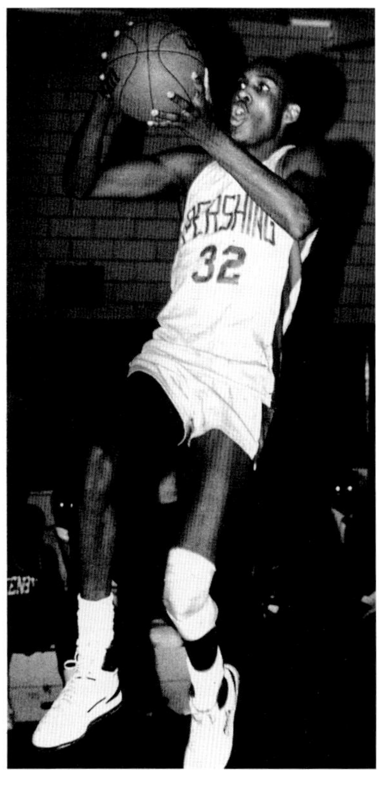

Detroit Pershing's Steve Smith earned his legendary status through his considerable on-court talent, engaging personality, and generosity. The former Pershing Doughboy became an All-Big Ten guard at Michigan State University for coach Jud Heathcote in the early 1990s. Smith made considerable gifts to Pershing and Michigan State University during his 18 years in the NBA. Both schools have retired Smith's No. 32 jersey for display from their respective rafters. (The Detroit News/Kirthmon Dozier.)

Jalen Rose learned to rise up on the basketball courts of Detroit's city parks. Rose, like Anderson Hunt and Antoine Joubert before him, led Southwestern to the MHSAA's Class A title game, but Rose helped deliver the only two state championships of coach Perry Watson's tenure in 1990 and 1991. Rose was issued a technical foul for hanging on the rim after this dunk in Southwestern's 77-63 win over city rival Detroit Northern. (MHSAA archives/Gary Shook.)

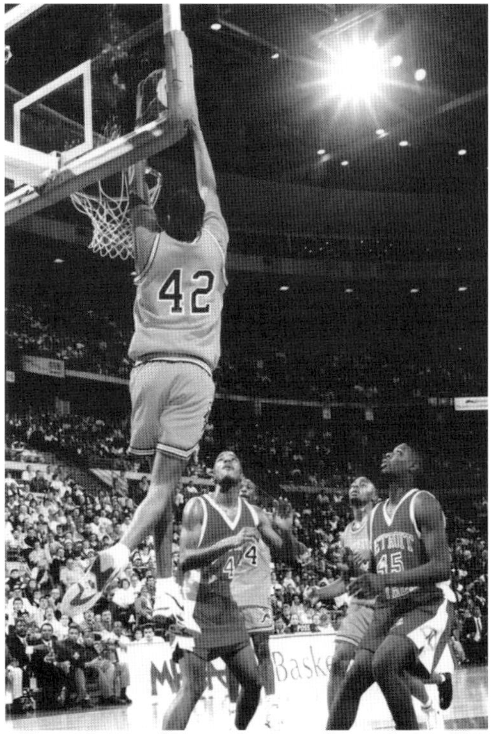

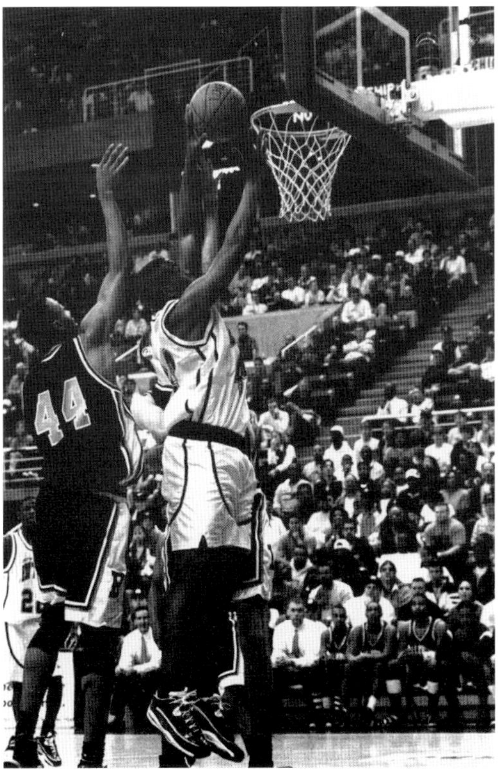

Antonio Gates puts Detroit Central two points closer to the Trailblazers' 63-47 victory over Belleville High in the 1998 Class A title game. Gates, an All-Pro tight end for the San Diego Chargers, first enrolled at Michigan State University to play both football and basketball. Gates tied Central High's single-game scoring record with 45 points versus Detroit Northwestern on February 7, 1998. (MHSAA archive/Gary Shook.)

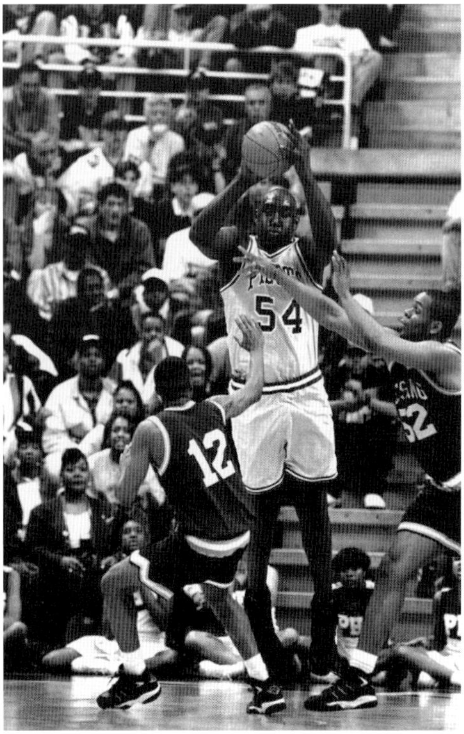

Pershing's Doughboys had no answers when it came to stopping Robert "Tractor" Traylor (54) in the 1994 Class A championship game. In yet another meeting of PSL rivals in the state's marquee championship, Detroit Murray-Wright marched to an 80-73 win. Traylor won the 1994 Mr. Basketball award before attending Michigan, winning the 1997 MVP of the National Invitation Tournament, and leading Michigan to the 1998 Big Ten tournament championship. (MHSAA archive/Gary Shook.)

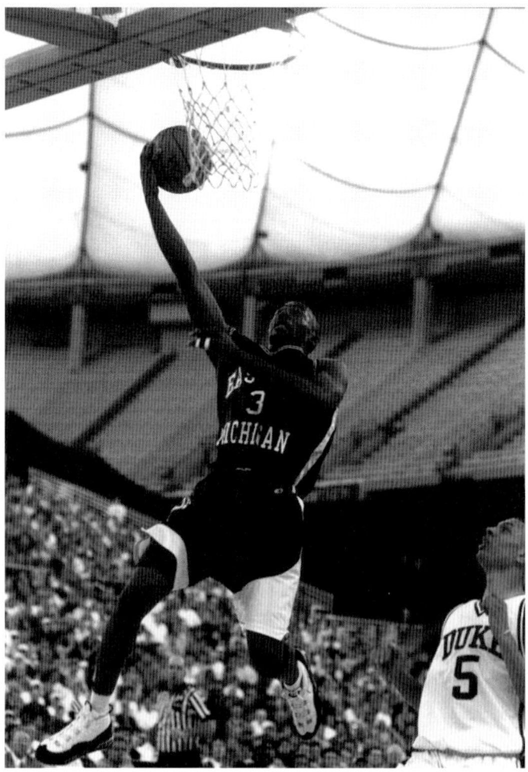

All-PSL guard Derrick Dial from Detroit Cass Tech blossomed at Eastern Michigan University with fellow Detroiters Brian Tolbert (St. Martin DePorres) and Theron Wilson (Detroit King/Royal Oak Dondero). Dial helped Eastern Michigan University reach four Mid-American Conference championship games, two Mid-American Conference titles, two NCAA tournament appearances, one National Invitation Tournament invite, and this 1996 upset of Duke University. Dial's 1,891 career points is third best all-time at Eastern Michigan University. (Eastern Michigan University Sports Information.)

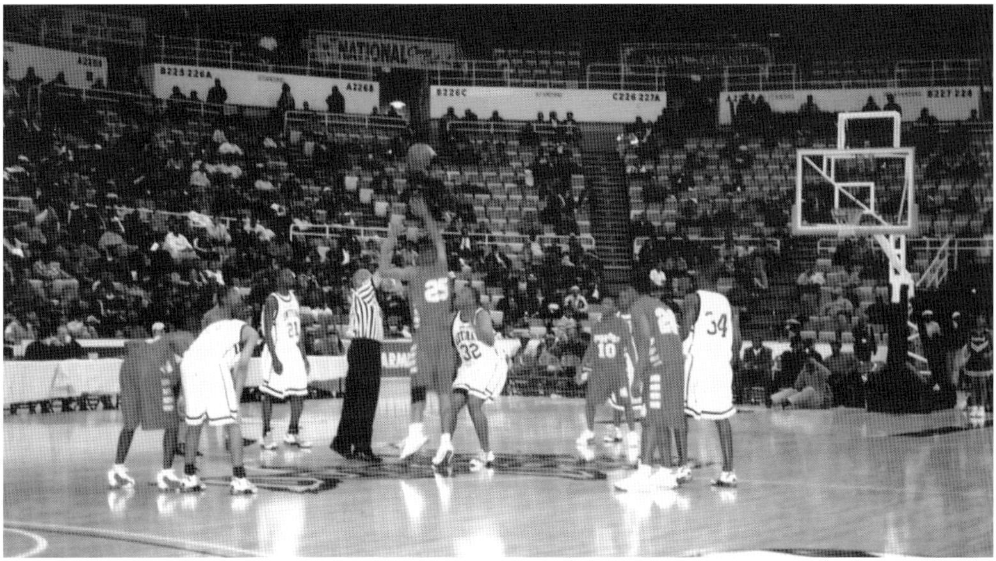

Detroit Redford made Detroit's Joe Louis Arena a championship home in the 2001 PSL final, a 56-43 win over Central High. Despite a near 80-year existence with no PSL titles, Redford became a city power in the school's final 12 seasons before closing in 2007. Dating back to 1995–1996, Redford made nine PSL Final Fours, seven championship games, and four PSL championships under coach Derrick McDowell or Ken Flowers. McDowell is an assistant at Eastern Michigan University; Flowers heads Detroit Henry Ford High. (Nancy Jewitt collection.)

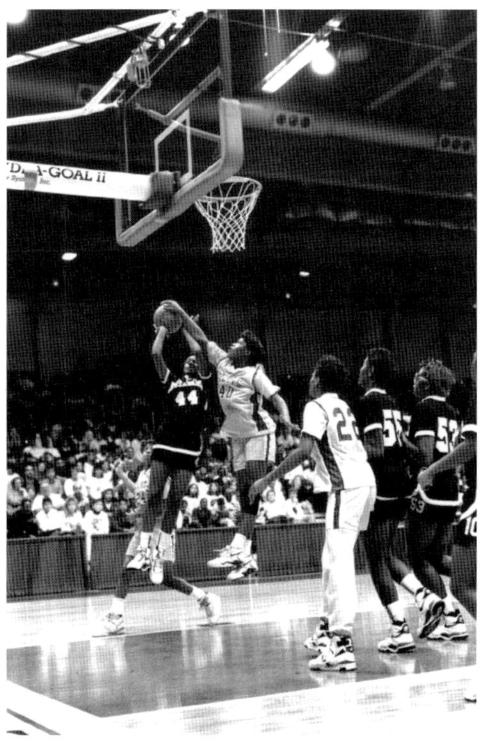

The 1990 Class A girls' final could have easily doubled as a routine PSL regular-season game. Murray-Wrights's Caryn Shinn blocks the shot of King forward Tamika Matlock but the Crusaders blocked Murray-Wrights's title dreams, defeating the Pilots 53-48 for their second of five Class A championships. PSL teams made seven finals in nine seasons from 1985 to 1994, with King earning three titles while Cass Tech gained the 1987 championship. (MHSAA archive/Gary Shook.)

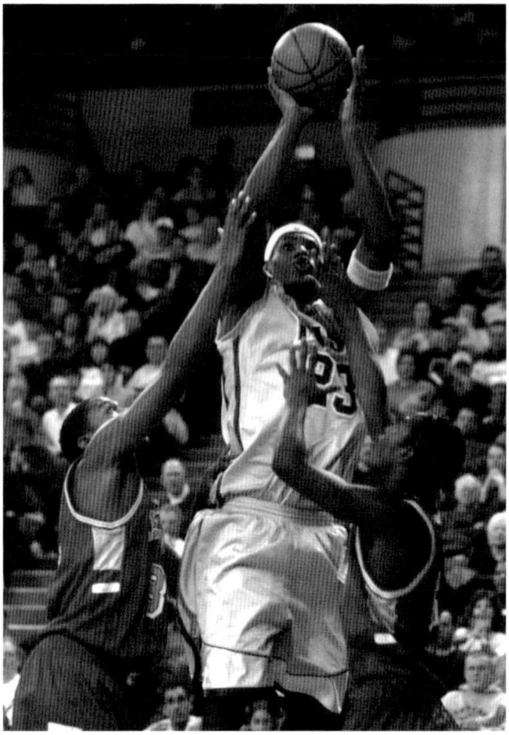

Detroit Redford faced Akron, Ohio's St. Vincent St. Mary's and LeBron "King" James four straight years under coach Derrick McDowell. The Huskies lost the first three games by 10, 5, and 3 points consecutively before losing by more than 30 in James's senior season. The last laugh, however, may have gone to another Detroit PSL prodigy. In 2009, Xavier University's Jordan Crawford, who prepped at Detroit Communication and Media Arts High, dunked on James at James's summer camp. James and Nike officials hurriedly tried to sequester all video of the play to avoid James, the most recognized sport star in the world, future embarrassment. The tape was eventually released; Crawford's dunk made worldwide headlines. (Akron Beacon-Journal.)

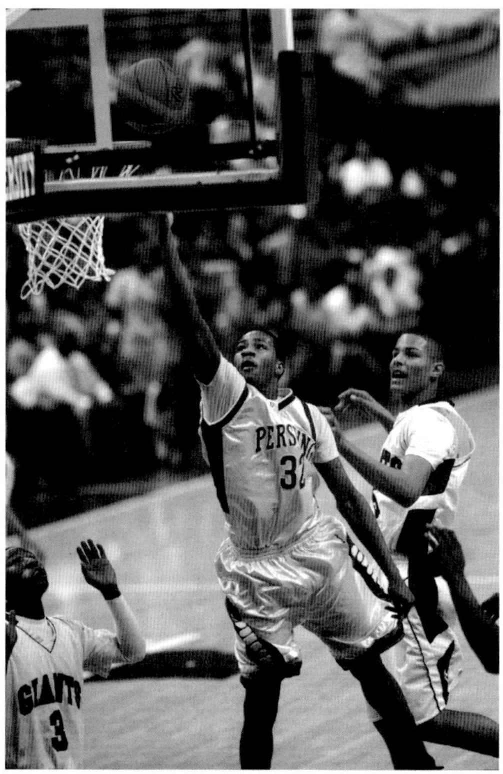

Detroit Pershing's Keith Appling scored 49 points in 2009's Class A finals at Michigan State University, breaking the MHSAA final game scoring record set when Antoine "the Judge" Joubert scored 47 for Detroit Southwestern in 1983. While Appling had never heard of Joubert when asked in the post-game press conference, Appling certainly heard the standing ovation at the Breslin Center from both Pershing and Kalamazoo Central's fans in the waning moments of Pershing's 90-73 victory over the Maroon Giants. (Terry McNamara/Crazy4Life Photography.)

2

Oakland County

Oakland County basketball success is equally distributed among schools big and small, public and private, within wealthy and working-class communities alike.

In 1958, Ferndale Lincoln closed and Ferndale High opened. The 4,000 Railsplitters-turned-Eagles students became Michigan's premiere Class A program. Coach Roy Burkhart marched Ferndale to the 1963 Class A title and took home the 1966 title too. Brother Rice opened in 1962 and Royal Oak Shrine's rivalry with Dearborn Divine Child was strong. Royal Oak Kimball and Royal Oak Dondero, powerhouse footballers, produced a handful of upsets. Troy dominated in Class B with several long tournament runs. Berkley and Southfield emerged as threats to Ferndale's dominance.

But the pride of Oakland County was a Native American chief's namesake town located midway between Ferndale and Clarkston. Pontiac's Central High advanced to an amazing 14 Class A quarterfinals, nine semifinals, and five title games from 1960 to 1979. Under coach Art VanRyzin and later Ralph Grubb, the Chiefs might claim the greatest teams in state history without a title trophy to mark their tremendous success. The annual battles with city rival Pontiac Northern were circled in blood—no county game will ever match the intensity and pride of Central-Northern.

Bill Norton's Brother Rice teams went to four semifinal games in 11 seasons while winning the 1974 crown. In 1977, Rice took Earvin "Magic" Johnson's Lansing Everett cagers to overtime before falling in the Class A title game. The 1975 Berkley Bears captured hearts. Coach Steve Rhoades and forward Bruce Flowers won 25 straight games before bowing in an oft-remembered quarterfinal to Terry Duerod and Highland Park.

Tim McCormick and Clarkston went to the Class A semifinals in 1980. Ferndale turned into a giant-killer, stunning No. 6 Dondero in the 1981 districts and halting Southfield's 31-game Southeastern Michigan Association (SMA) winning streak in 1983. Ray Kelser led Southfield High to the Class A finals in 1983. Clarkston became an annual contender for league, district, and regional crowns. And Detroit Country Day, with Chris Webber and later Shane Battier, emerged as the face of Oakland basketball in the late 1980s.

In 2001–2002, Pontiac Northern won back-to-back Class A titles, Oakland County's first public school since Ferndale to bring the big title home. Northville, Novi, and Detroit Catholic Central became neighbors and subsequent bitter rivals. Rochester Hills Stoney Creek and South Lyon East opened to the north; Kimball and Dondero closed to the south. Pontiac's Northern and Central shuttered in 2009.

The county's face changed; its hardwood history remains etched in the hearts of metro fans everywhere.

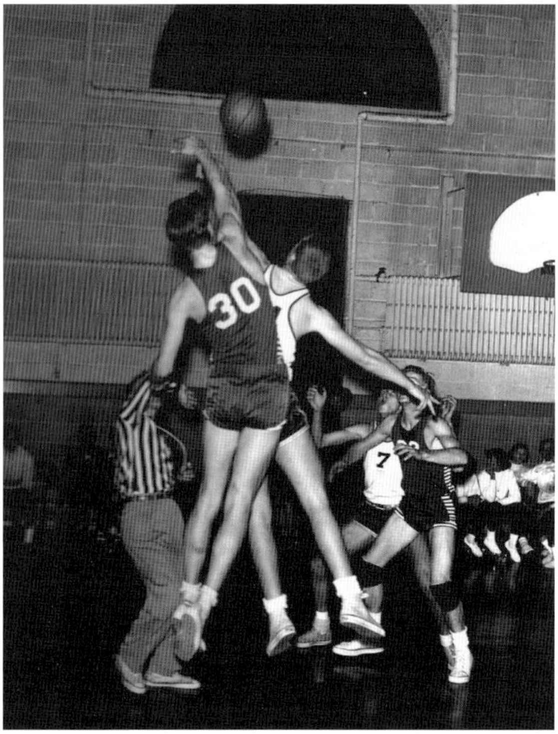

In the 1950s, Detroit Country Day was located on Seven Mile Road near Wyoming Street in Detroit. While the opponent is unknown, the referee has smartly avoided contact at the game's start. Most of Michigan's referees wore the white Converse Chuck Taylor and grey slacks until the early 1960s, when belted black pants and black leather shoes phased out the grey slacks and canvas shoes. (Detroit Country Day archive.)

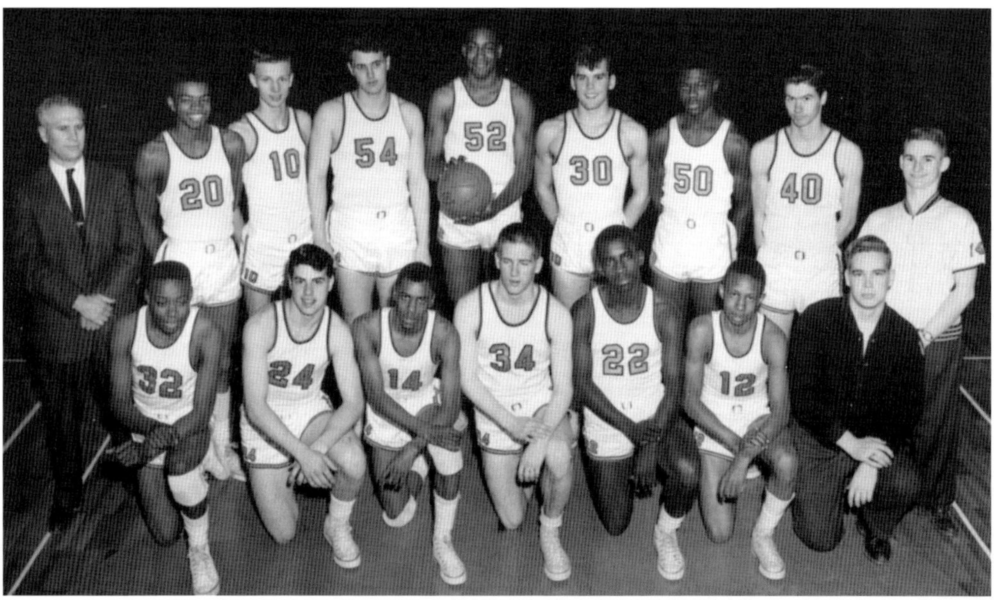

Pontiac High's 1958 Chiefs reached the regional final before falling to now-closed Livonia Bentley in the MHSAA regional final, 50-49. These Chiefs swept Detroit Catholic Central and split a home-and-home with Saginaw High, Michigan's all-time winningest prep basketball program, before entering tournament play. Bill Davis, wearing No. 24, became a longtime MHSAA basketball official. (Bill Davis collection.)

Here is the program from Pontiac High's important game with Flint Central's Indians on February 14, 1958. Every Pontiac High home game was broadcast from a tiny catbird seat in Pontiac's gym on WPHR. In 1994, the Chiefs joined city rival Northern in the Oakland Activities Association (OAA), where both schools played until their 2009 consolidation into a new Pontiac High, with new purple colors and Pheonix nickname at the former Northern High building. (Bill Davis collection.)

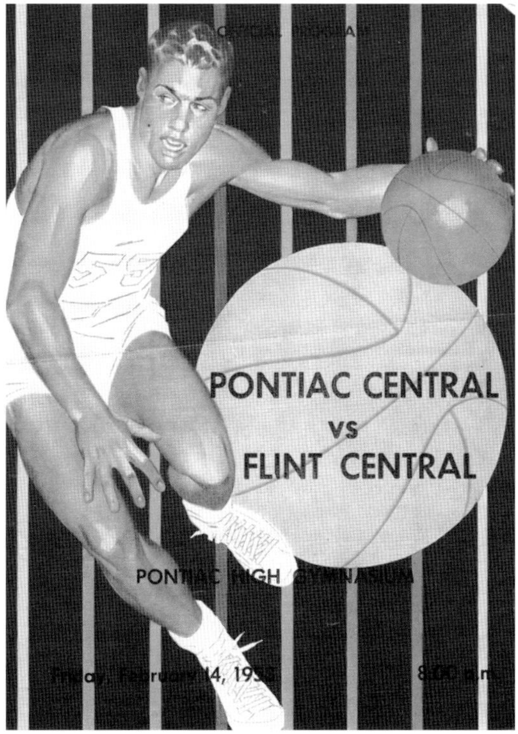

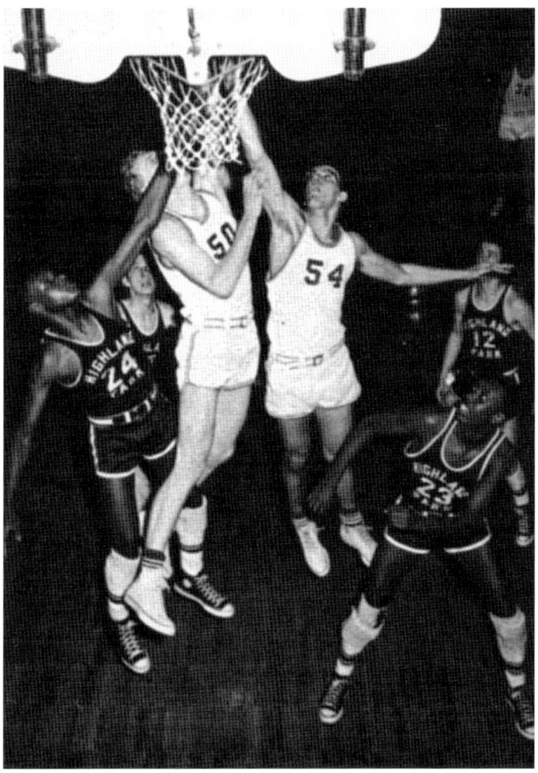

During the sock-hop era, schools were aligned in various leagues based on the friendships of school athletic directors. Here Royal Oak Dondero's Oaks, three years removed as Royal Oak High Acorns, battle the Polar Bears of Highland Park High. Tom Goodman (54) watches John Meadows (50) score, but it was Highland Park that netted a 66-59 win in this Border Cities League game from 1959–1960. Dondero closed in 2006. (Dondero *Oak*, 1960.)

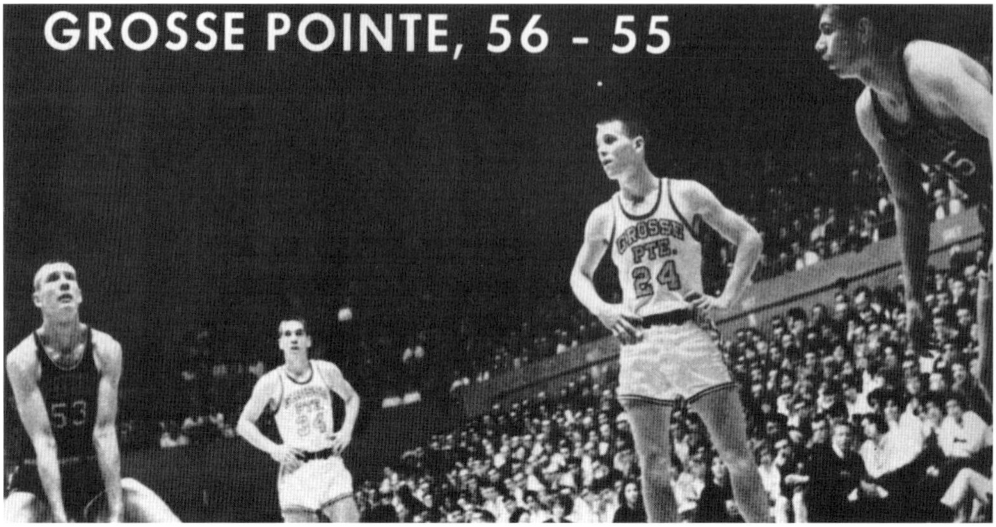

The undefeated Grosse Pointe Blue Devils were considered the best team in metro Detroit when the Pointers faced Ferndale in this 1963 Class A quarterfinal. Ferndale, however, was battle-tested, having outlasted Highland Park the previous Friday by a 43-42 count when Bruce Rodwan, shown here shooting free throws, scored a basket with 37 seconds to play. Jeff Hicks finished off Grosse Pointe with two clutch free throws, pushing Ferndale into the Class A semifinal versus PSL power Detroit Northwestern. (Ferndale Historical Museum/Ferndale *Talon*, 1963.)

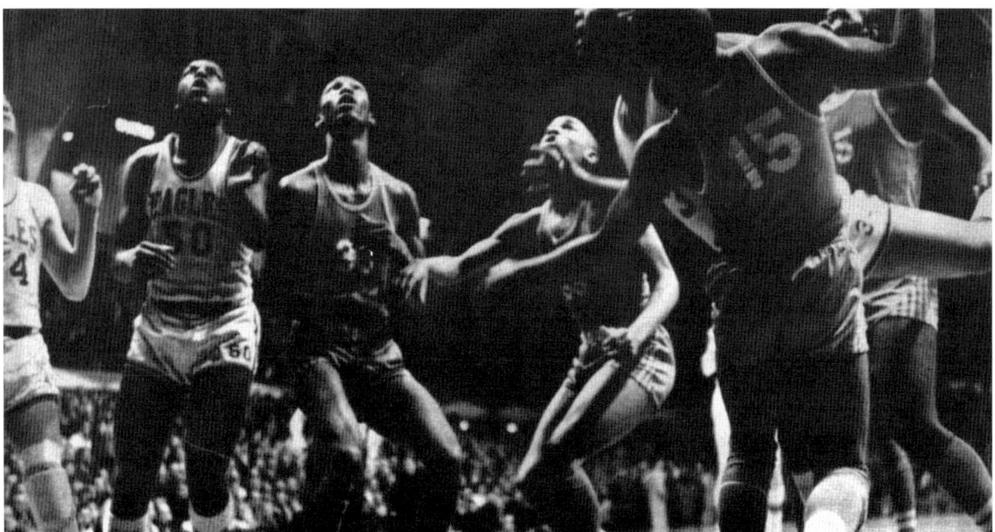

The Ferndale Eagles remembered Hal "Swami" Schram's prediction about the 1963 Class A semifinal in the *Detroit Free Press* on Thursday, March 21: "There is no school for (Detroit) Northwestern Friday . . . there will be no basketball on Saturday for Ferndale." Above is Bob Falardeau's late shot (obscured by No. 15) that downed the regular season PSL champion Northwestern by a 52-51 margin to advance to Saturday's Class A showdown with the Adrian Maples. (Ferndale Historical Museum/Ferndale *Talon*, 1963.)

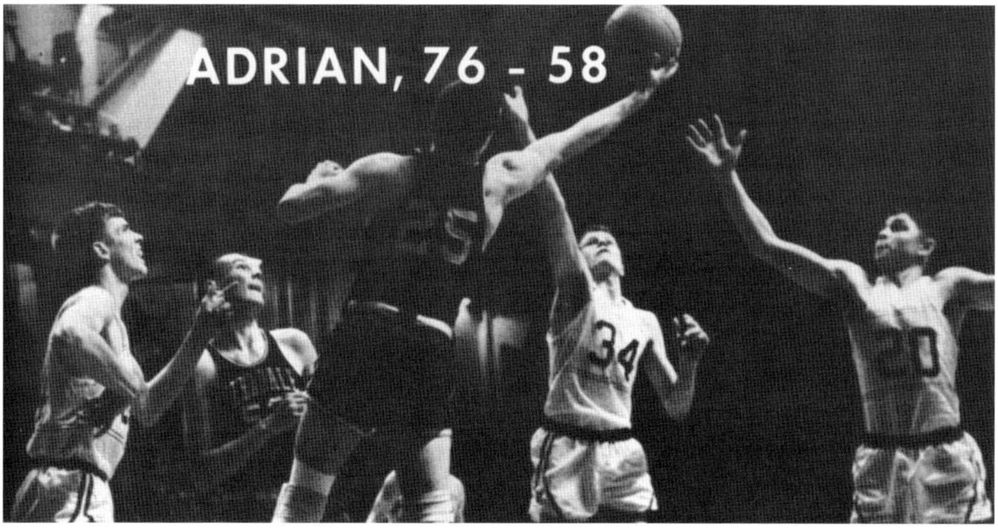

After three grueling gut-check wins worthy of the movie *Hoosiers*, Ferndale's Eagles soared above Adrian's Maples in a 76-58 blowout of the 1963 MHSAA Class A finals. Ferndale bruiser Bruce Rodwan, left of teammate Don Brooks (25), scored 25 points and pulled down an astounding 24 rebounds to earn a spot on the all-tournament first team, while Ferndale earned Oakland County's first Class A championship of the post–World War II era. MHSAA icon Vern Norris officiated Ferndale's title-winner. (Ferndale Historical Museum/Ferndale *Talon*, 1963.)

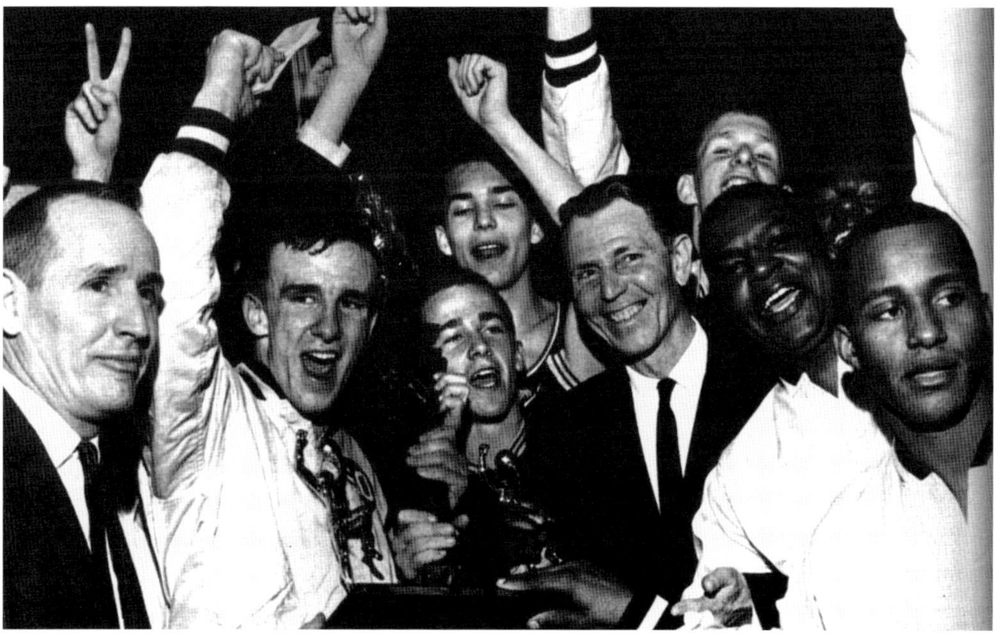

Ferndale stepped onto the hardwood pines of Michigan State University's Jenison Field House for the 1963 Class A finals an undefeated league champion, winners of 21 straight games. The Eagles stepped off as MHSAA champions after trouncing Adrian 76-58. The game was witnessed by over 12,000 fans and broadcast statewide. (Ferndale Historical Museum/Ferndale *Talon*, 1963.)

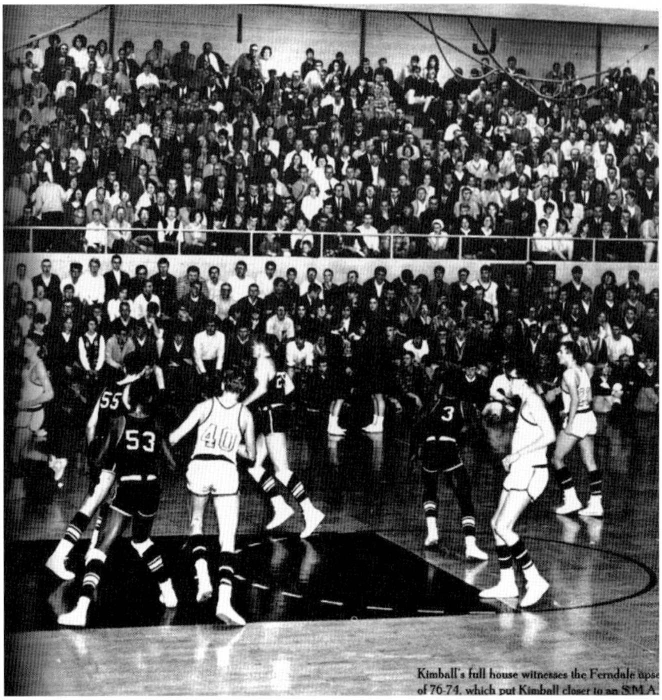

Royal Oak Kimball was a thorn in Ferndale's 1965 feathers. Kimball claimed the first SMA cage crown by upsetting No. 1 ranked Ferndale, 74-72. Kimball's best teams played in the 1960s and 1970s and were known for occasional upsets like this one and the 1963 district upset of Detroit Pershing. Despite marginal overall success, Kimball owned an 8-3 record versus Detroit's public league schools in MHSAA bracket play. (Royal Oak Kimball *Lancer*, 1965.)

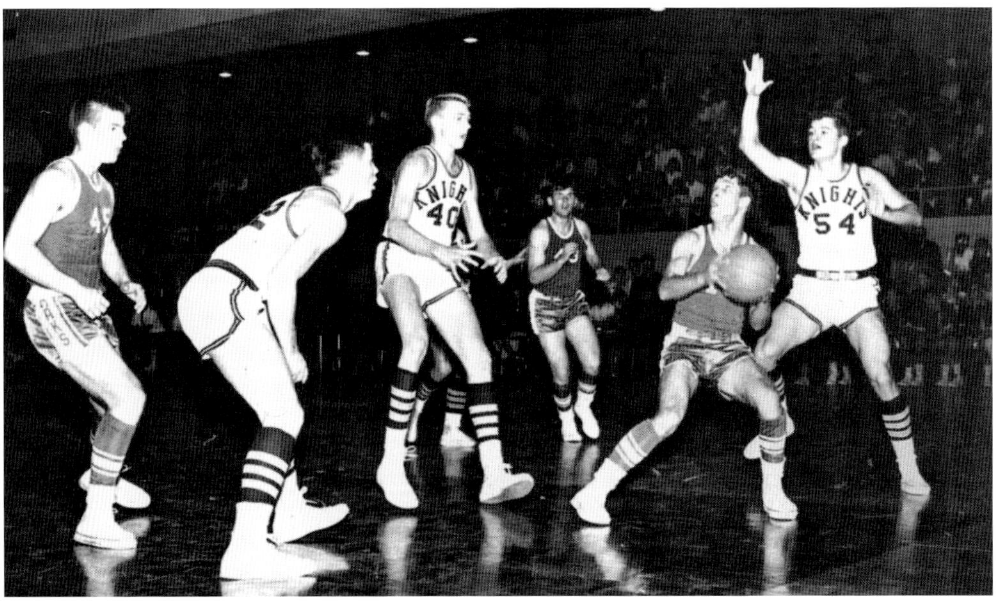

Royal Oak's Kimball-Dondero game was always intense, as Kimball's Roger Peltz (40) and Bob Weed (54) surround Dondero's Doug Goulait (42) in 1965. The south Oakland County rivals enjoyed an outstanding football game for 35 years, and three weeks after the climatic Oak Stump football game, basketball's season opener was played against each other. Packed gyms and crowd chants like Dondero's "Remember November!" and Kimball's "Just Like in Football!" were born from this scheduling. (Royal Oak Kimball *Lancer*, 1965.)

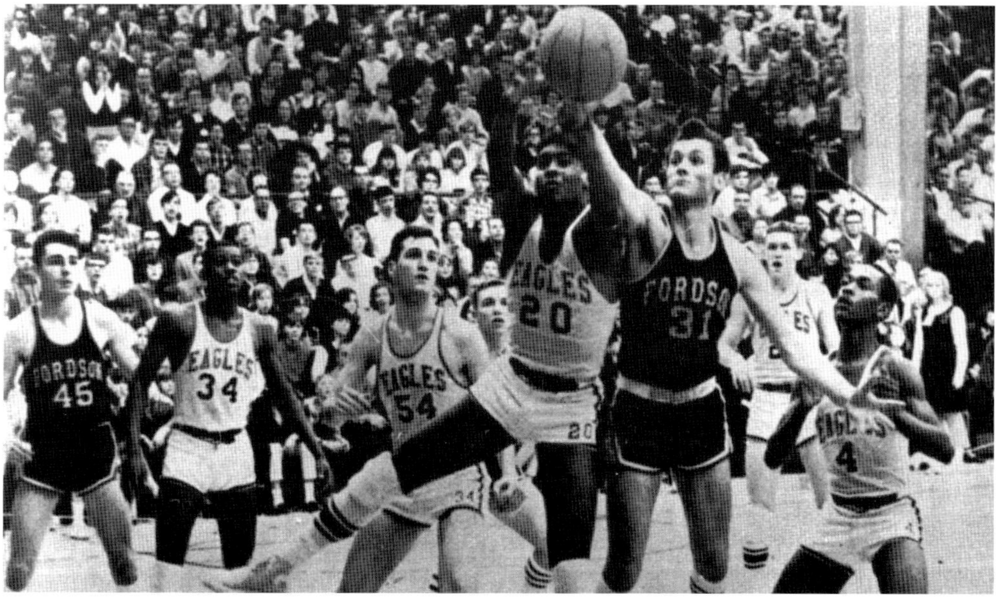

March's magic returned to Ferndale's Pinecrest Avenue campus in 1966. After defeating Oak Park, Southfield, and hated Hazel Park in the districts, Ferndale disposed of Birmingham Groves 61-57 and Pontiac Central 52-46 in the regionals. Ferndale trucked the Tractors of Dearborn Fordson in this quarterfinal, 72-59, and survived the East Detroit Shamrocks by a single point, 63-62 in the semifinals to earn a chance at a second Class A title in four years. (Ferndale *Talon*, 1966.)

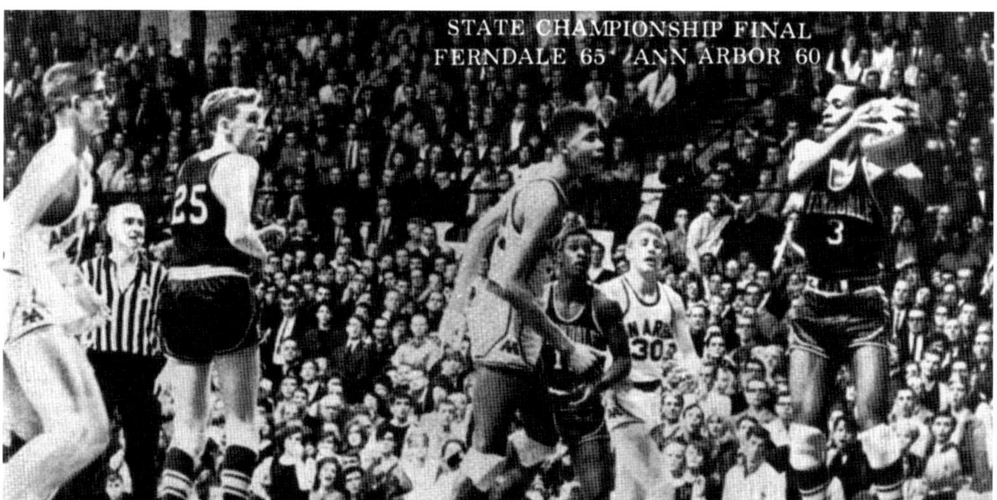

Ferndale's 1966 Class A title, the school's second in four years, did not come without a fight from Ann Arbor High's Pioneers. Down 44-37 in the final quarter, the Pioneers forced overtime but could not stop Sam Dunlap, wearing No. 3 in this photograph. Scoring six of his game-high 31 in the extra stanza, Dunlap helped deliver coach Roy Burkhart's second title in his 20th season at Ferndale. The Eagles went 9-1 in the SMA, reclaiming the SMA crown Kimball had upset Ferndale for the year previous. (Ferndale Historical Museum/Ferndale *Talon*, 1966.)

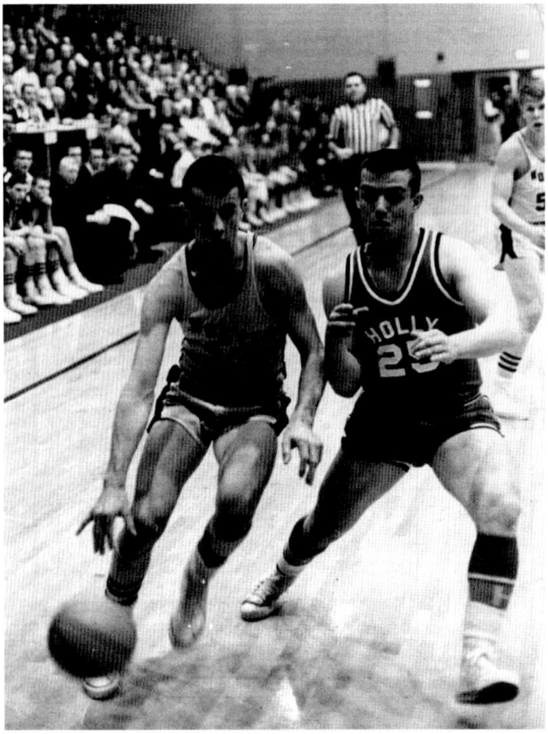

Dan Fife, varsity boys' coach at his alma mater since 1982, his familiar No. 33 revered for many years, had his jersey ultimately retired at Clarkston High. Fife scored 1,589 points for the Wolves, shown here in this 1954 game with a longtime rival, the Holly High Bronchos. Fife earned All-State honors as a prep player and later starred at the University of Michigan with Detroit Northern/Cass Tech star Bill Buntin. (The Oakland Press.)

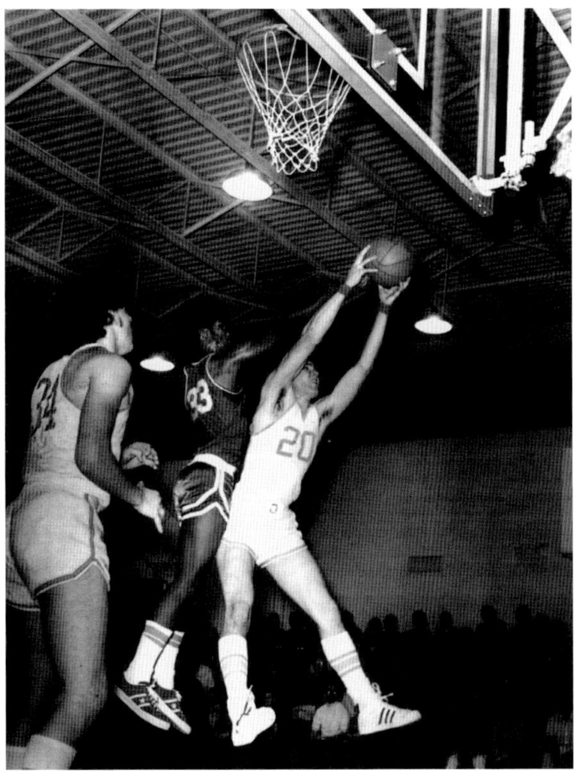

Affluent Oakland County has more than its share of private schools, two being Detroit Country Day and Bloomfield Hills Roeper, located just a few miles from one another. This is from a December 18, 1971, game at Country Day, as Country Day's Bob Zinkelm (20) wrestles a rebound away from Roeper's Jim Teasley (33). Yellowjacket Todd Rich (34) closes on the play. (Detroit Country Day.)

Lonnie Moncrief and Pontiac Northern's Huskies never failed to fight the good fight versus city rival Campanella Russell (44) and Pontiac Central's Chiefs. The two schools played in 33 MHSAA tournament games, including 18 district finals, often serving as the rubber match to a pair of thrilling regular-season meetings. Northern won 18 of the 33 tournament games; the two rivals split 18 district finals. (The Oakland Press/Ed Vanderworp.)

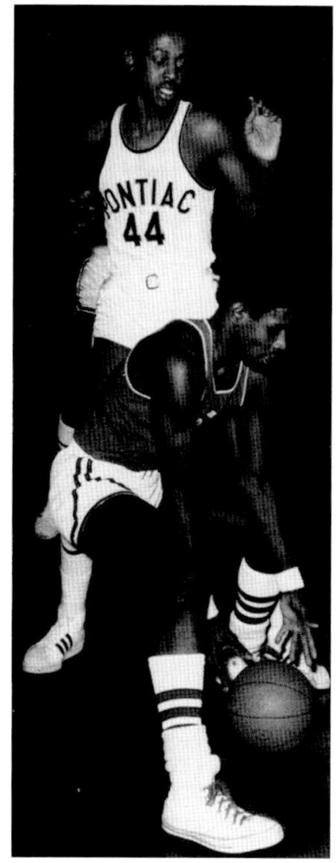

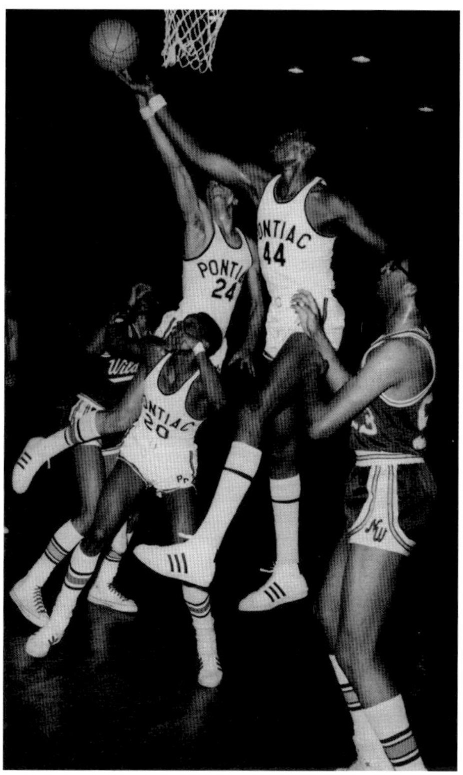

Campy Russell and the Pontiac Central Chiefs battle Saginaw Valley rival Flint Northwestern in this February 5, 1971, game. The Chiefs played in arguably the toughest league in Michigan, the vaunted Saginaw Valley Conference, better known as "the Valley" to basketball fans statewide, and earned a perfect 8-0 Valley ledger before winning the district, regional, and quarterfinal. A loss in the Class A semifinal to Detroit Kettering ended the Chiefs' season (The Oakland Press/Rolf Winter.)

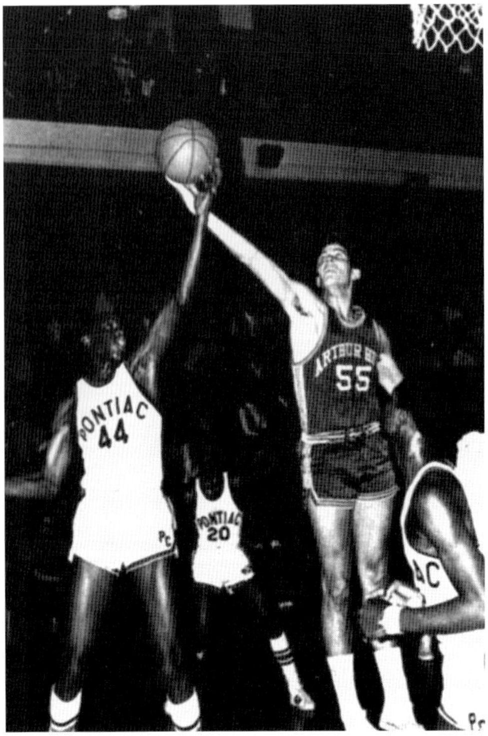

Playing in the toughest league in the entire state of Michigan paid dividends that resulted in every possible success—save for a state championship—for Pontiac Central's mighty Chiefs. Saginaw Valley Conference foe Robert Becker (55) and Saginaw Arthur Hill found their hands full with Campy Russell (44) in this 1970 game at Central. From 1950–1951 to 1980–1981, the Chiefs were an outstanding 215-96 in the Valley and 109-31 in MHSAA tournament play. (Pontiac Central *Quiver*, 1970.)

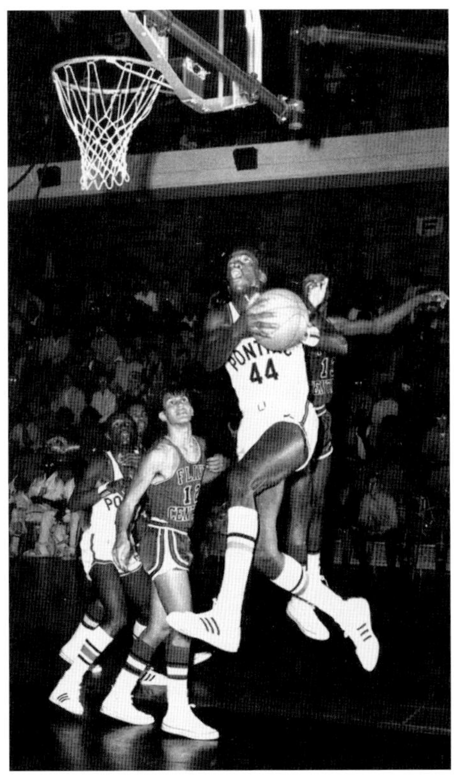

Pontiac Central star Campanella "Campy" Russell drives for two during this Saginaw Valley Conference game with Flint Central in 1971. Russell attended the University of Michigan, was an All-American, and played the majority of nine seasons with the NBA's Cleveland Cavaliers, where he currently works. (The Oakland Press/ Rolf Winter.)

Berkley's Bruce Flowers battles Royal Oak Kimball's Louis Gervais as referee Don Phillipe closes down in the 1975 district championship at sold-out Kimball High. During Berkley's magical 1975 campaign, the Bears marched to 25 straight wins, sweeping powerful Ferndale and beating archrival Kimball three times, surviving the Knights on this night, 61-59, including a controversial half-court shot attempt at the buzzer. Terry Duerod and Highland Park ended Berkley's dreams, defeating the Bears 84-59 in the Class A quarterfinals. (The Daily Tribune.)

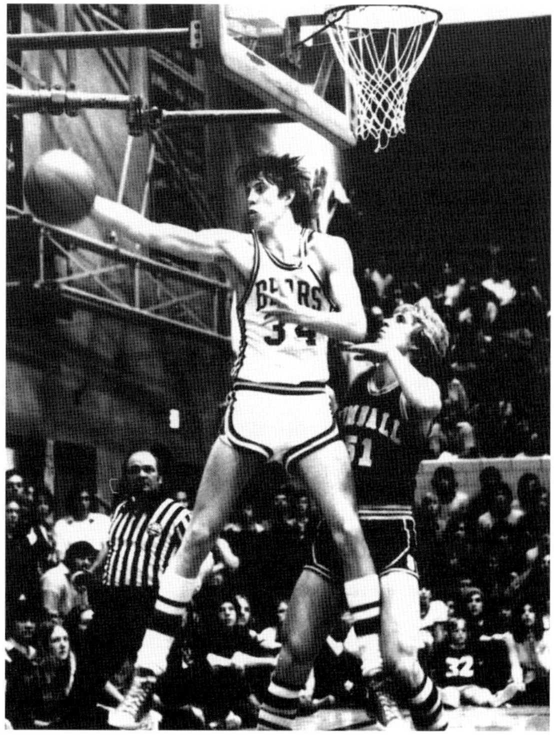

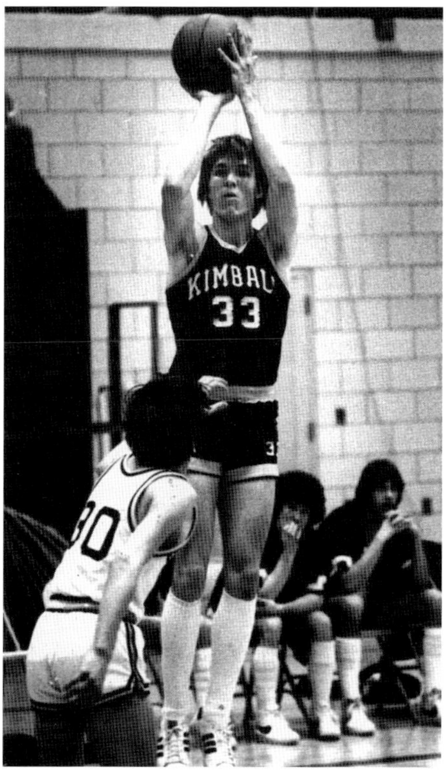

Royal Oak Kimball was a stubborn, gritty opponent in the 1970s with the Gervais brothers, Kevin Friesen, Ken Hallberg, and brothers John and Bruce Brownie, Bruce shown here shooting for two at Birmingham Seaholm in a 1975 game. Coach Chuck Jones guided Kimball to 51 wins in three years (1974–1977) and went to the 1978 quarterfinal before losing to coach Ralph Grubb and Pontiac Central. (The Daily Tribune.)

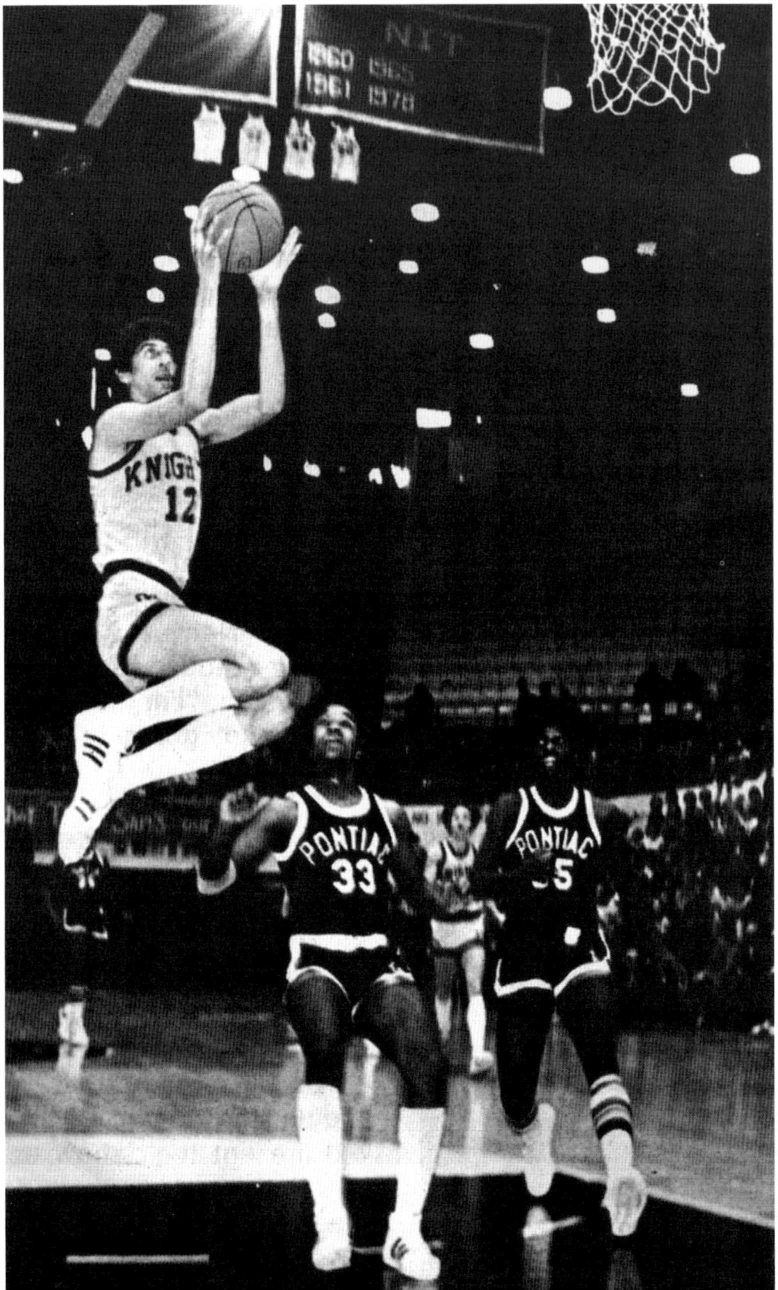

Royal Oak Kimball's only All-State player, John Gervais, scores two in a 1978 Class A quarterfinal loss to Pontiac Central, 54-46, at Calihan Hall. Kimball's playoff nemesis in the 1970s was Pontiac Central. Four times Kimball met Central in the MHSAA tourney; four times the Chiefs won, including three regional games and this quarterfinal. Central's tough luck was the state finals, where the Chiefs advanced to 10 Class A semifinals and 5 title games from 1960 to 1979 without winning a state title. (Kimball Herald/Chuck Jones collection.)

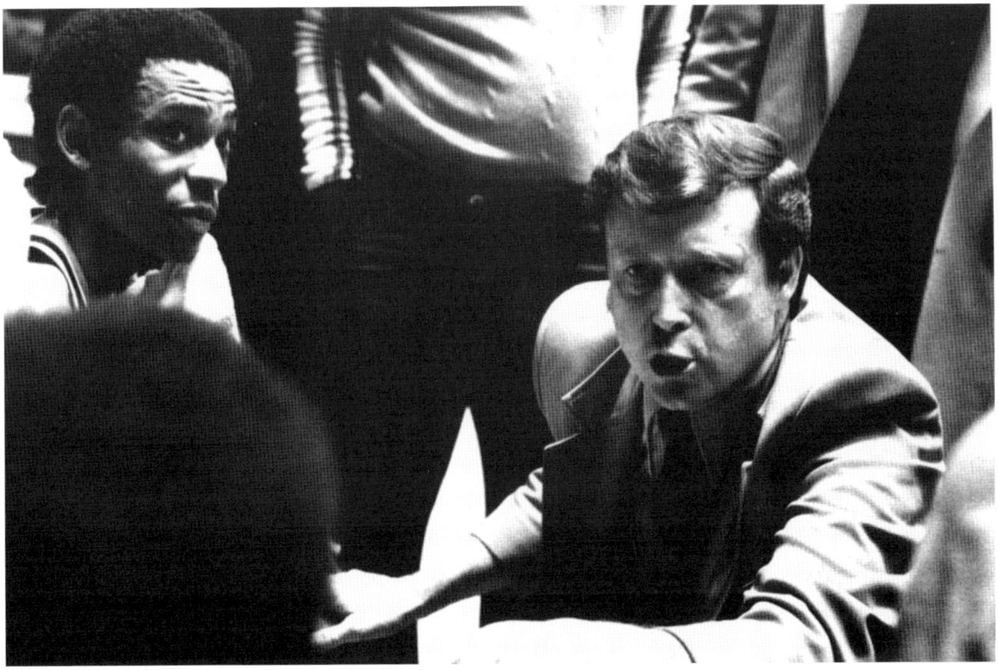

A valiant, final attempt to win the elusive state title that escaped Pontiac's favorite sons came in the 1979 Class A finals, a 72-64 loss to Detroit Mackenzie's Stags. One can see the Central player to the left of coach Ralph Grubb gazing at the scoreboard, the potential loss staring the Chiefs in the face late in the fourth quarter. (The Oakland Press/Rolf Winter.)

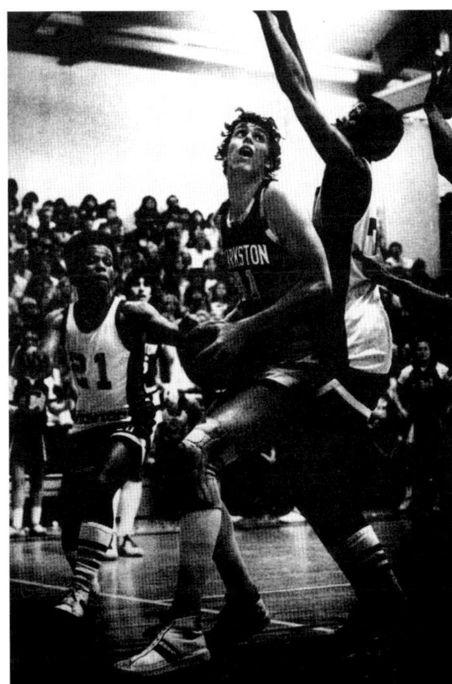

The year 1980 was Clarkston High's most successful tournament run until 2009, a march that was officially christened with this 80-45 victory over Pontiac Northern in the district final. Clarkston center Tim McCormick scores two in a season that earned McCormick an All-State appointment and inclusion on nearly every county and regional first team. (The Oakland Press/Tim Thompson.)

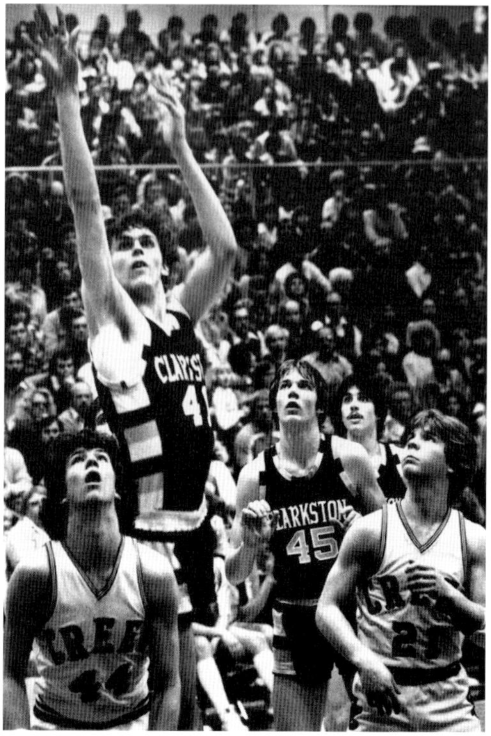

This 73-56 Clarkston victory over Swartz Creek High in front of a sold-out crowd in the 1980 regional triggered tournament fever. The Wolves advanced to the Class A quarterfinals and defeated Saginaw High's Trojans before bowing to Highland Park High, 51-50, in the Class A semifinals at Jenison Field House. (The Oakland Press/ Tim Thompson.)

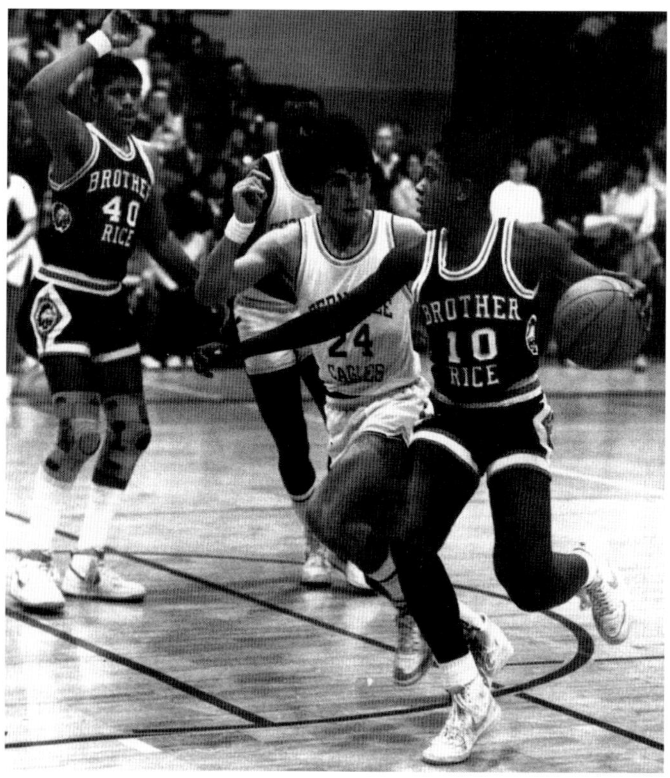

Rice forward Ray Wheelock (40) and B. J. Armstrong battle Ferndale's Mike Hammerle (24) in a 1984 regional final won by Rice, 61-36. Rice and Ferndale would meet in four regionals in eight seasons in the 1980s, including three finals. The Warriors advanced to the state semifinal before losing to Detroit Southwestern. Ferndale would avenge this loss in the regional final of 1985 by a 43-40 count. (The Oakland Press/Rolf Winter.)

Chris Webber and Detroit Country Day advance to the Class B title game of 1990 at the Palace of Auburn Hills with this 70-50 win over Grand Rapids Northview. Webber and his Yellow Jackets won the Class C title in 1989 and captured the Class B title the day after this photograph was taken. During Webber's four years at the Beverly Hills school, only Detroit St. Martin De Porres defeated Country Day in MHSAA tournament play. (The Oakland Press/Mitchell.)

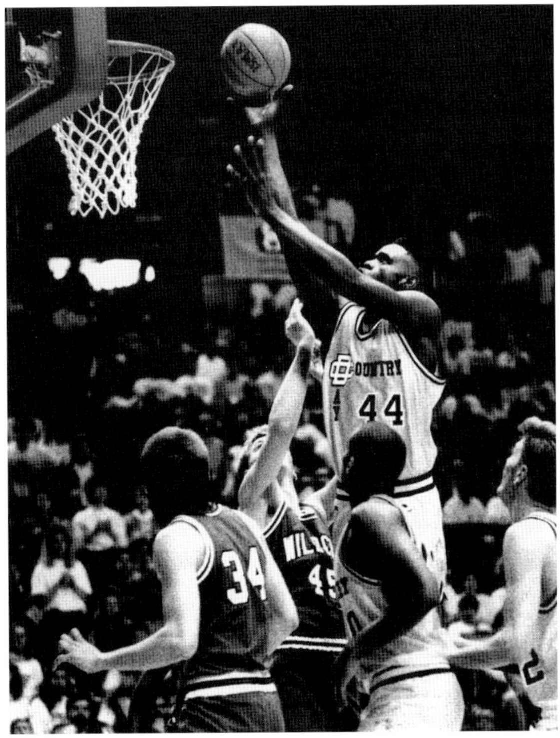

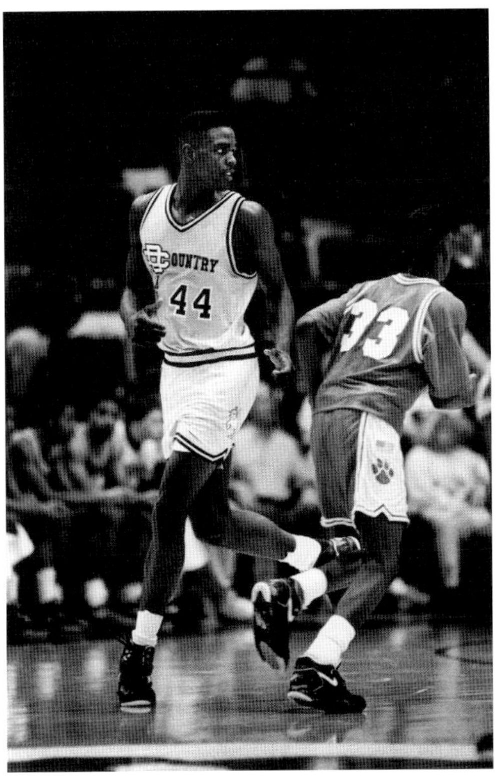

Michigan's Mr. Basketball winner from 1991 was perhaps the most ballyhooed player in state prep basketball history. This is Webber leading Detroit Country Day to a 78-44 win over outmanned Bridgeport High in the 1991 MHSAA Class B semifinal. Webber's No. 44 was the first number retired in Country Day history. (The Oakland Press.)

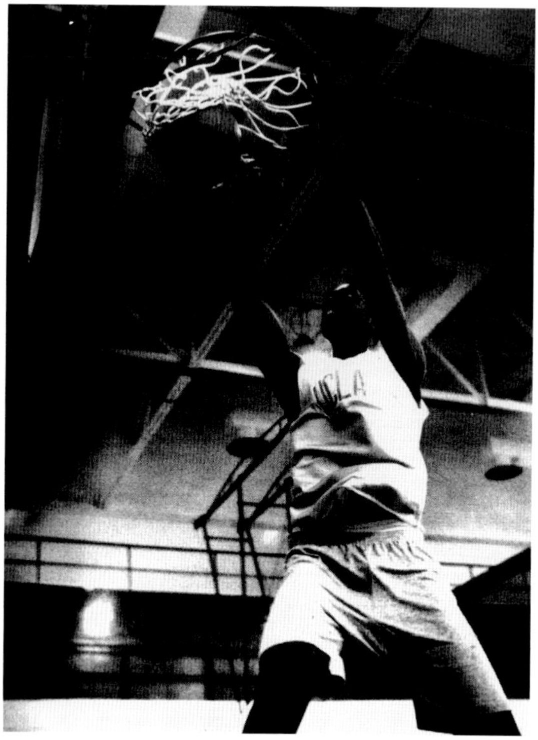

Royal Oak Dondero coach Jerry Barich did not minimize Theron Wilson's impact on his Oaks: "He's the greatest Dondero player ever and the only first team All-State player in school history." A Detroit King transfer, Wilson led Dondero to a Metro Suburban title (1989–1990). Wilson played for Eastern Michigan before knee injuries curtailed his professional basketball career. (The Daily Tribune.)

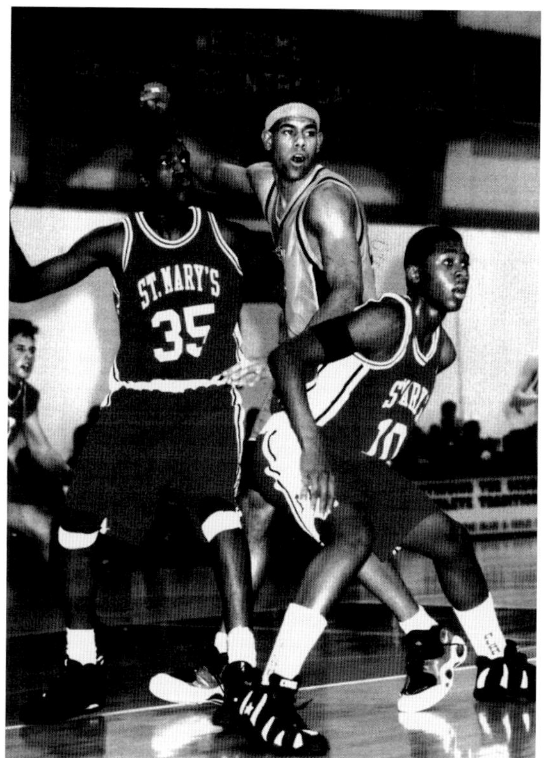

Detroit Country Day's Shane Battier battles for position versus Orchard Lake St. Mary's defenders Juan Pegues (35) and Brad Mitchell (10) in this 1996 MHSAA district game won by Detroit Country Day, 70-59. Battier matched fellow Country Day alumnus Chris Webber by winning a Mr. Basketball award (1997) and led the Yellow Jackets to three MHSAA titles from 1995 to 1997. Battier won the John R. Wooden Award, four ACC regular season titles, and the 2001 championship at Duke University. Battier has played eight NBA seasons since 2001. (The Oakland Press.)

3

Wayne County

The glare emanating from the trophy cases in the city of Detroit's public high schools and River Rouge High might lead one to believe Wayne County's basketball tradition is only found in the county's largest city, Detroit, and its most industrial city, River Rouge. While it is true the incredible legacy in Detroit's public school leagues and the dynasty at River Rouge high school is unrivaled statewide, cities like Dearborn, Livonia, Grosse Pointe, and a select number of Catholic schools have added to the luster that makes up the county's considerable hardwood history.

In the well-to-do lakeside community of Grosse Pointe, the annual North-South game is one that still provides a sold-out crowd and the school spirit of two generations ago. The gymnasium at South High, formerly Grosse Pointe High, has hosted Highland Park, Fordson, Monroe, and Royal Oak Dondero in addition to Dr. Martin Luther King and a nationally televised Detroit Pistons playoff game in 1960. Dearborn's football fever easily transfers to the hardwood. Dearborn Fordson's 1953 Class A title ensured the Tractors remained a red-letter game before winter's cabin fever ended. Dearborn High and newly opened Edsel Ford High combined with Fordson to make the late 1950s and 1960s memorable. Even today, the public schools in Dearborn command a crowd when the intercity rivals play.

In Livonia, city schools Franklin and Stevenson were annual contenders in regional play in the 1970s, Birmingham's Brother Rice and Pontiac Central often the roadblock to title dreams. While annual tournament success has been limited to regional rounds with few exceptions in Livonia, their yearly game and the addition of Livonia Churchill remain dates to circle. Detroit Catholic Central's time on Breakfast Drive in Redford added to the Livonia lore of rival's bragging rights. The Shamrocks often paired with their Livonia neighbors until they moved to Oakland County a few years ago.

Finally, in several downriver communities, basketball can seem like an afterthought compared to the passion that hockey provides, but do not say that on the island community of Grosse Ile, in Allen Park High, or at neighboring Cabrini. It is the same at Riverview High and neighboring Gabriel Richard and a handful of other industrial towns like Melvindale and Southgate populating the shadows of Ford Motor Company.

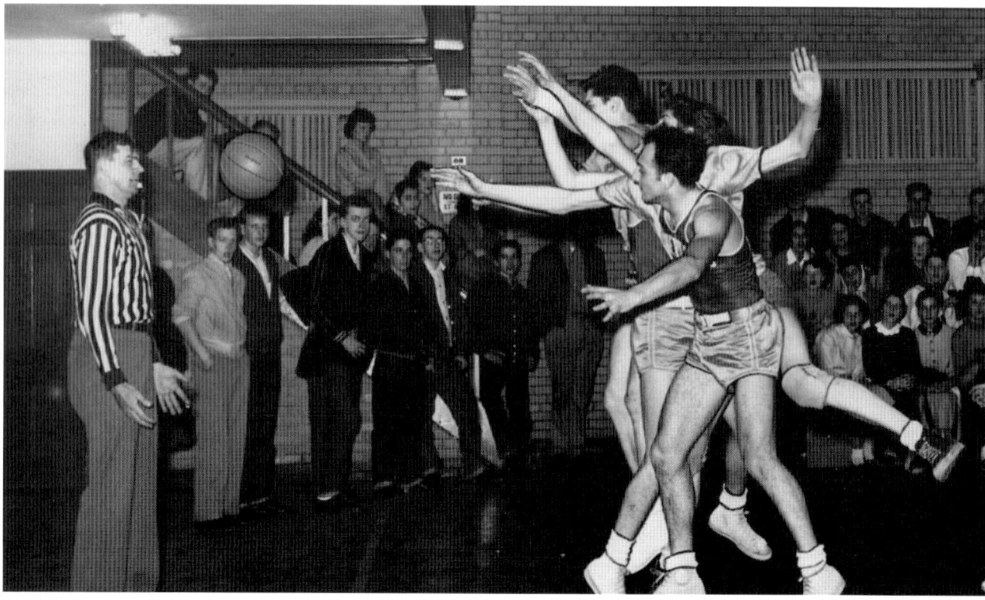

Referee Casimir "Casey" Lopata will decide who touched the ball last in this game between Dearborn High and Detroit's now-closed Holy Redeemer High. As photographer John Kenny from the Michigan Catholic Company wrote in his cutline, "Either way he decides, he'll make enemies." (Stan Lopata family collection/John Kenny.)

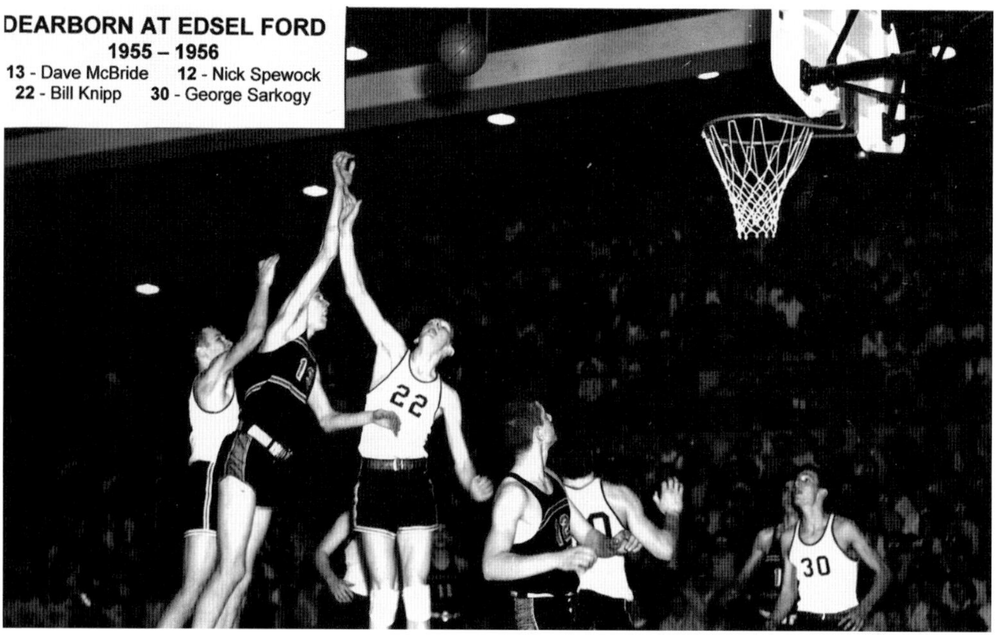

Dearborn High's first-ever visit to rival Dearborn Edsel Ford in 1956 attracted a huge throng, a norm in the 1950s sock-hop era. Dearborn's love-to-hate relationship with longtime adversary Dearborn Fordson High made Edsel's emergence a welcome respite for the Pioneers. Dearborn earned a 6-2 ledger in their first season in the newly formed Huron-Rouge League. (Patrick Stagg collection.)

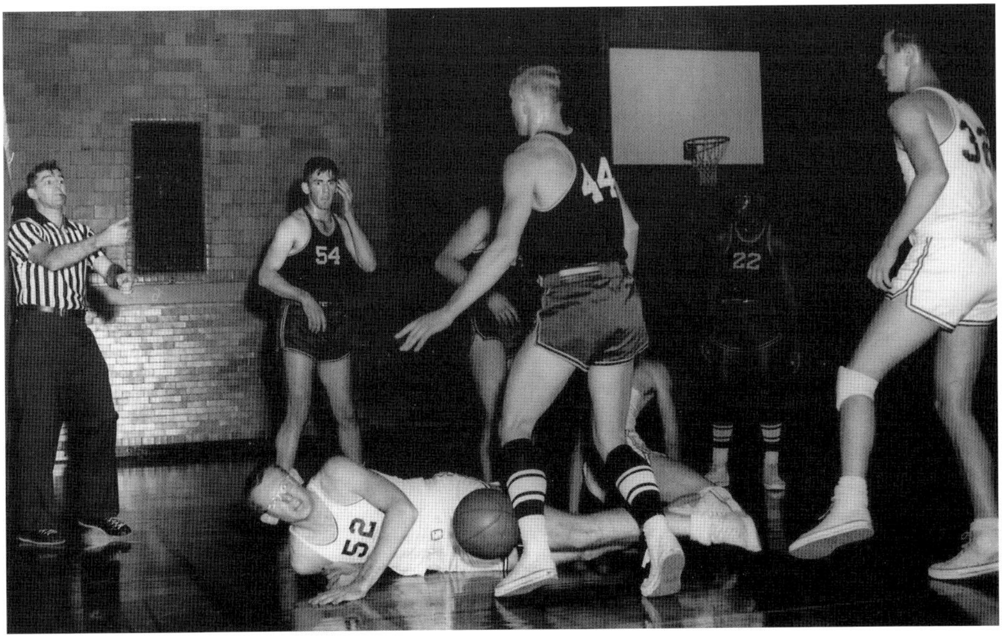

"No I didn't!" was the response to referee Casey Lopata's whistle and bird dog mechanic, which imparted the message, "Oh yes you did!" after watching an Edsel Ford bruiser crash to the floor with a helpful push from his defender from Dearborn Fordson High. (Patrick Stagg collection.)

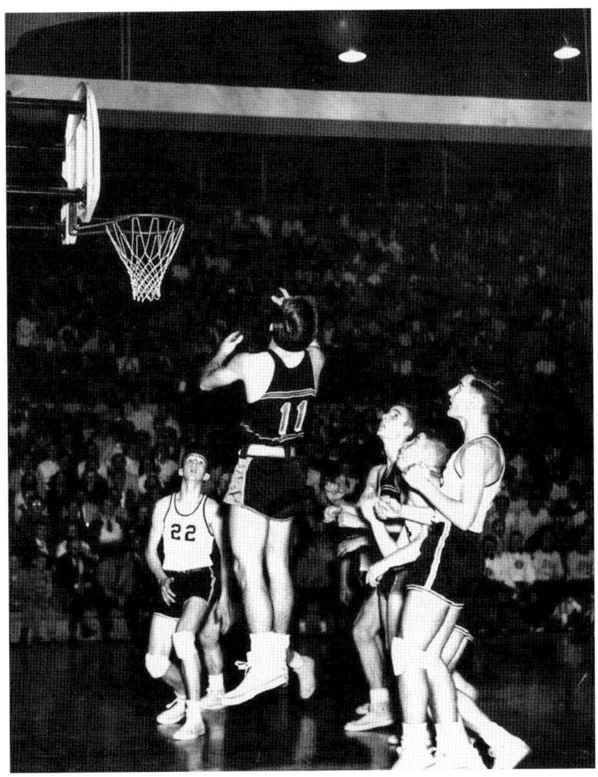

Alex Tannas (11) leaps for visiting Dearborn High in a 1956 visit to a sold-out Dearborn Edsel Ford. Teammates Bill Knipp (22), Bob Winkworth (25), and Don Kaminski congregate around the basket to await the try's result. In the 1950s, Dearborn High often battled for supremacy of the now-defunct Twin Valley Conference with city rival Dearborn Fordson, who was a contender in the former Border Cities League. Edsel's Thunderbirds, playing their first season ever in 1956, was a member of the Huron-Rouge, also since shuttered. (Patrick Stagg collection.)

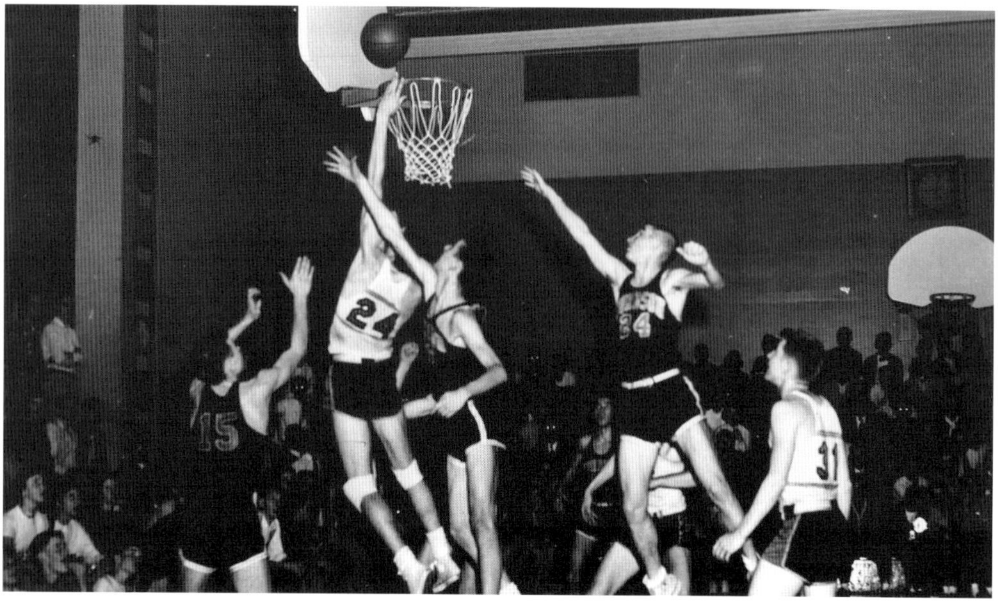

Dearborn's Bob Dunlap (24) drives for two as Fordson's No. 24 and an unidentified teammate are rendered helpless to defend. Fordson, led by coach Jim Vanderhull, won the 1953 Class A title by defeating Lansing Sexton, 53-47. (Patrick Stagg collection.)

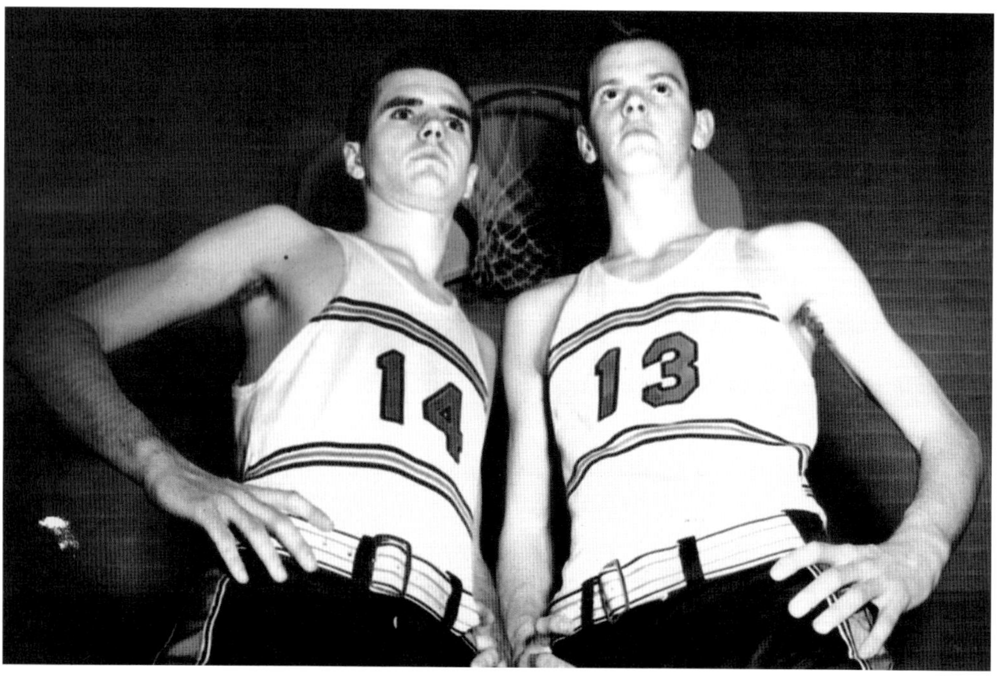

Dearborn captains Paul Kinder (14) and David McBride pose before the start of the 1955–1956 season, the school's first season in the now-defunct Huron–Rouge Conference. The Pioneers went on to earn a 6-2 mark in their new league, but success in the MHSAA tournament escaped the Pioneers, who dropped the district opener to rival Dearborn Fordson, 67-50. (Patrick Stagg collection.)

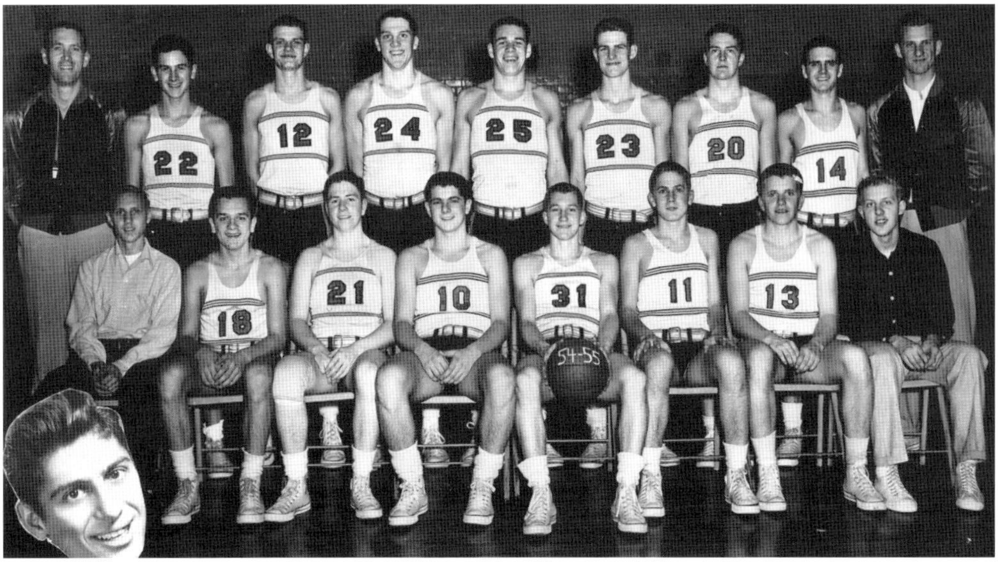

Dearborn's 1954–1955 team went 14-2 and captured the Twin-Valley Conference championship. The orange and black was coached by Carl Flegle, who guided these Pioneers to the district title before dropping a regional matchup with Detroit Catholic Central by a 54-49 count. The inserted headshot is identified as Paul Kachaturoff. (Patrick Stagg collection.)

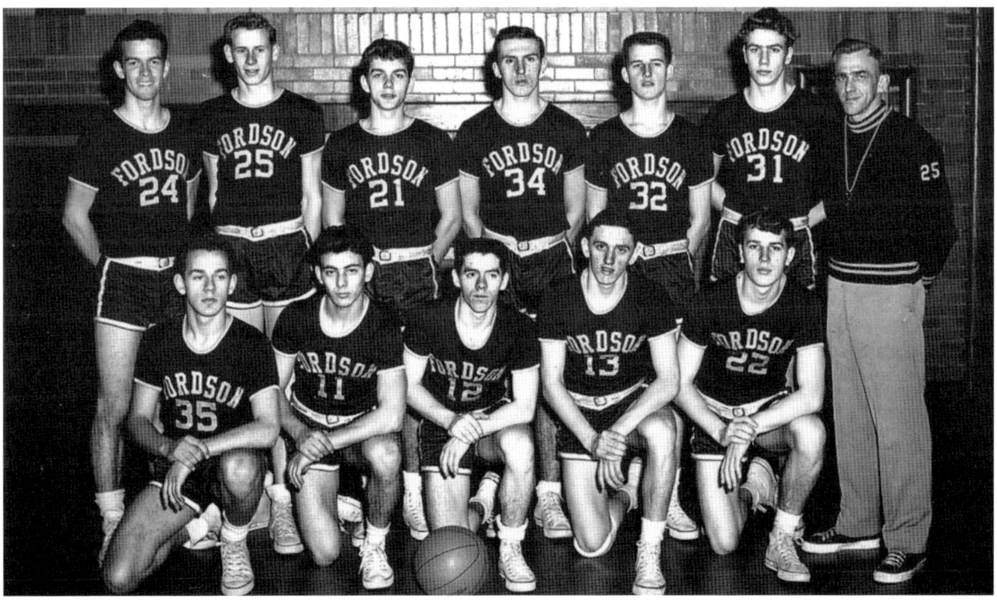

The 1951 Tractors of Dearborn Fordson High had a fruitful season, going 7-3 in the old Border Cities League and winning the district title. After besting Wayne Memorial by 12, the Tractors were felled by an ironic city rival, Dearborn Ford Trade, 48-46. The Craftsman would defeat Wyandotte High the following Friday in the regional final, 41-22, before bowing to Lansing Eastern in the quarterfinal. Ford Trade, along with Dearborn Edison High, closed that spring. (Arella Studios.)

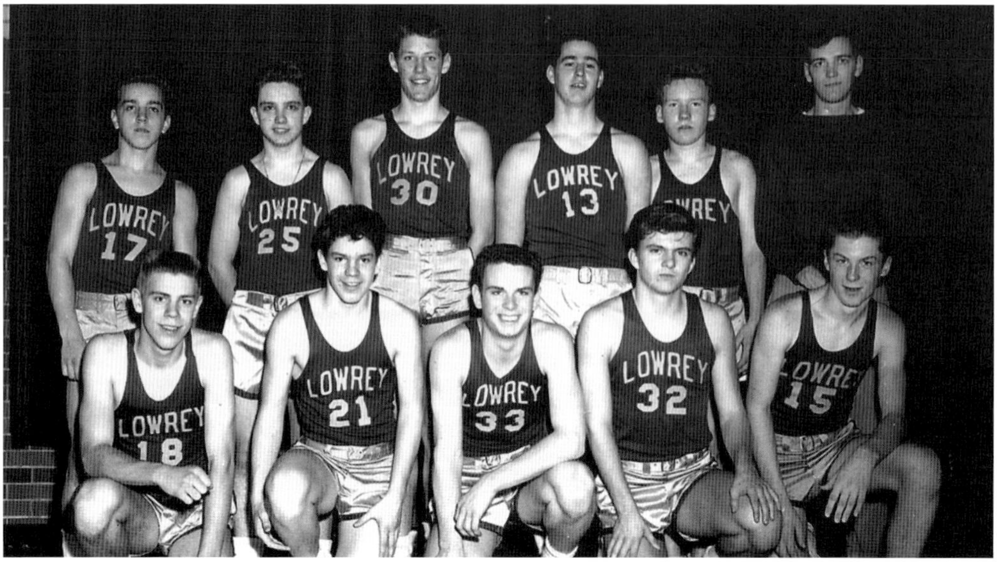

Another Dearborn school of years past is Dearborn Lowrey. Its best season might have come in 1966–1967, when the Polar Bears earned a 10-4 mark in the Tri-River Conference, a district title with victories over city rivals Dearborn and Edsel Ford and a gritty effort in defeat to Detroit Catholic Central in the regional. This is the 1958–1959 squad that failed to earn a win in eight Twin-Valley Conference games. (Patrick Stagg collection.)

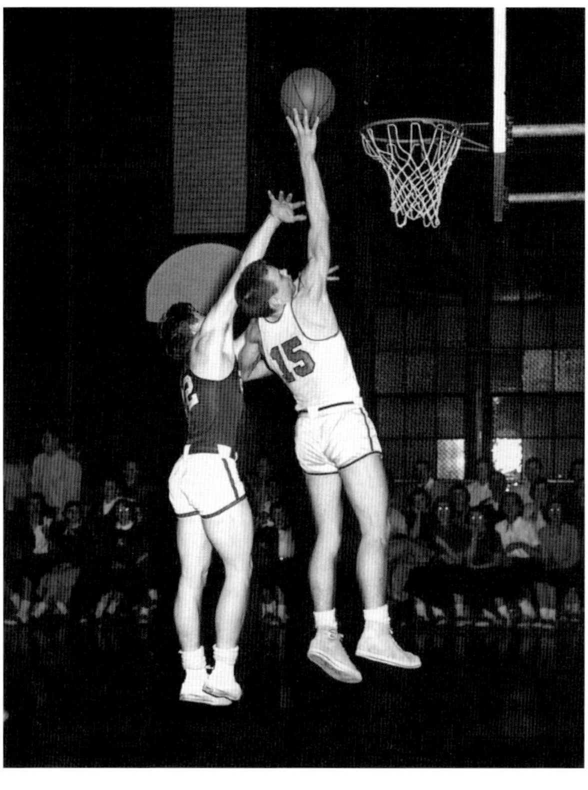

Edsel's visit to Huron-Rouge rival Dearborn High in 1958 was trademarked by the usual passion that was a staple of prep sports in the 1950s and 1960s. A Dearborn guard (15) drives as Edsel Ford's unidentified defender tries in vain to stop the score. Neither school enjoyed a long run in the MHSAA tournament of 1958. (Arella Studios.)

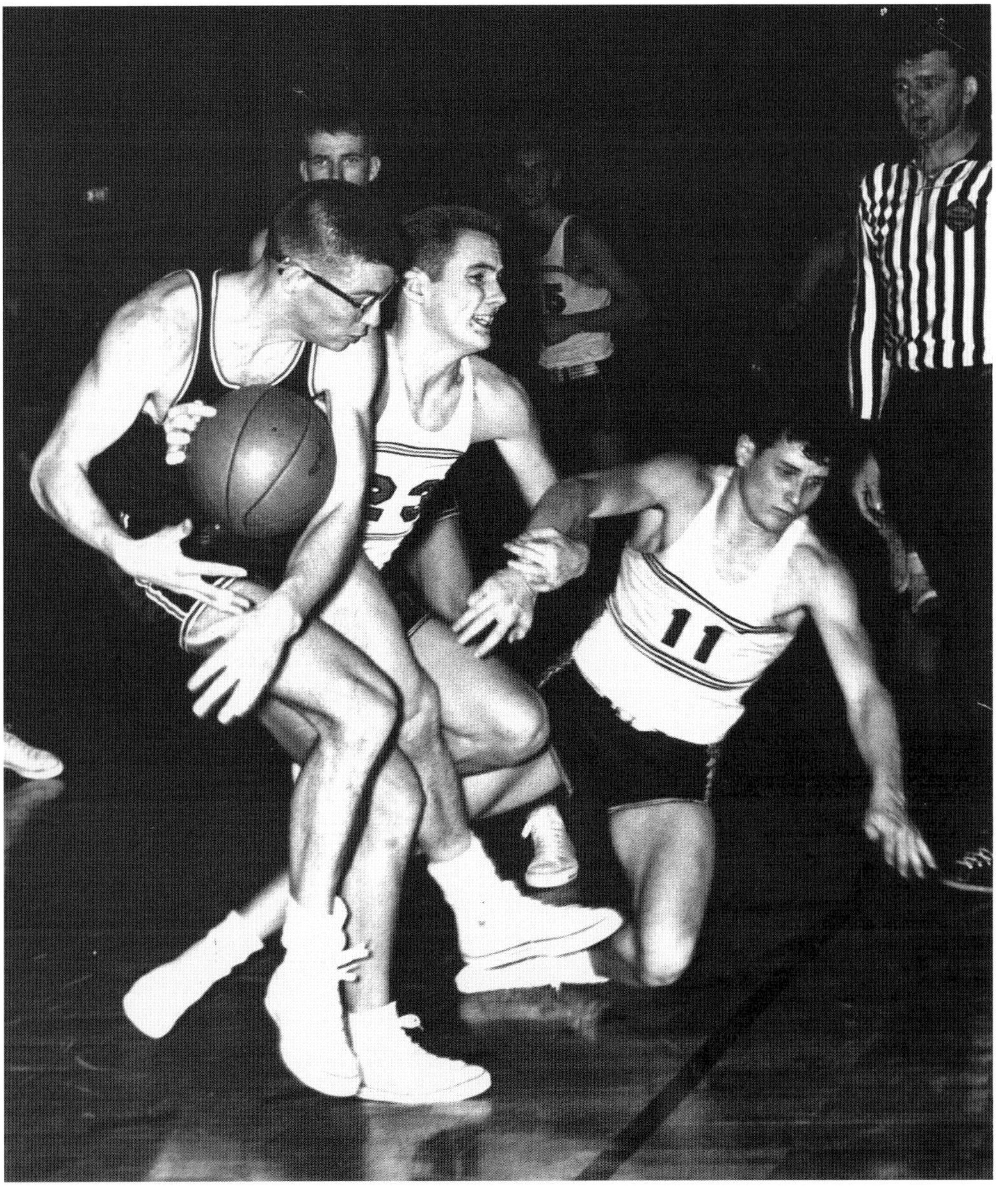

Dearborn Pioneer Howie Winkworth (23) reaches for the ball as John Christianson (11) is floor-bound in Dearborn's 1958 battle with new rival Dearborn Edsel Ford. Winkworth's brother, Bob (25) can be seen in the background as Casey Lopata (right) officiates. Both Dearborn and Edsel Ford were eliminated in the state tournament by Melvindale. Edsel dropped the district final to the Cardinals, who bested Dearborn in the first round of the regional. (Patrick Stagg collection.)

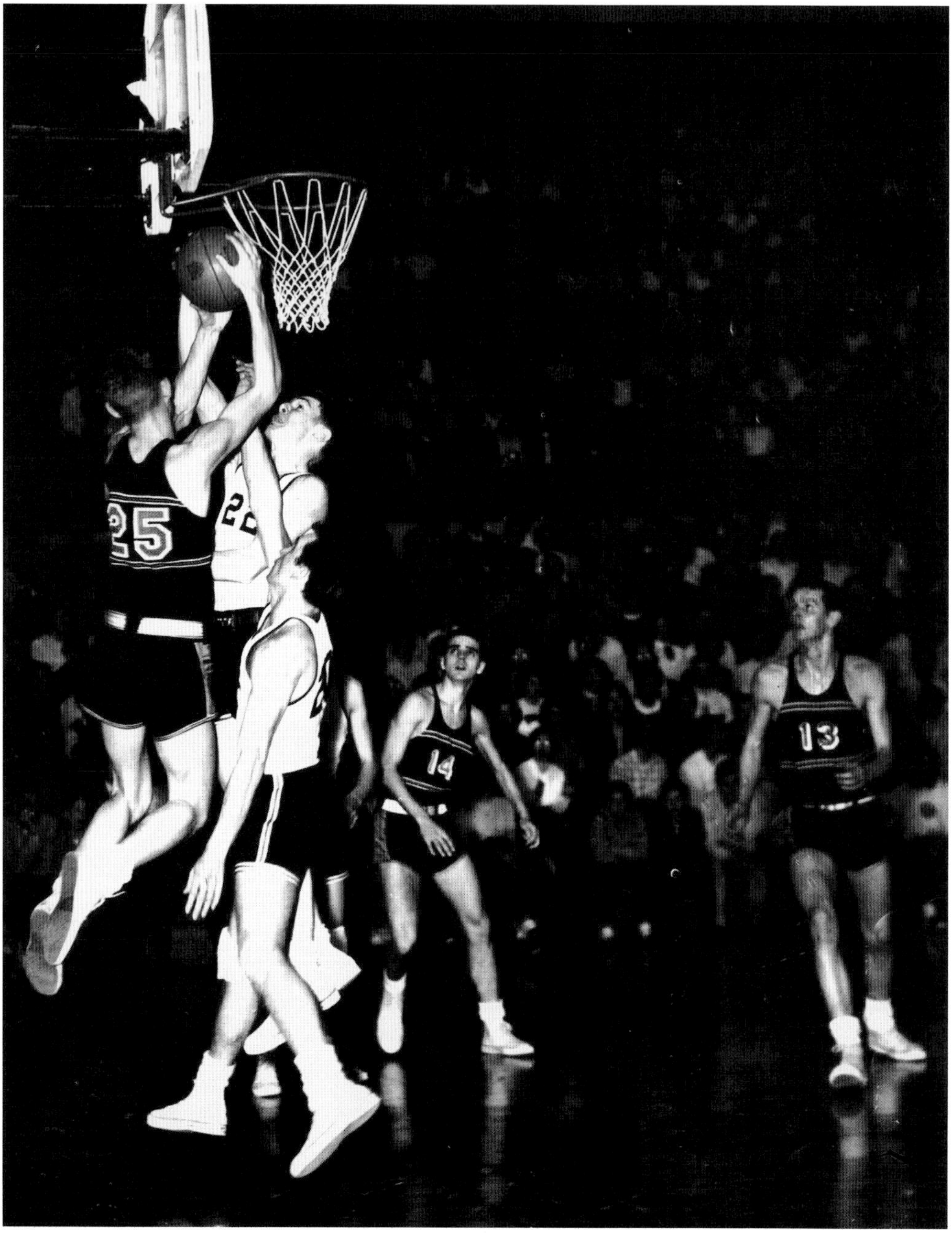

Outnumbered but undeterred was Dearborn Edsel Ford's rally cry in the early years of the school's existence. Here Pioneer Bob Winkworth (25) attacks the basket as Thunderbird Bill Knipp (22) blocks his shot. Dearborn captains Dave McBride (13) and Paul Kinder (14) watch as an unidentified Edsel Ford player helps in the 1958 battle of city rivals. The gym was sold-out and potential fans were turned away by the Dearborn fire marshal. (Patrick Stagg collection.)

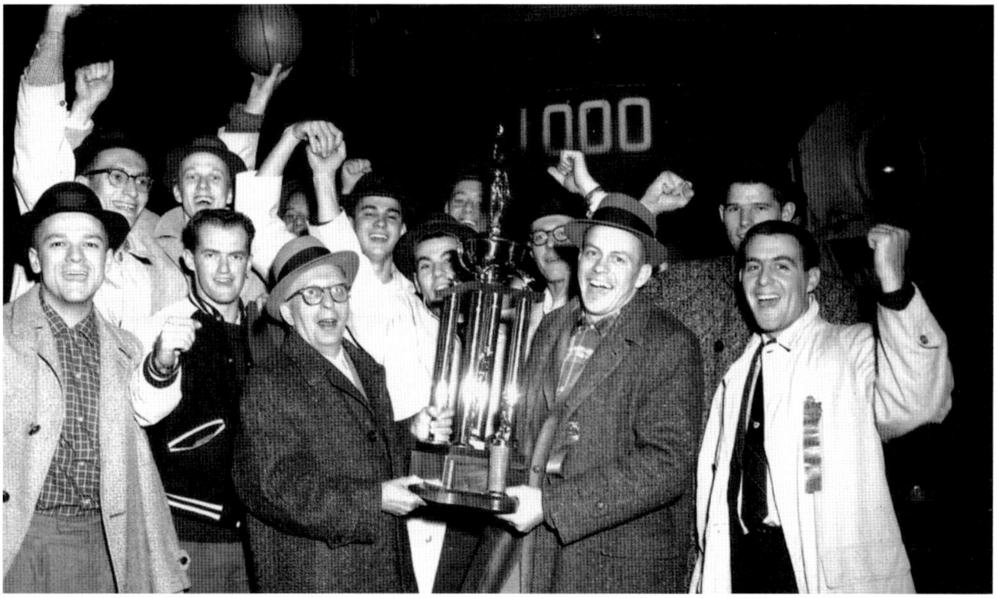

Henry Ford Community College's teams in the 1950s were stocked for the most part by players from the local Dearborn high schools. Here Henry Ford's team is met with a grand welcome after garnering a championship either at the state or national level. This scene at the now-abandoned Michigan Central Depot, located at Michigan Avenue and Vernor, is just minutes from the Dearborn border of Detroit. (Arella Studios.)

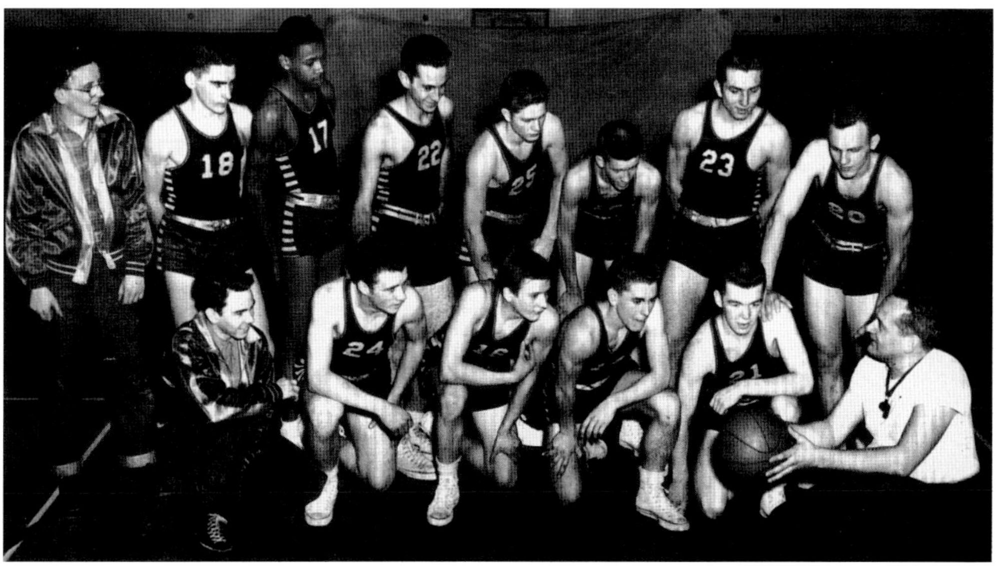

Henry Ford himself chartered Dearborn Ford Trade High. Here the Craftsmen pose as a team in 1951, the season Ford Trade nipped city rival Fordson 48-46 in the regional semifinal and crushed Wyandotte Roosevelt 41-22 to advance to the Class A quarterfinal. Lansing Eastern's Quakers delivered a 58-38 defeat to Ford Trade. In 1952, the Craftsmen dropped the regional final 54-47 to Detroit Catholic Central and closed the following spring. (Patrick Stagg collection.)

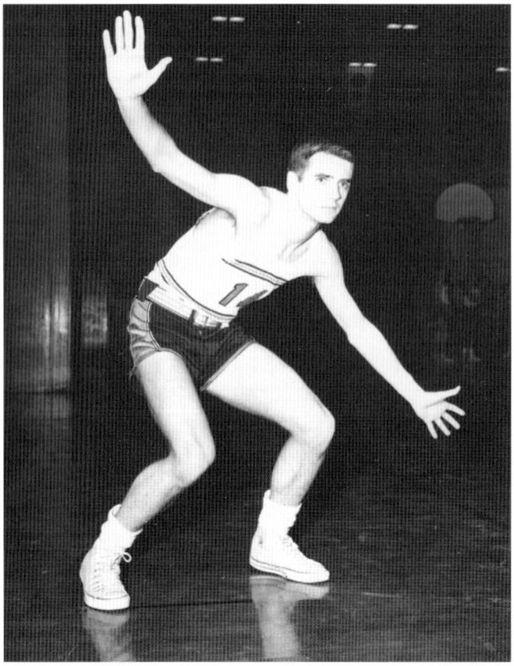

Paul Kinder was a Dearborn High captain in the 1955–1956 season, but his claim to fame would come after he traded these horizontal stripes of his players' uniform for the vertical stripes of an official. An accomplished official in basketball, softball, baseball, and football, Kinder lived in Oakland County and worked finals in softball and basketball before retiring from prep and collegiate officiating. (Patrick Stagg collection.)

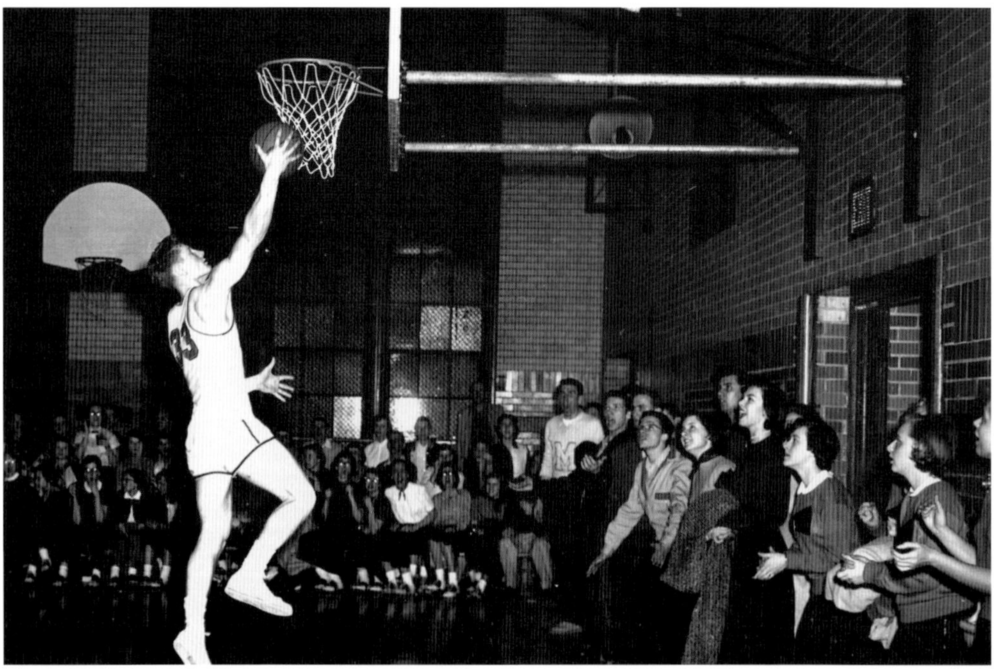

This unidentified game from the 1950s at one of the many high schools in Dearborn illustrates the passion local communities had for prep basketball in post–World War II Detroit and the surrounding metropolitan areas. Public schools Dearborn, Edsel Ford, and Fordson join Dearborn's Divine Child as survivors of an era when 10 different public, private, and trade schools operated in Dearborn proper. (Patrick Stagg collection.)

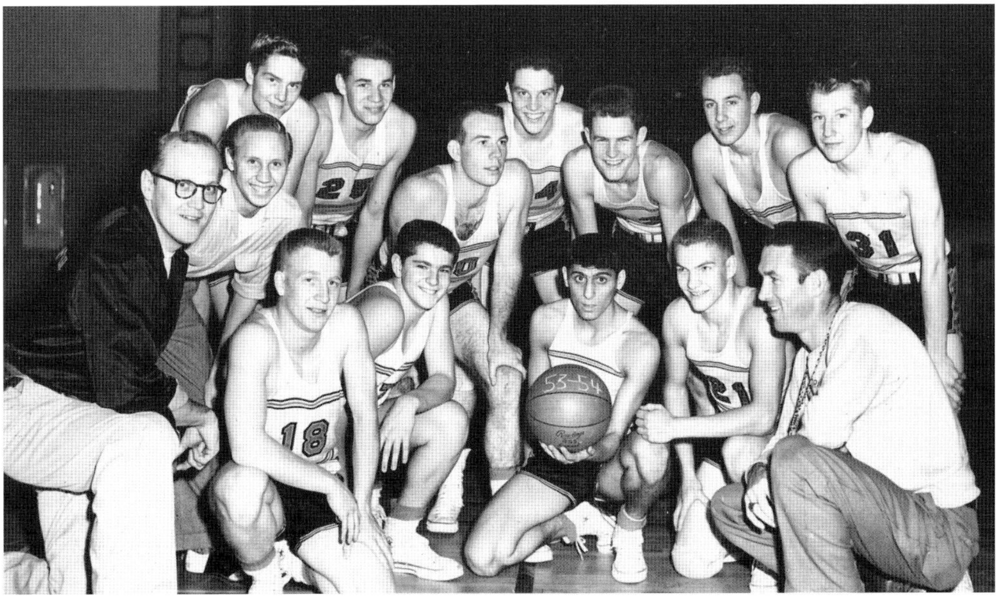

Dearborn High's 6-4 mark in the Twin-Valley Conference for 1953–1954 also garnered a district championship for the Pioneers before falling in the regional to Detroit St. Joseph High, 47-45. St. Joe's would defeat fellow Detroit Catholic Leaguer Detroit St. Anthony 35-34 before falling to Dearborn archrival and defending Class A champion Dearborn Fordson, 61-50, in the regional final. St. Joe's later consolidated into Detroit De La Salle High.

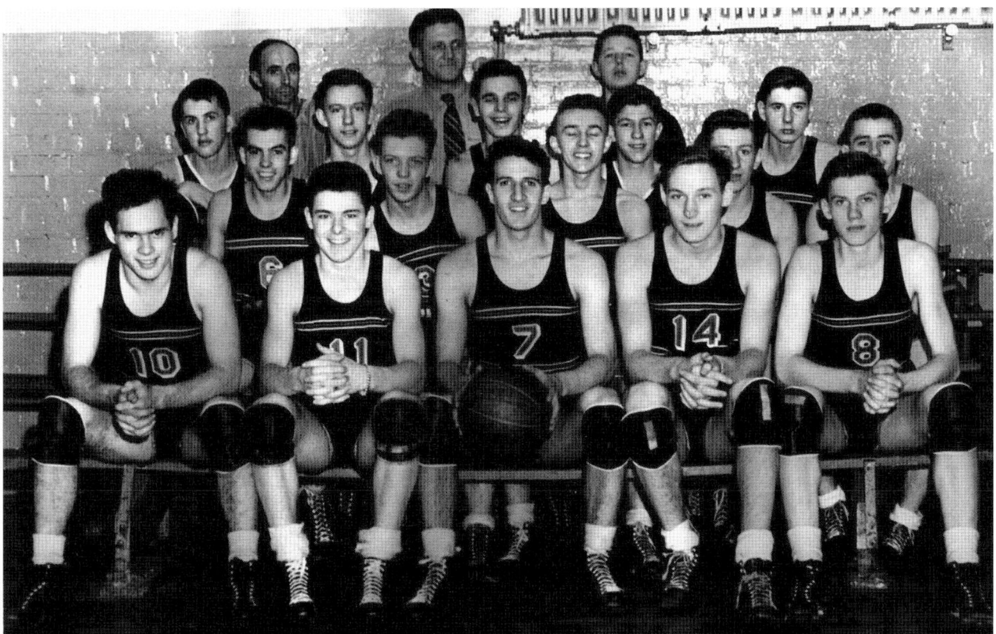

Black boot basketball shoes were the rage before a single pair of canvas Chuck Taylors were ever laced up, as evidenced by the 1945–1946 Dearborn Pioneers. (Patrick Stagg collection.)

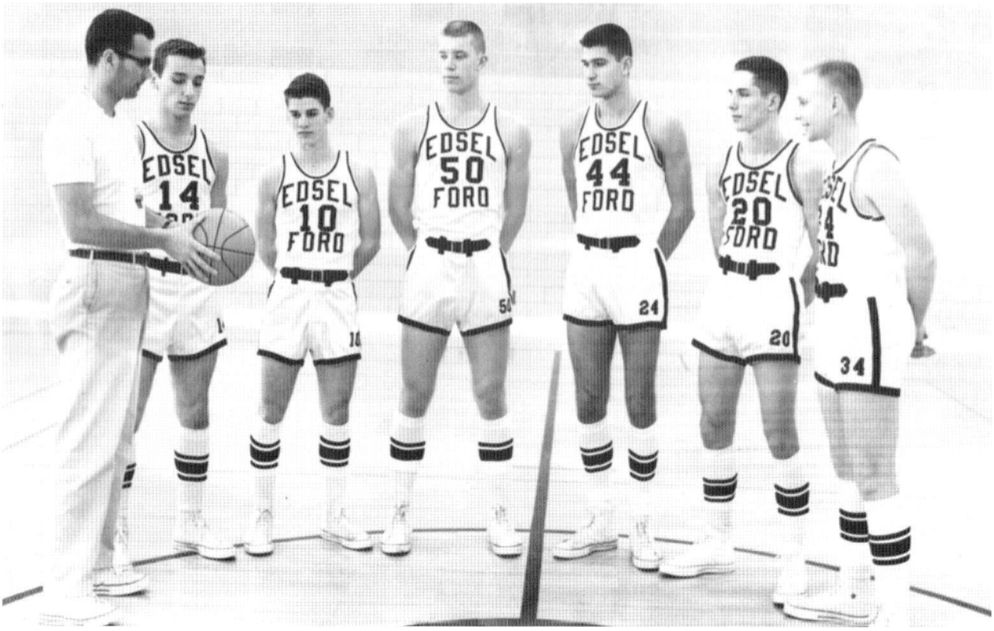

Dearborn Edsel Ford's starting five and sixth man pose with their coach in this team photograph from around 1960. Edsel is nicknamed the Thunderbirds, matching Dearborn Divine Child's Falcons and Dearborn Fordson's Tractors with an obvious nod to a famed Ford Motor Company product. What might not be obvious is No. 44 being the odd man out—the number on his shorts does not match the number on his jersey. (Patrick Stagg collection.)

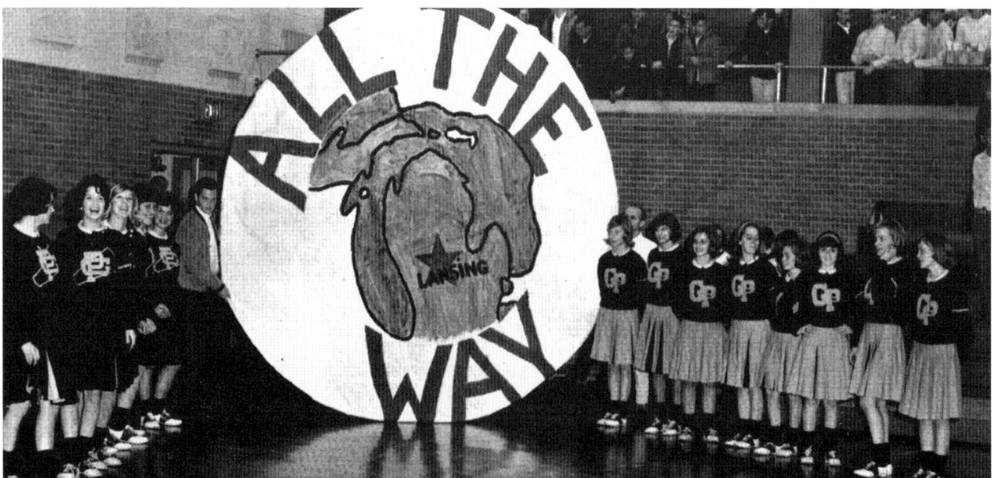

Perhaps the most famous prep gym in the metropolitan Detroit footprint could be Grosse Pointe South High's iconic hardwood home. In addition to being the home of the Blue Devils, the Detroit Pistons played a nationally televised playoff game versus the Minneapolis Lakers on March 12, 1960. Coach Chuck Hollosy left Detroit Austin for Grosse Pointe High in the early 1960s and the Blue Devils soon entertained the championship dreams pictured here. (Grosse Pointe *View Pointe*.)

4

THE CATHOLIC LEAGUE

The first rule of social etiquette is simple—never discuss politics or religion. But when discussion centers upon Detroit's Catholic High School League (CHSL), the league's players, coaches, officials, and fans politic with reverence about which parochial school they believe to be best.

The schools that recite the Lord's Prayer before each league game and mandated home teams show colors in dark jerseys for many years are the same schools and league responsible for an army's worth of quality collegiate players, thrilling league and championship games, and a mountain's worth of memories for nearly 100 years.

Perhaps no league has done for Detroit's community of players, coaches, and officials what the CHSL has. The basketball is outstanding, the players are well schooled. Catholic League coaches remain as detailed and driven and the league's top tier of officials remains as accomplished as any public high school league's staff.

It is true some league facilities were less than desirable, but the basketball—oh, the basketball! Catholic League gyms oozed spirit, passion, and energy. Birmingham Brother Rice and Detroit Catholic Central made football an afterthought, the two rivals being the last private schools to win Michigan's Class A crown. Detroit's DePorres and Benedictine high schools staged quite the grudge match. University of Detroit High, now known as University of Detroit-Jesuit High, played in and hosted some of the biggest games the Catholic League ever played. Detroit East Catholic was a gritty Class D contender annually. Orchard Lake St. Mary's, with 1,300 wins in nearly 100 years of basketball, ranks behind only Saginaw High as the state's winningest high school cage program. Not many leagues, save for Detroit's PSL or Saginaw's Valley, can boast the merits the Catholic League can.

The league's annual playoffs often served as rubber match to a season's rivalry. Culminating at the University of Detroit-Mercy's Calihan Hall, formerly Memorial Arena, championship Sunday remains a date to circle in red on metro Detroit calendars. A final marquee match-up annually pits the champions of the Catholic League and PSL in the Operation Friendship Game, known 60 years ago as the city championship game.

Many a state champion or title contender has called the Catholic League home. Above all else, Detroit's Catholic League, both in metro Detroit and statewide circles, is best defined by one word: worthy.

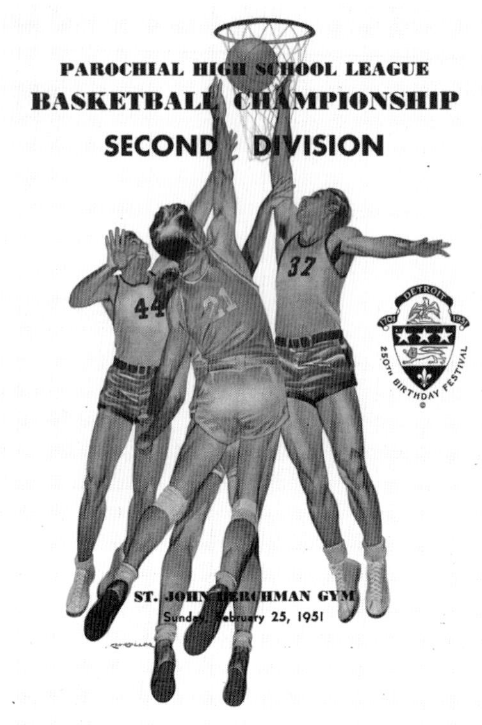

Detroit's St. Andrew won the second of four consecutive CHSL titles from 1950 to 1953 when the Flyers defeated Detroit St. Charles 53-38 at St. John Herchman gym. Over 40 Catholic League high schools competed for the Parochial School League crown in the 1950s. (CHSL archive.)

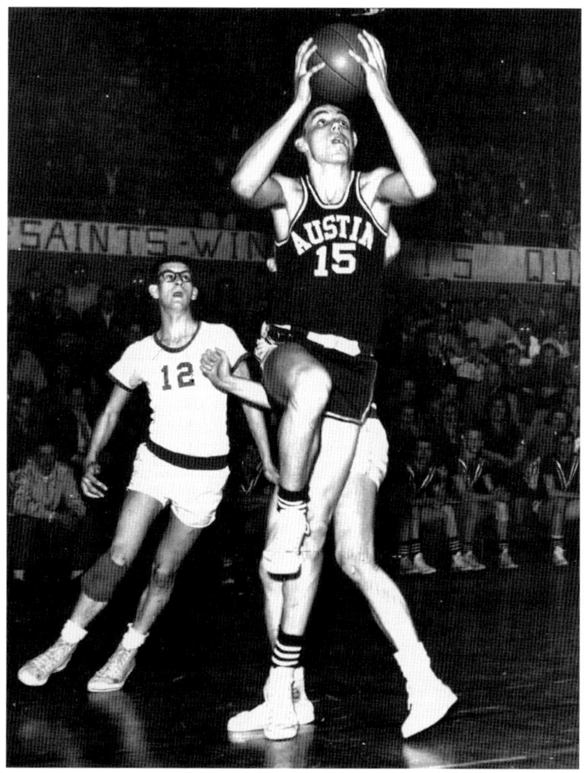

No Catholic League athlete is more accomplished and revered than Detroit Austin's Dave DeBusschere, shown here in the 1957 Catholic League title game played on March 9 at University of Detroit-Jesuit's Calihan Hall. DeBusschere went on to play for the University of Detroit-Jesuit's Titans. The Detroit Pistons signed DeBusschere and traded him to the New York Knicks in 1968, where he led the Knicks to NBA titles in 1970 and 1973. Named to the NBA's 50 Greatest Players in 1997, he suffered a heart attack in 2003 and died at 62 years of age. (The Detroit News/Rollie Ransom.)

Dearborn Fordson met Dave "Big D" Debusschere and Detroit Austin High in the 1957 Class A quarterfinals. The Tractors had little defense for DeBusschere and his Friars from advancing to the MHSAA Final Four in a 62-52 Austin win on March 21. After defeating East Detroit High 66-62 in the semifinal, the Friars dropped a 61-49 decision to Muskegon Heights in the title game. (The Detroit News/Alan L. Deneau.)

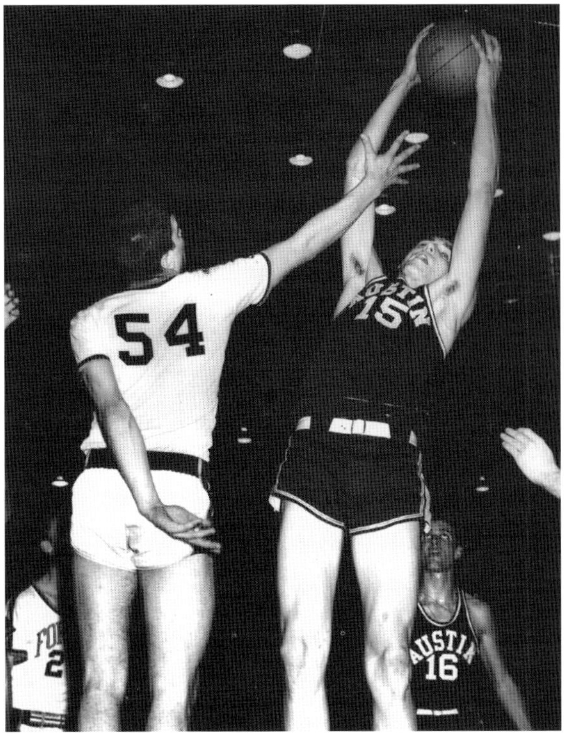

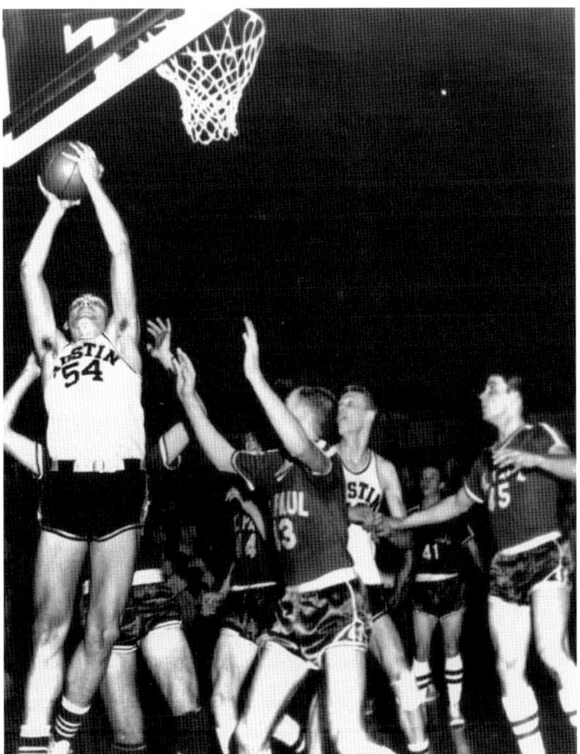

While Austin is remembered as DeBusschere's alma mater, Grosse Pointe St. Paul was a Catholic League and MHSAA tournament power in its heyday. The Lakers went 150-21 in CHSL play, winning nine crowns from 1951 to 1971, the school's final season. St. Paul was an amazing 83-19 in MHSAA tournament games in that same period, winning 15 districts, seven regionals, and two state titles. (The Detroit News.)

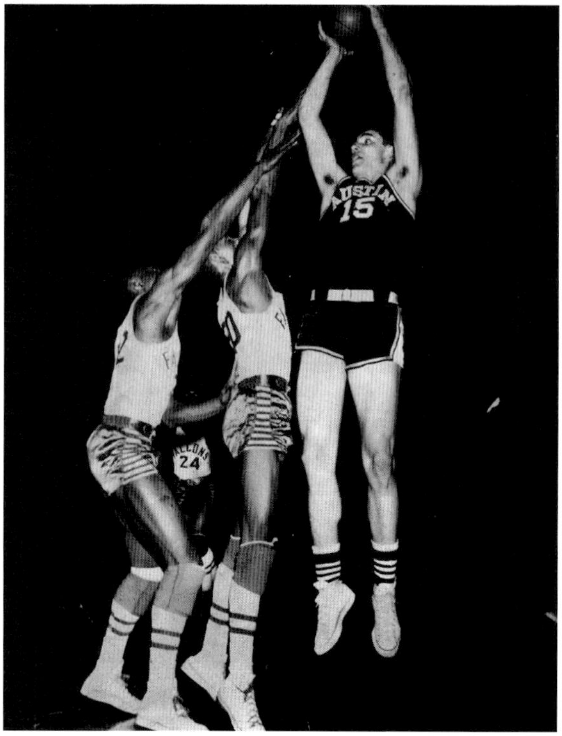

Before entering the MHSAA tournament, Dave DeBusschere and his Austin Friars battled the PSL one final time, facing Detroit Northeastern in the city championship. Austin and runner-up Grosse Pointe St. Paul earned the Catholic League a rare sweep, with the Friars winning 63-40 and St. Paul beating Detroit Northwestern 61-51. Only Northwestern remains open today. St. Paul closed in 1971, followed by Austin (1978) and Northeastern (1982). (The Detroit News.)

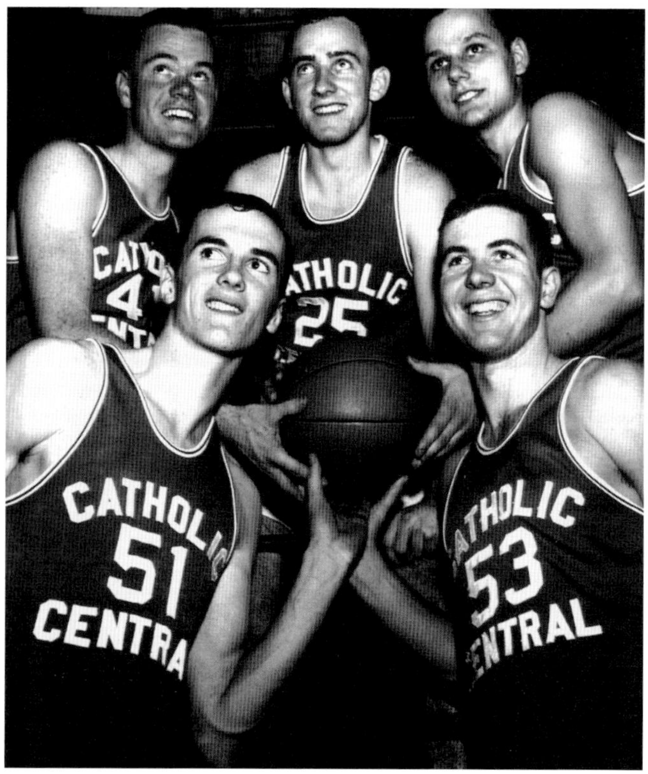

Catholic Central's starting five for 1961, Bill Maher (41), Bill Downs (25), Walt Lipeic (33), John Goetz (51), and Brian Motter (53) led the Shamrocks to the CHSL title and the MHSAA's highest honor with the Class A title in March. (Catholic Central archive.)

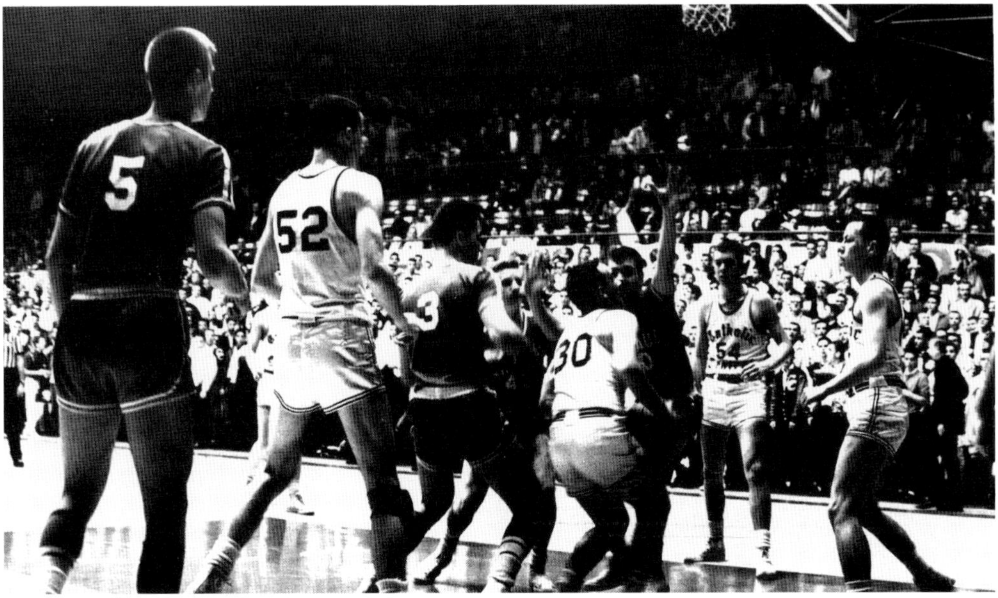

The 1961 Catholic League title game was a battle of the future MHSAA Class A and C champions. Catholic Central's John Goetz (52) and Bill Downs (30) helped the Shamrocks down Glen Cross (5) and Ken Wujek (3) at Grosse Pointe St. Paul's, 61-41. Catholic Central marched to the Class A title while St. Paul's won the Class C title, defeating four league rivals before stomping Parma Jackson County Western in the finals. (Catholic Central archive.)

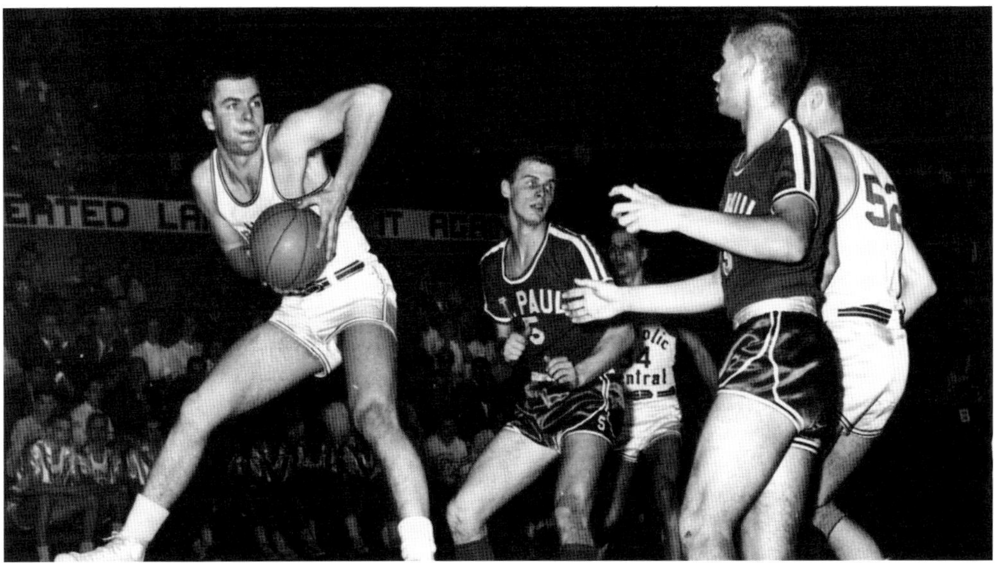

Shamrock forward Brian Motter takes the rebound in the 1961 Catholic League title game. Shamrock teammates are John Goetz (52) and Walt Lipiec (54); Joe Ayrault and Glen Cross (5) are pictured for St. Paul's. Both Catholic Central and St. Paul's dropped the 1961 Operation Friendship Games. The Shamrocks were nipped by PSL champion Detroit Eastern 56-53; PSL runner-up Detroit Northwestern handled the Lakers 59-37. (Catholic Central archive.)

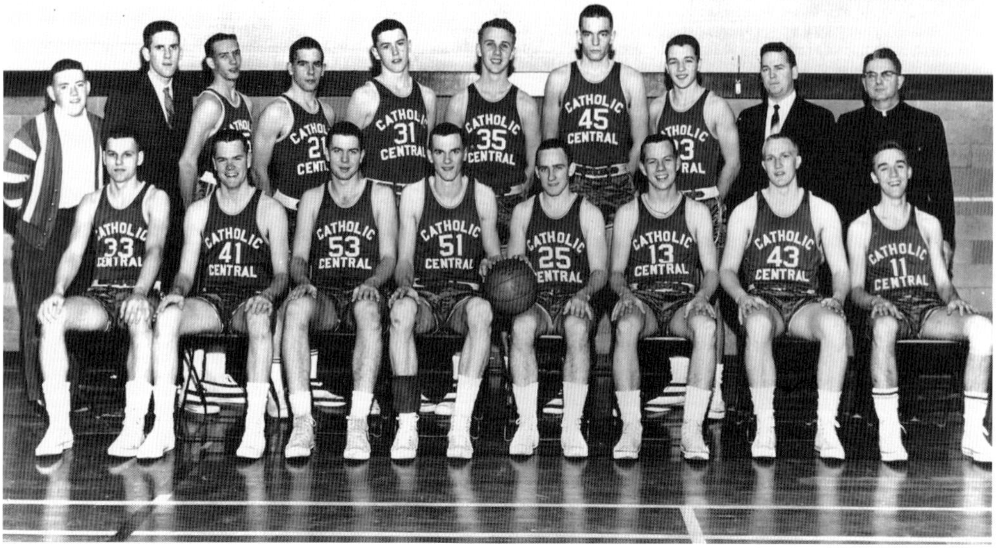

The 1961 Shamrocks marched to the Class A title by defeating every MHSAA tournament opponent they faced by at least 10 points, save for Lincoln Park in the quarterfinal. They blew out Muskegon heights, 72-53, in the finals at Michigan State University's Jenison Field House. Walt Lipiec, Bill Maher, and Brian Motter combined for 50 points in the finals. (Catholic Central archive/McNutt.)

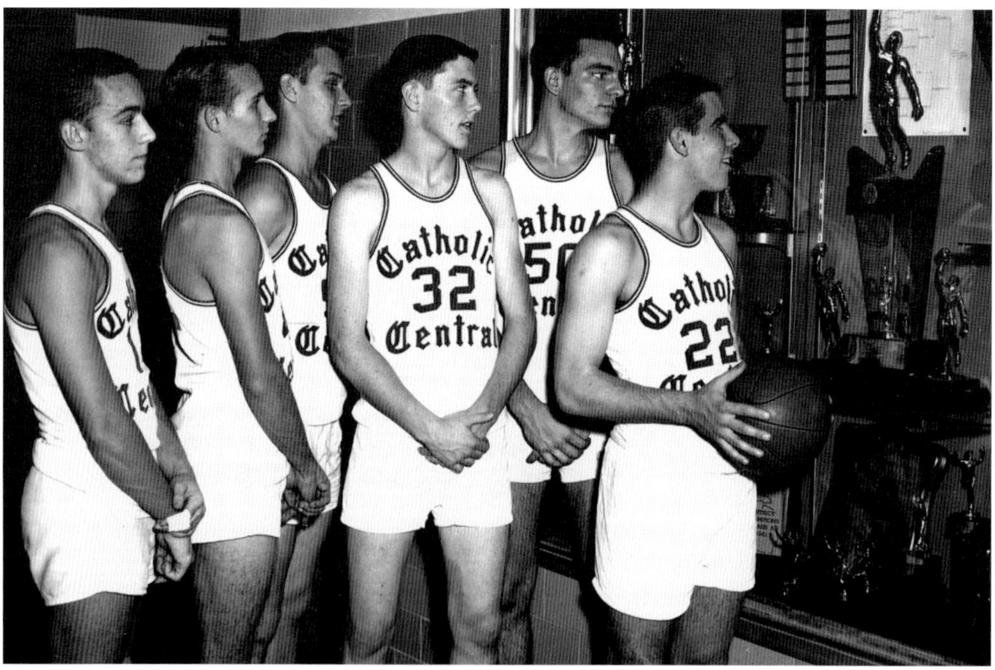

The 1961 Class A title won by Catholic Central was a source of pride and joy to the team. Catholic Central's 1961 championship would not be duplicated by a CHSL school until Brother Rice did it in 1974. (Catholic Central archive/Elaine Studios.)

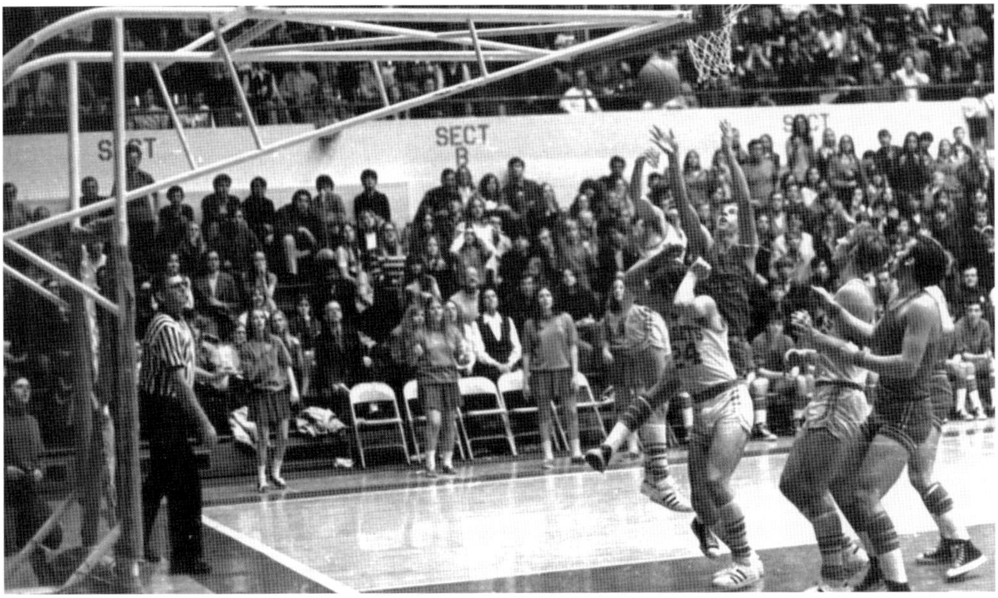

Orchard Lake St. Mary's greatest season since 1933 included a disappointing 54-44 loss to now-closed Dearborn St. Alphonsus in the 1971–1972 Catholic League title game at Calihan Hall. The Eaglets, 22-3 overall, tied for the regular season Catholic title with St. Alphonsus but gained revenge for the Calihan Hall loss by eliminating the Arrows, 52-49, in the regional final at Birmingham Seaholm. (Stan Lopata family collection.)

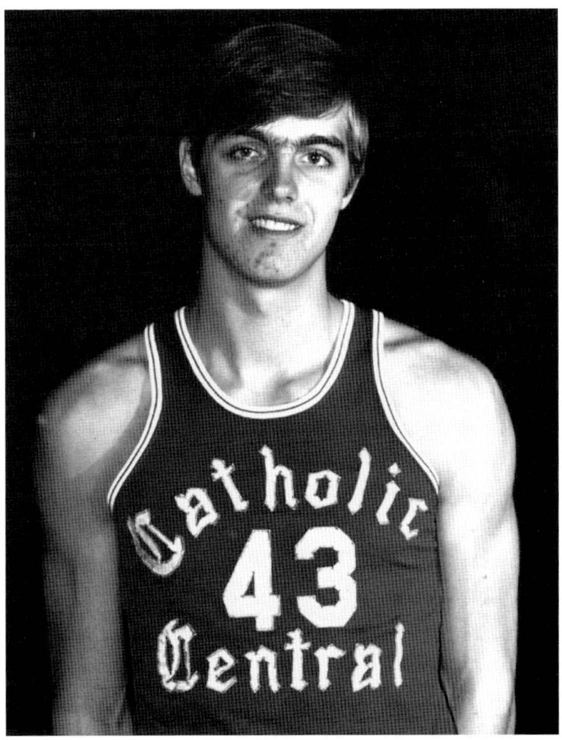

Before he was a fireballing major leaguer, Frank Tanana was a Class A All-State basketballer for Detroit Catholic Central. In 1970, the forward earned third team from the *Detroit Free Press*, second team from the *Detroit News*, and a first-team selection from both papers as a 1971 senior (pictured here). Tanana's father, also named Frank, scored 214 points in the 1951 Class C tournament as Detroit St. Andrew doubled Marlette, 52-26, for the Class C crown. (Catholic Central archive/McNutt.)

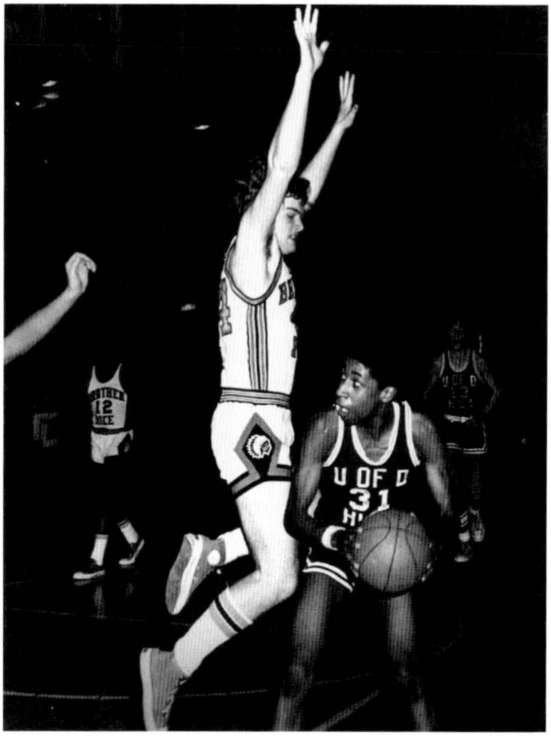

Birmingham Brother Rice senior Mike Brielmaier limits the offensive options of his University of Detroit-Jesuit High opponent in Rice's 56-51 win at the University of Detroit-Jesuit's Seven Mile Road campus in Detroit. The Rice–University of Detroit-Jesuit High game featured Rice coach Bill Norton, who earned a 273-106 record in his first stint at Rice, coaching against his University of Detroit-Jesuit High alma mater. (Bill Norton collection.)

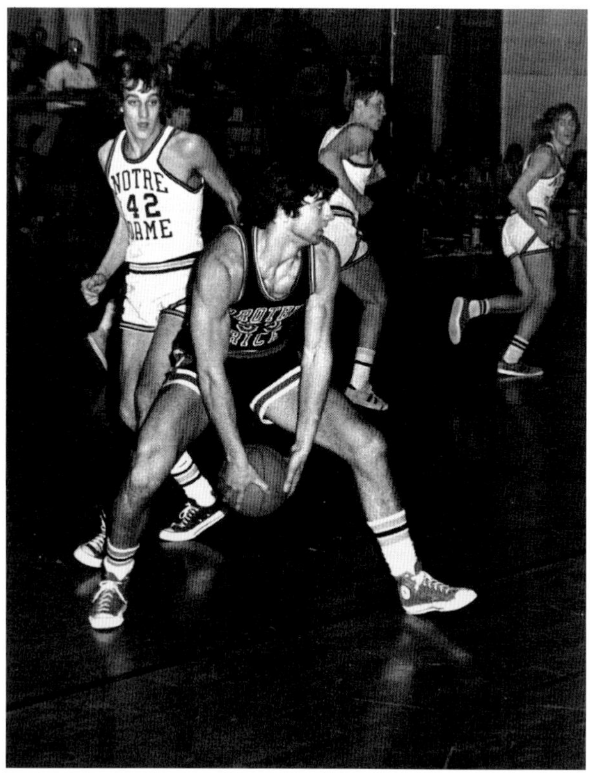

The No. 7 ranked team in Class A had little trouble with Harper Woods Notre Dame, a longtime Catholic League rival that represented Detroit's east side parochials with Bishop Gallagher and De La Salle, in their 1973–1974 meeting at Rice. The Warriors moved to 14-2 overall with this 69-53 win on February 8, 1974. Kevin Hart (55) and Rice earned a Catholic League playoff berth with this victory. (Bill Norton collection.)

Rivalries usually eliminate predictable results, making Catholic Central's fifth straight win over Brother Rice on January 18, 1974, a lesson in frustration. Rice's hopeful bench watches the waning moments of Catholic Central's 72-62 win at Rice after the Shamrocks won the first meeting, 60-54. The last laugh of 1974 belonged to the Warriors, who whipped Catholic Central 71-65 in the Catholic League semifinals to avenge the regular season sweep. (Bill Norton collection.)

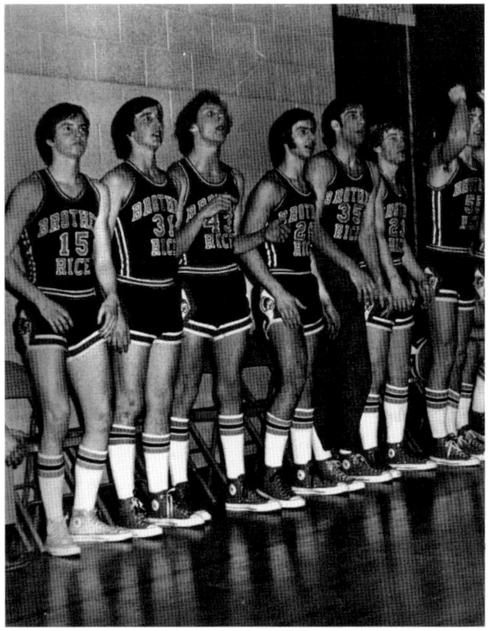

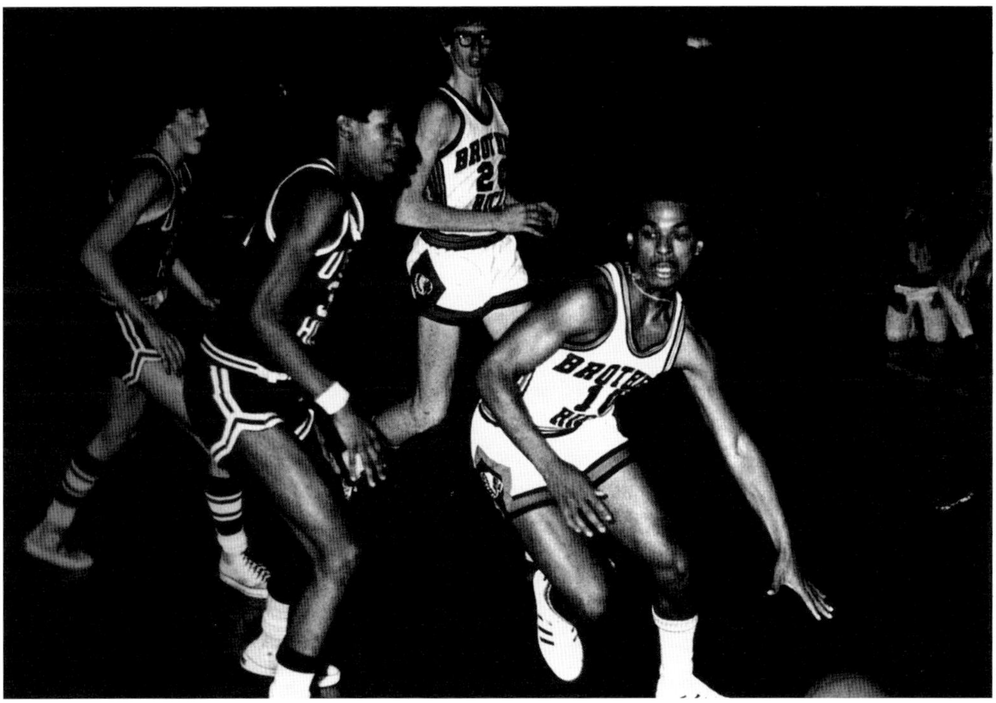

Senior Same Washington, eldest of Brother Rice's "band of Washington brothers," drives around rival University of Detroit-Jesuit High in this January 11, 1974, game. The Cubs rallied from a 47-35 deficit with just minutes to play, outscoring Rice 16-9, but the Warriors' stall tactic survived the rally for a 56-51. University of Detroit-Jesuit won its first CHSL title by upsetting Brother Rice in 1971–1972. (Bill Norton collection.)

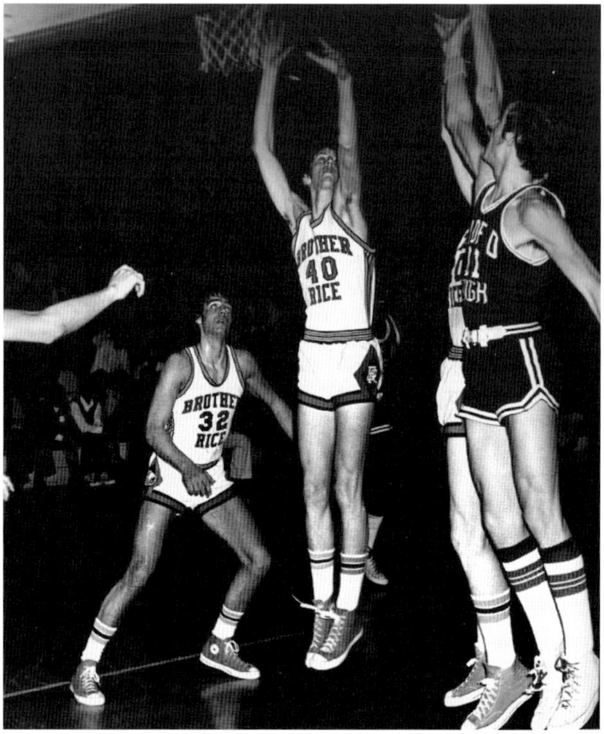

Warrior Bill Lelich (32) watches teammate Jim MacGuidwin score his only points of the game in a Brother Rice 56-51 win over University of Detroit-Jesuit High. The Cubs posted a furious rally, outscoring Rice 16-9 in the final stanza, to finish 8-2 in the Catholic League behind Catholic Central (10-0). Both the Cubs and Catholic Central's Shamrocks spent a stint outside of the Catholic League in the 1950s. (Bill Norton collection.)

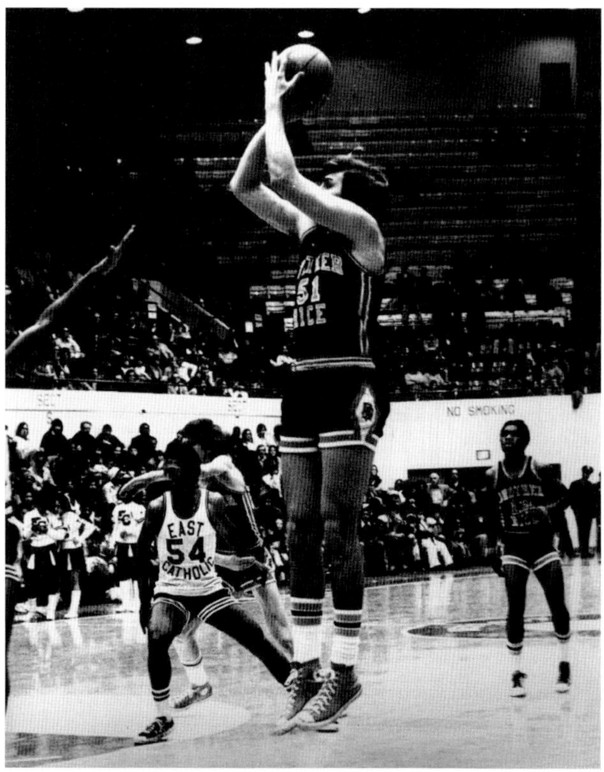

The first Catholic League title for coach Bill Norton and Birmingham Brother Rice came at the expense of a legendary metro Detroit coach, East Catholic High's Dave Soules. Rice's 10-year existence was void of a cage title until 1974 and this 69-61 win in front of over 4,500 at the University of Detroit-Mercy's Calihan Hall. (Bill Norton collection.)

Will Franklin (53) made eight field goals and scored 18 points for Birmingham Brother Rice in the 1974 regional final versus Pontiac Central, but his two free throws with six seconds remaining eliminated the Chiefs, 55-54. Central and Rice met in five regionals and one quarterfinal in the MHSAA tournament in the 1970s; Central won four of these six meetings. (Bill Norton collection.)

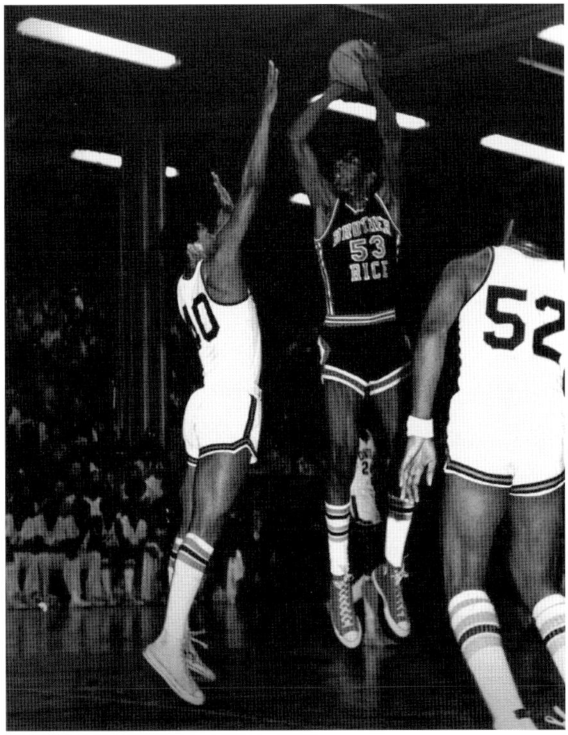

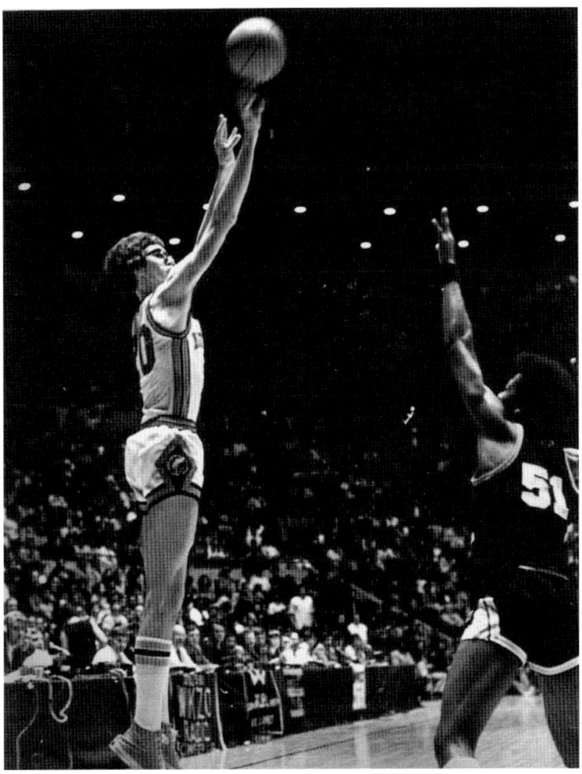

Before Frank Rourke (20) and Brother Rice could battle for a state title, they had to first defeat the Saginaw High Trojans in Michigan's Crisler Arena. Rourke's 17 points carried Rice to a 64-53 win over Michigan's winningest prep basketball program and into the final with Detroit Cass Tech. In the final, Rice overcame an 11-point deficit to force overtime and then outscored the Technicians 6-2 to win the Class A title. (Bill Norton collection.)

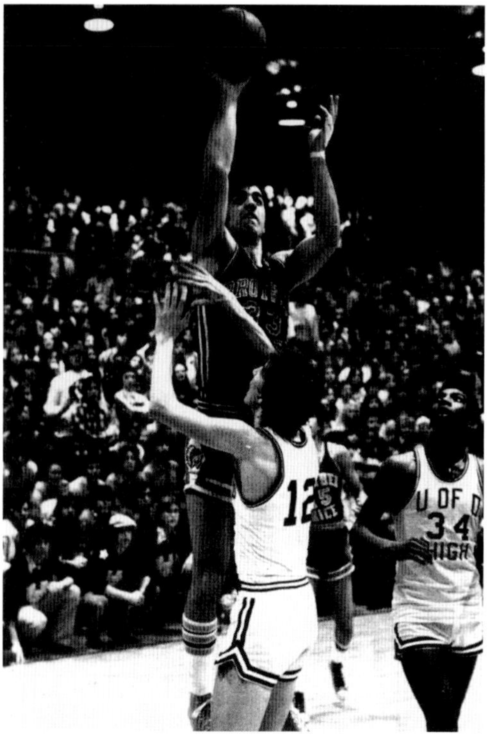

Kevin Hart (33) shoots for two in Brother Rice's annual rivalry game with University of Detroit High in the 1974–1975 season. The defending state champs found the bull's-eye to be a difficult target to wear. While the Warriors won this game, University of Detroit-Jesuit High earned the 1975 Catholic League title. No Operation Friendship Game was played in 1975, and University of Detroit-Jesuit High was drubbed by Ferndale 73-51 in the district. (Bill Norton collection.)

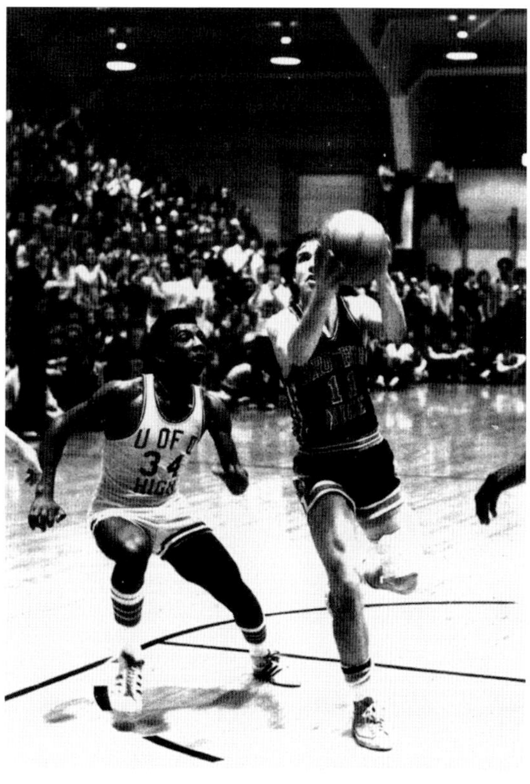

Brother Rice's Don Henricks (11) drives past University of Detroit-Jesuit High's Ed Moultrie (34) in the 1974 game at Brother Rice. Brother Rice and University of Detroit-Jesuit enjoy an intense home-and-home basketball game annually. The University of Detroit-Jesuit Cubs won the Catholic title in 1972 over Rice and again in 1975, lost the 1981 title game to Rice in overtime, won the 1992 title, and played in the 2007 title tilt. Rice has captured Catholic titles in 1979, 1981, 1982, and 1990 while losing the championship games of 1980 and 1999. (Bill Norton collection.)

David Washington (13) drives and Will Franklin (53) crouches as Brother Rice carried the ball as mythical state football champs and official basketball champions (top right) in the same calendar year. Orchard Lake St. Mary's would officially win both titles in the 1977–1978 school year. (Bill Norton collection.)

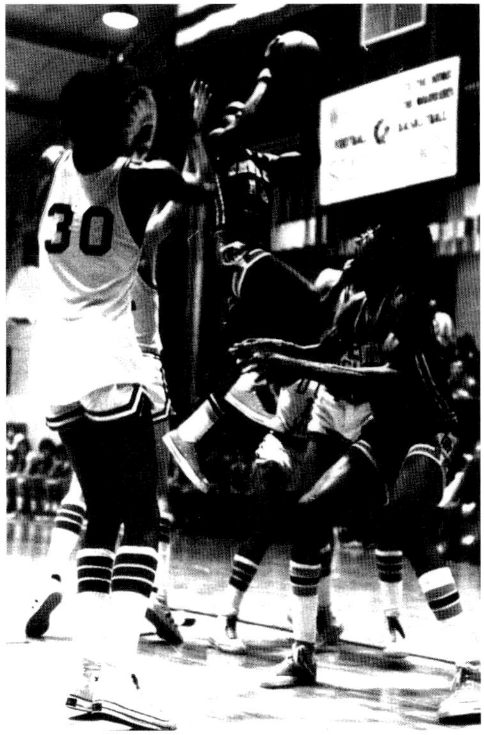

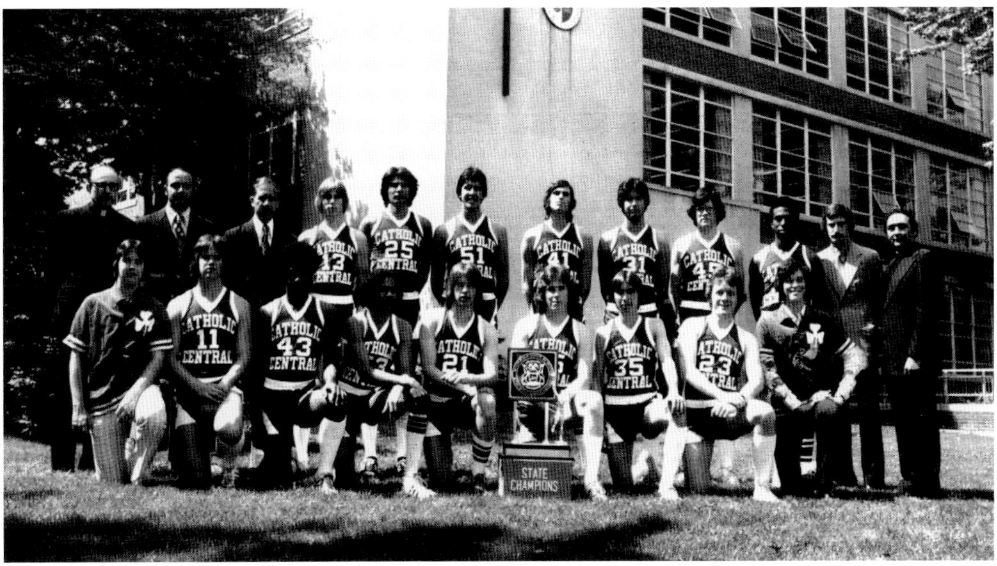

The 1976 Shamrocks managed to elicit the school's famous "6565 Outer Drive" cheer for all of Michigan to hear when Catholic Central won that season's Class A title. Thirty-three years later, these Shamrocks represent the last year a private school has won Michigan's Class A basketball championship. Catholic Central defeated PSL members Chadsey, Henry Ford, and now-closed Mackenzie before defeating Magic Johnson and Lansing Everett 68-60 in the semifinals on their way to the title. (Catholic Central archive.)

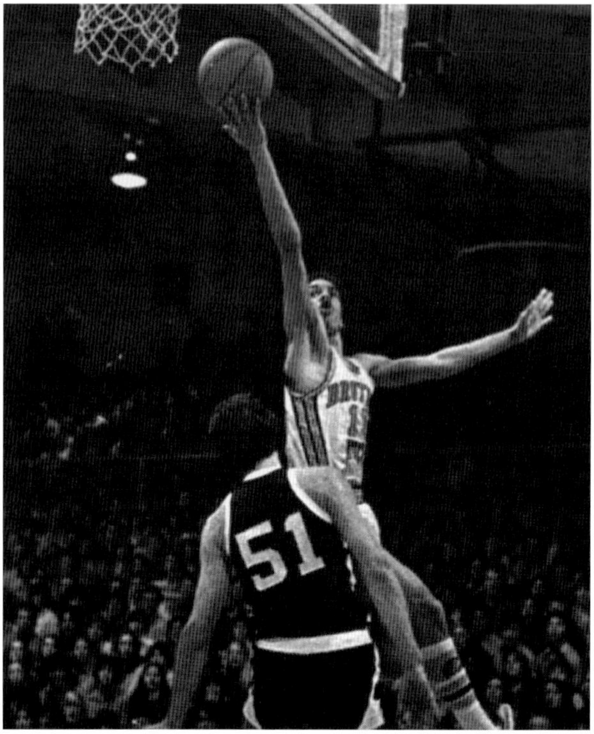

Kevin Smith evokes memories of one of Michigan's revered 1977 Class A finals, when Smith made a half-court heave at the buzzer to force Magic Johnson's Lansing Everett Vikings into overtime before succumbing, 62-56. Here Smith scores two versus archrival Detroit Catholic Central, defending Class A champion from 1976, in the 1977 semifinals. Before dropping the 1977 finals, Bill Norton's 1974 team won the Class A title in overtime over Detroit Cass Tech, 60-56. (MHSAA finals program, 1977.)

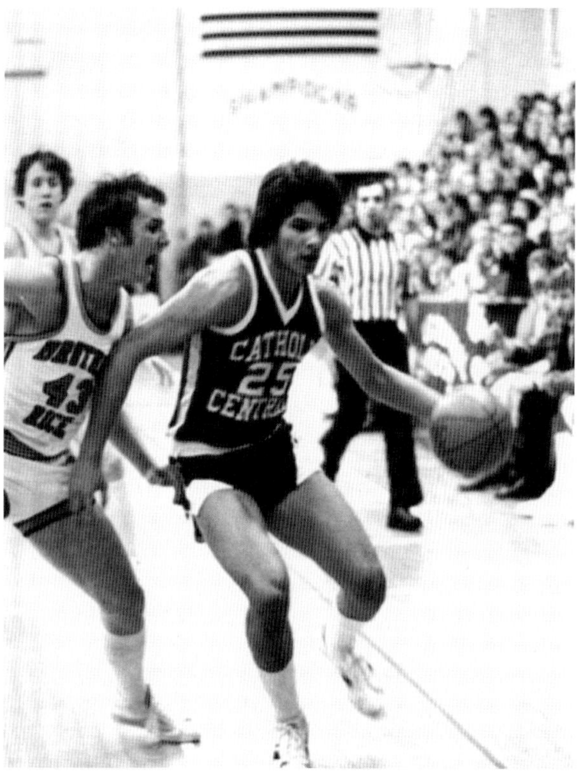

It is win at all costs for Birmingham Brother Rice guard Mike Henry, shouting at Catholic Central's Rob Gonzalez as the Shamrock forward tries to drive past Henry. Gonzalez would score the winning basket with five seconds remaining. Ever since Rice football coach Al Fracassa and Catholic Central gridiron leader Tom Mach ignited the football rivalry, cage coaches Bill Norton (Rice) and Bernie Holowicki (Catholic Central) kept the fire hot in winter basketball. (Catholic Central archive.)

Catholic Central's Mr. Everything of 1977–1978, forward Rob Gonzalez (25), shook free for this lay-up at the buzzer to lift Catholic Central to a stunning 51-49 upset of Class A's No. 3–ranked team, rival Birmingham Brother Rice. Picked fifth in the preseason predictions, Catholic Central won the regular season CSHL title and eliminated Rice from making the league playoffs with a 59-57 win in the second meeting. (Catholic Central archive.)

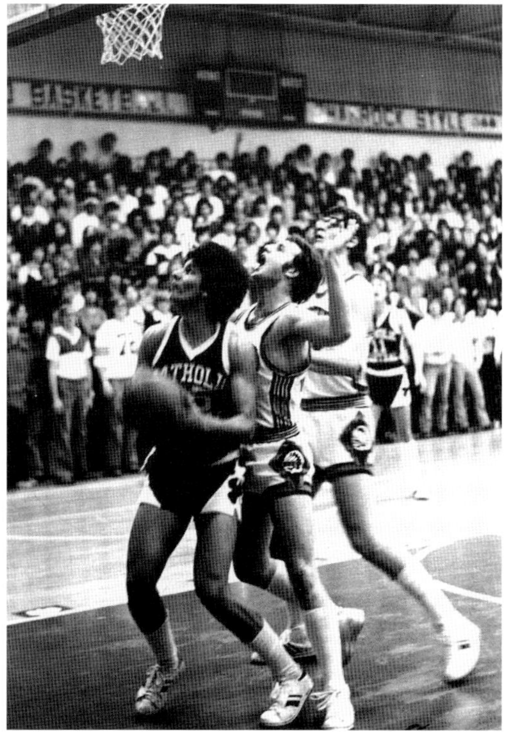

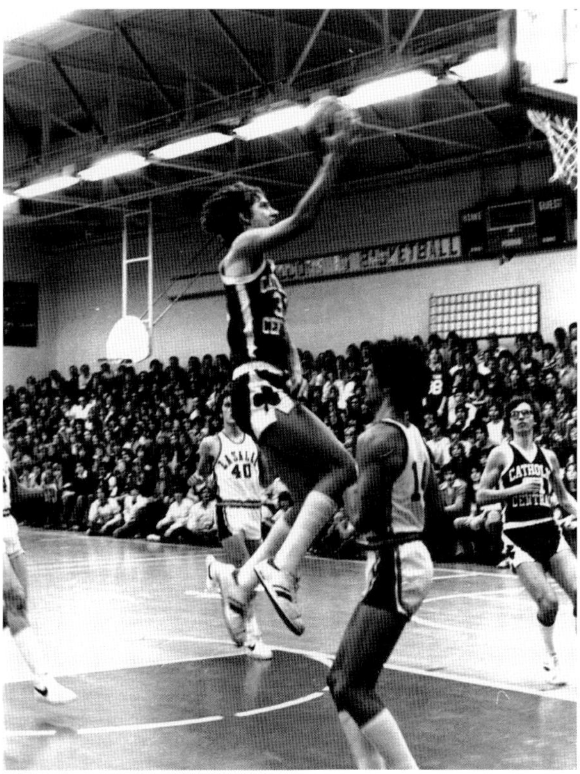

Catholic Central's Jeff Blanzy picks up a charging foul as his Detroit De La Salle defender is braced for collision in the final game played on West Outer Drive. Joe Chop (21) is observing from the play's back side. De La Salle has played in nine Catholic League title games, winning in 1988, 2001, 2002, and the 2009 crown over Catholic Central. (Catholic Central archive.)

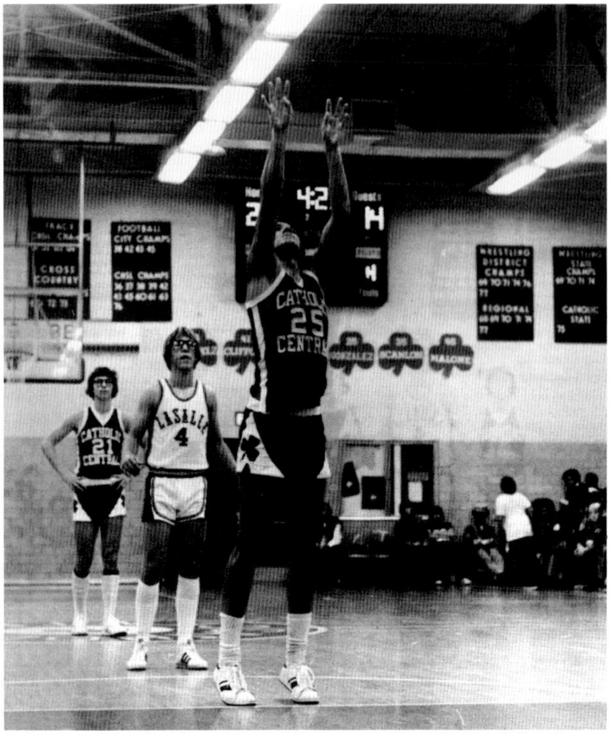

Rob Gonzalez shoots free throws with teammate Joe Chop (21) in the background during the final game at Catholic Central's famed 6565 West Outer Drive gym versus Detroit De La Salle. The school's "6565 West Outer Drive" cheer is still recited by Catholic Central grads over 30 years after the school played its last game there. After Catholic Central left Detroit for its Redford location on Breakfast Drive in 1978, De La Salle followed suit four years later and left the shadows of Detroit's City Airport for suburban Warren. (Catholic Central archive.)

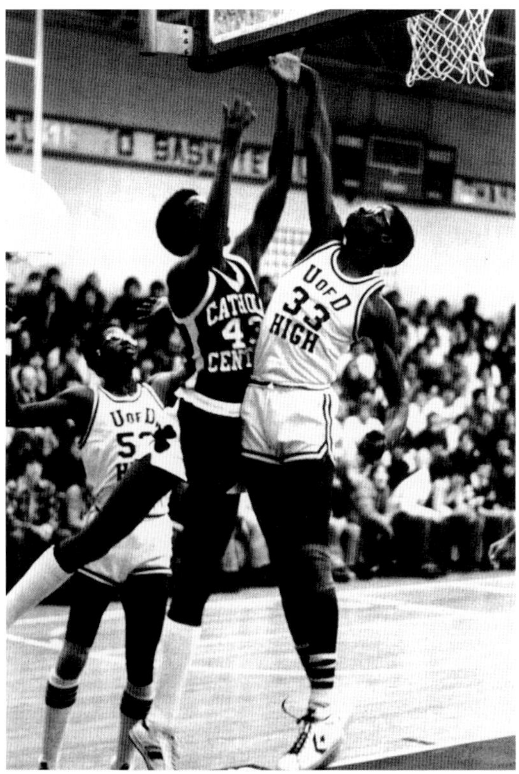

Barry Spenser was Catholic Central's super sophomore in the 1977–1978 season that produced a regular season Catholic League title for coach Bernie Holowicki and the Shamrocks. Spencer combined with senior Rob Gonzalez to score 44 points in the title clincher, a 59-57 thriller over Birmingham Brother Rice. Catholic Central was served revenge by Highland Park in the 1978 district final, 70-62, for the previous season's defeat in the Class A quarterfinal. (Catholic Central archive.)

Terry Malone (45) did not play a huge role in this 1977–1978 game with rival University of Detroit-Jesuit High, but his jumper from inside the free throw line in the final seconds of Catholic Central's February 1, 1978, rematch with Brother Rice was a Warrior dagger. The 59-57 win over archrival Rice clinched the regular season title for the Shamrocks and eliminated Rice from making the league playoffs. University of Detroit-Jesuit High and Catholic Central enjoyed a more spirited rivalry when the Shamrocks were located just minutes from University of Detroit-Jesuit High. (Catholic Central archive.)

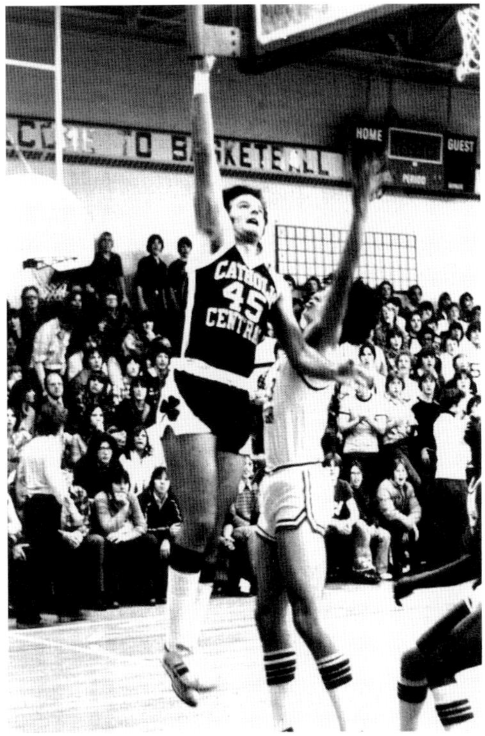

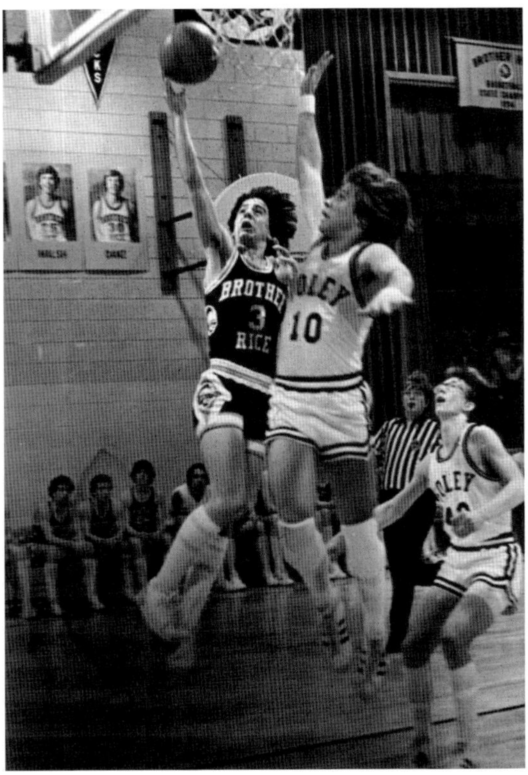

Junior Michael Dietz flings himself fearlessly toward the goal for two of his four points in Brother Rice's 77-51 win over Madison Heights Bishop Foley in a Catholic League crossover game during the 1977–1978 season. Dietz opened DietzTrott Sports and Entertainment Management in 2004. (Bill Norton collection.)

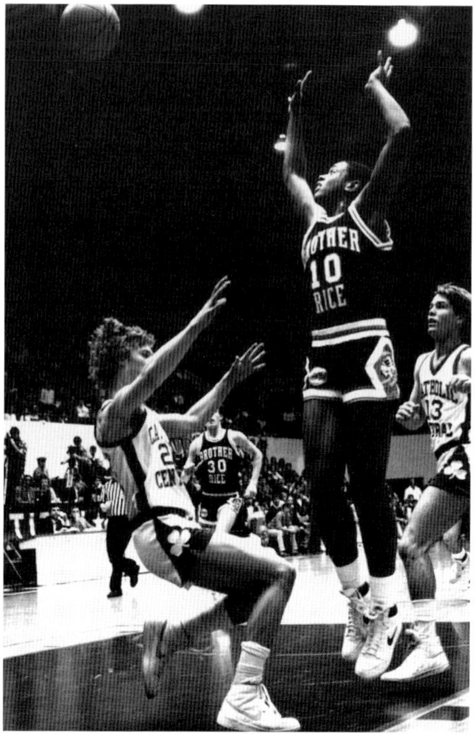

This is the 1985 Catholic Central home game of the annual home-and-home rivalry, between Brother Rice and Catholic Central, played at the University of Detroit-Jesuit's Calihan Hall to manage the overflow crowd and maximize the gate profit. B. J. Armstrong (10) won three NBA titles in the 1990s as Michael Jordan's backcourt mate with the Chicago Bulls. (Oakland Press/Tim Thompson.)

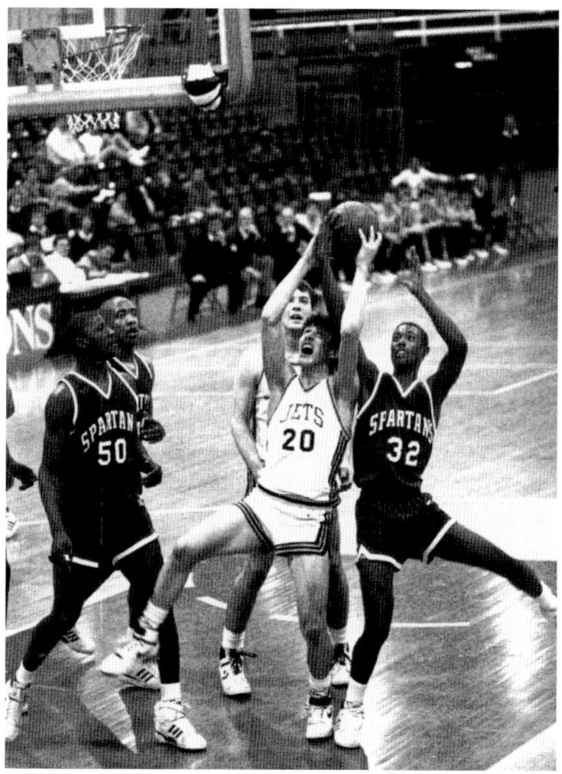

Before Shawn Respert was a Michigan State University Spartan, he was a Redford Bishop Borgess Spartan playing in the 1988 Class B regional final at the home of the Hurons, Eastern Michigan University. Borgess defeated Carleton Airport High 77-60 in Bowen Field House and went on to earn the first finals berth in school history before losing the 1988 finals to Grand Rapids South Christian, 69-66. Borgess won the 1997 Class C title before closing in 2005. (MHSAA archive.)

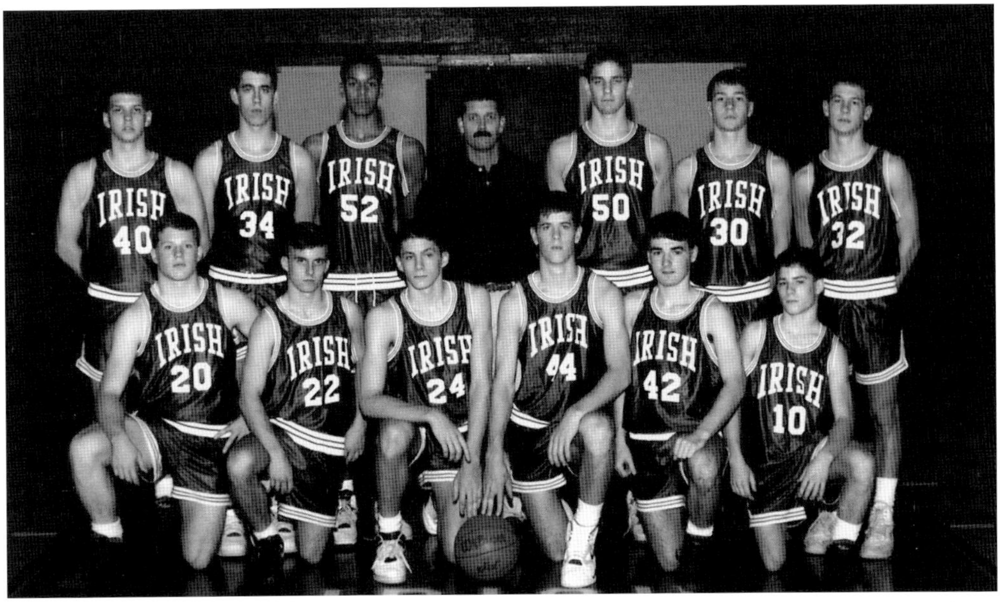

The only coach from Michigan's storied basketball tournament history to win state titles in both girls' and boys' basketball with the same school is Ann Arbor Gabriel Richard's Tom Kempf. Shown here in the middle of the second row, Kempf first guided this 1991 Fighting Irish team to a 62-48 conquest of Allendale in the Class D boys' title tilt. Two years later, his Lady Irish outlasted Mio High, 43-42, in two overtimes to take that year's Class D title game. Kempf is now a men's assistant coach at Aquinas College in Grand Rapids. (MHSAA archive.)

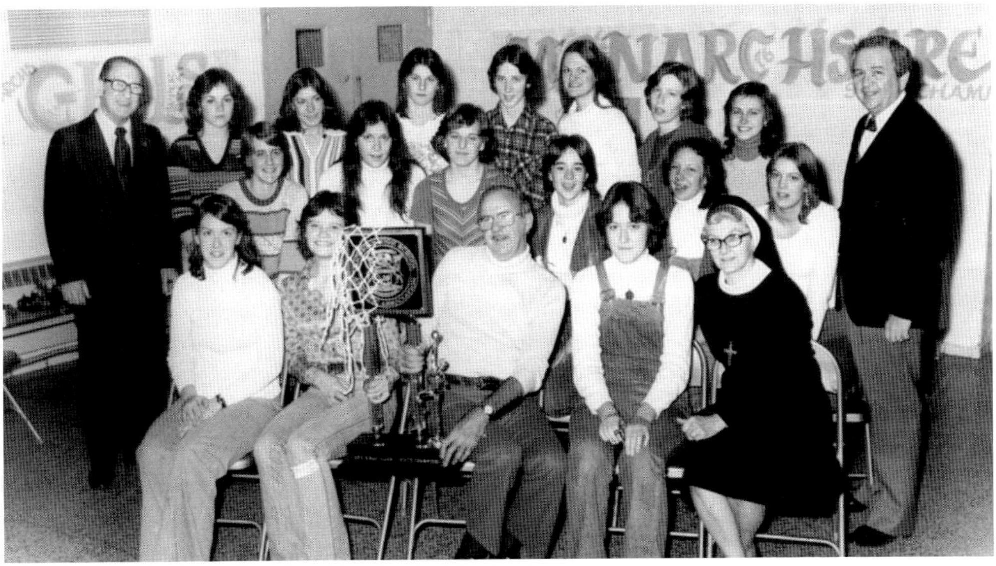

Allen Park Cabrini's long tenure in the rugged Catholic League was rewarded with the 1978 Class C title after coach Shelly Oliva's Monarchs, shown here celebrating the trophy, defeated Norway, 50-43. Cabrini also took home the 1976 Class C title, coached by Ken Quire. The Catholic League dominated the first few years of the MHSAA finals in all classes in the 1970s.

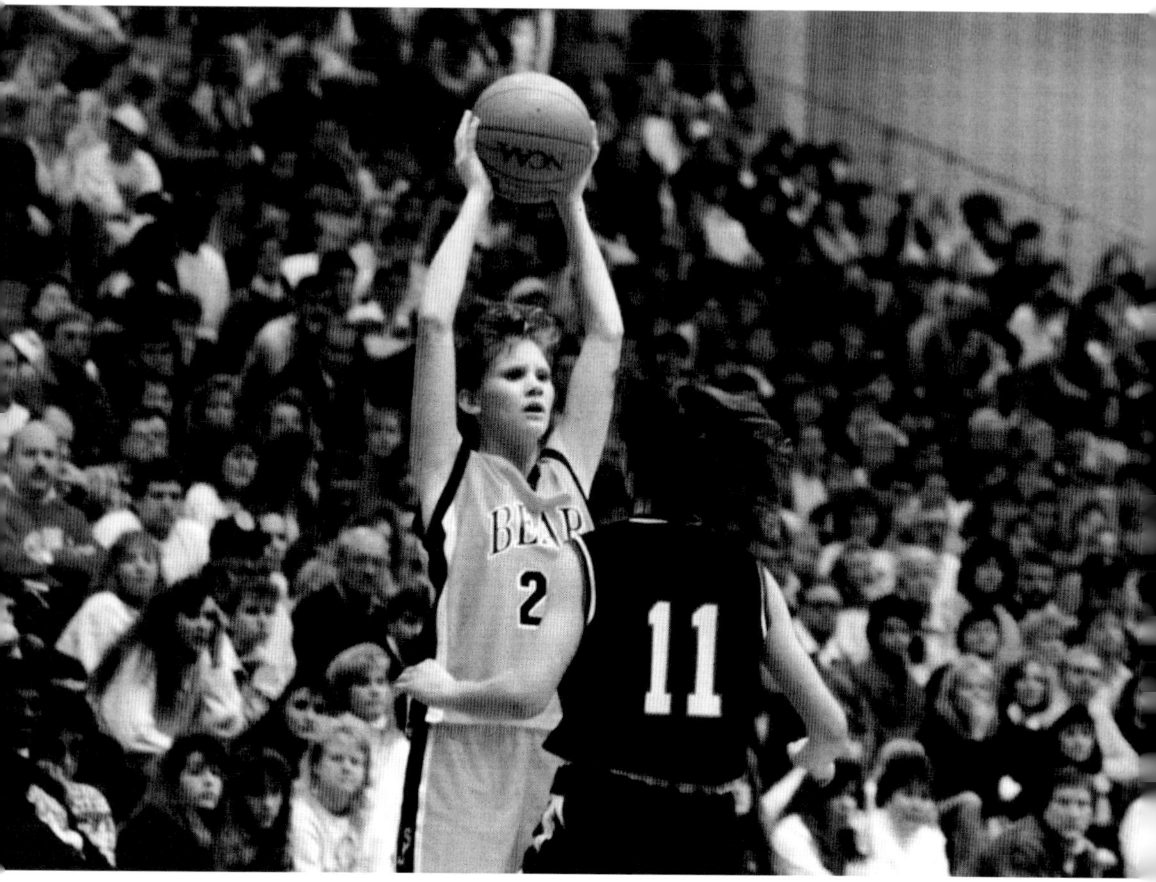

St. Joseph's Tracy Bloodsworth passed over Dearborn Divine Child's Shawn Bannon (11) in the 1989 Class B title game, but Bannon and the Falcons earned the bragging rights. After Bloodsworth scored 12 first-quarter points, Bannon tied a then MHSAA title game record with four triples in leading Divine Child to a 44-36 victory at Grand Valley State University. This victory represented the second of four Falcon Class B titles in nine seasons and five Class B title game appearances from 1985 to 1994. Their only loss in the championship game was a 45-41 defeat to fellow Catholic League rival Livonia Ladywood. (MHSAA archive/Gary Shook.)

5

River Rouge

When River Rouge High School retired the No. 12 at the school's historic Frank "Buck" Webber gym almost a decade ago, no single player was honored, but no one questioned why No. 12 was retired, either.

The greatest dynasty in Michigan prep basketball history—River Rouge High's 12 MHSAA Class B titles won from 1954 to 1972—has never been duplicated. Born in Barlow, Kentucky, and raised in Jackson, Michigan, the self-described old Kentuckian, coach Lofton Greene won 710 games against 200 losses in 40 years as head coach of the Great Lakes' most dominant high school basketball program. The Panthers won 12 Class B championships, appeared in 16 title games, and won 20 regional titles from 1943–1944 to 1983–1984.

Ironically, the 49-42 loss to Coldwater High coach Floyd Eby's Cardinals in the 1949 finals was the catalyst to Rouge's dominance. Eby's defensive press—not the 8 of 25 free throw shooting by River Rouge—had cost Greene's Panthers. "He [Eby] sold me on the man-to-man press," Greene was quoted in one of MHSAA historian Ron Pesch's several articles about the Rouge legacy. "We installed one starting that next year."

Thus was born "Loftonball." Greene's undefeated Panthers lost the 1951 finals but his 1954 Mighty Mites earned the school's first title. Rouge repeated in 1955, went to the finals in 1958, and took home the 1959 title too. Buffered by a 48-game MHSAA tournament winning streak, the Panthers earned five consecutive Class B titles from 1961 to 1965, set the finals team scoring record in back-to-back years (64-65), and featured the only player in Michigan history to start four consecutive title games, Willie Betts. Their amazing winning streak was snapped in 1966 during their sixth straight finals appearance.

Rouge won another 33 straight tournament games during the four-title stretch from 1969 to 1972. The 12th title came to be known as "Leighton Moulton's Miracle." Down 64-57 to Muskegon Heights High with 45 seconds to play, Ralph Perry was fouled on a layin. Byron Wilson scored the missed three throw. After a Tiger turnover, Leighton Moulton nailed a 22-foot jumper. With 23 seconds remaining, there was another Tiger turnover. Moutlon was fouled while shooting with two seconds remaining. Two free throws later, Greene, tears streaming down his face, had his final title.

No Michigan high school has a basketball history like the Rouge.

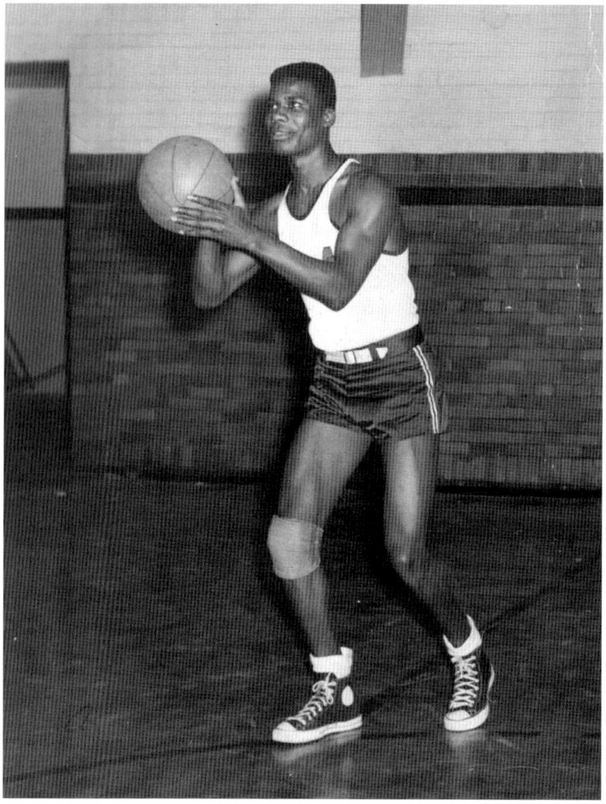

Al Driscoll was coach Lofton Greene's first All-State player and scored a then state record 24 points in the 1949 Class B state final, a 49-42 loss versus coach Floyd Eby's Coldwater Cardinals. The game changed prep basketball in Michigan forever. Coldwater's win justified Eby's brand of racehorse basketball; Rouge's loss prompted coach Lofton Greene to adapt the Coldwater style of defensive pressure and fast-break offense. Rouge lost in the 1951 finals but returned to win the 1954 Class B finals, the beginning of Rouge's 12 titles in the next 19 years. (River Rouge Historical Museum.)

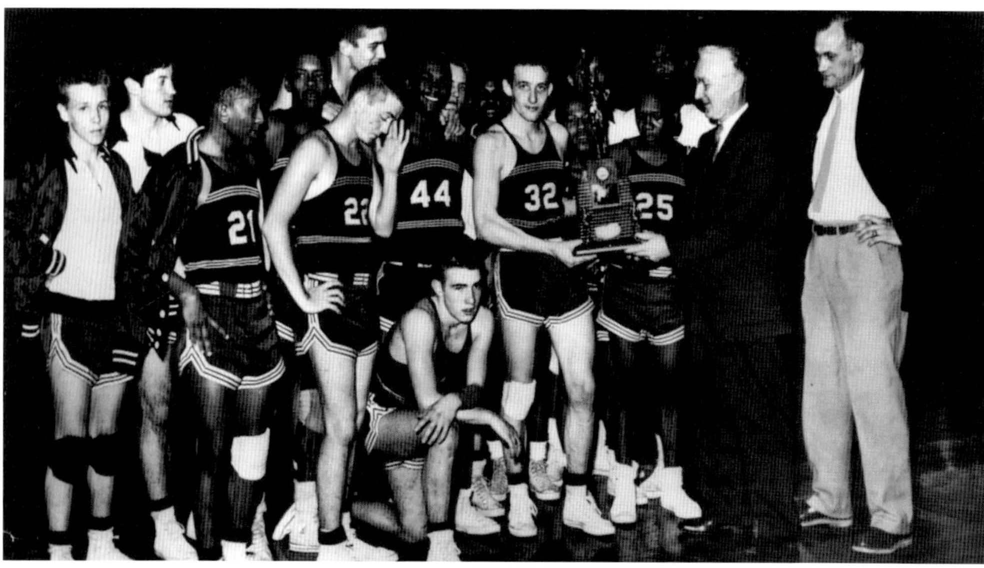

The third trip to the finals proved to be the charm for coach Lofton Greene (right), who oversees the MHSAA title trophy presentation to his Panthers by Michigan education superintendent C. L. Taylor. River Rouge won the Twin-Valley Conference with a 9-1 record and earned a 22-2 overall record in 1954. (River Rouge Historical Museum.)

River Rouge All-Tournament selections Herbie Woods (21) and Blanche Martin (44) exalt the 1955 Class B trophy above the hardwood pines of Michigan State University's Jenison Field House. Woods missed all but three games of the regular season due to a surgical procedure but scored 16 points, including two free throws with four seconds remaining to ice the 51-48 final over Buchanan. Martin scored a game-high 21 points. (River Rouge Historical Museum/ Ross H. McGregor.)

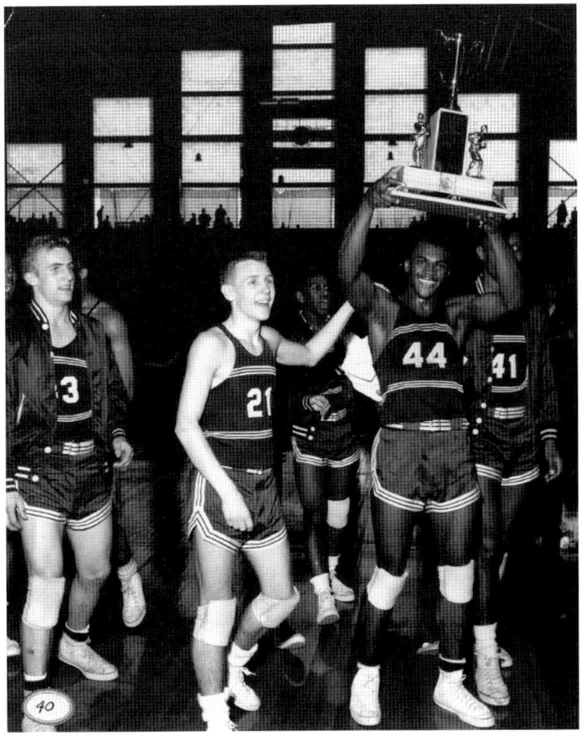

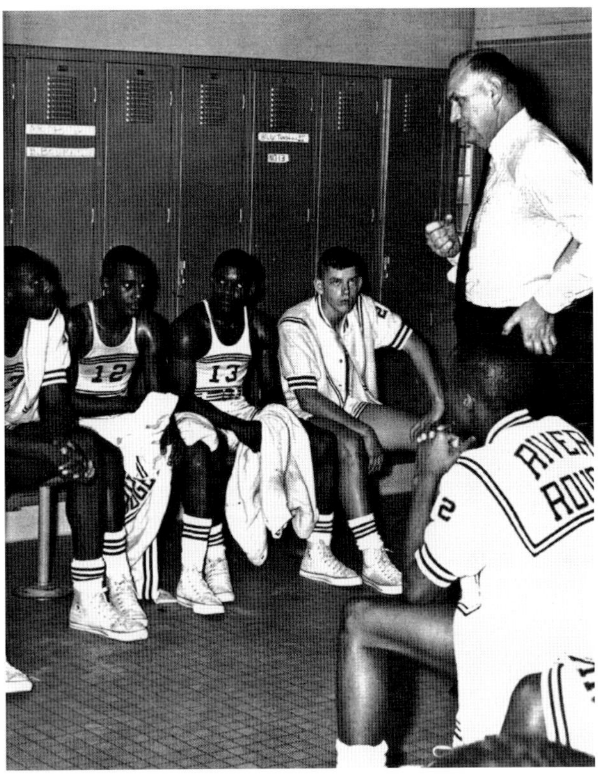

This is coach Lofton Greene at halftime in a 1963–1964 game at River Rouge's Frank Buck gym. Greene's career records of 739-231, 12 Class B titles in 16 appearances in the MHSAA finals, and 20 or more wins in 19 different campaigns earned the "Old Kentuckian" a place in the National Federation of High Schools Hall of Fame, an honor only five other Michiganians share. (River Rouge *Vigilant*, 1964.)

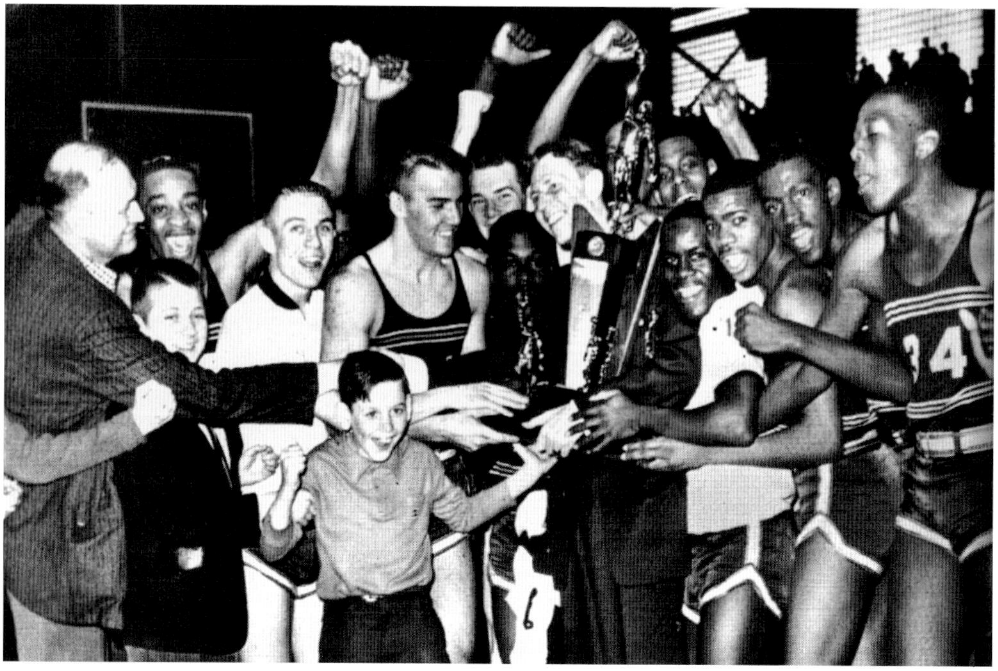

This is the 1961 afterglow for the Rouge after a 79-44 thrashing of Holland Christian in the Class B title. Dating back to the 1939 Class B semifinal loss, River Rouge won an amazing 28 games in 33 games at the home of the Big Ten's Spartans. Even more amazing is River Rouge's 26-year record in tournament games from 1951 to 1976: 143-14. (River Rouge *Vigilant*, 1961.)

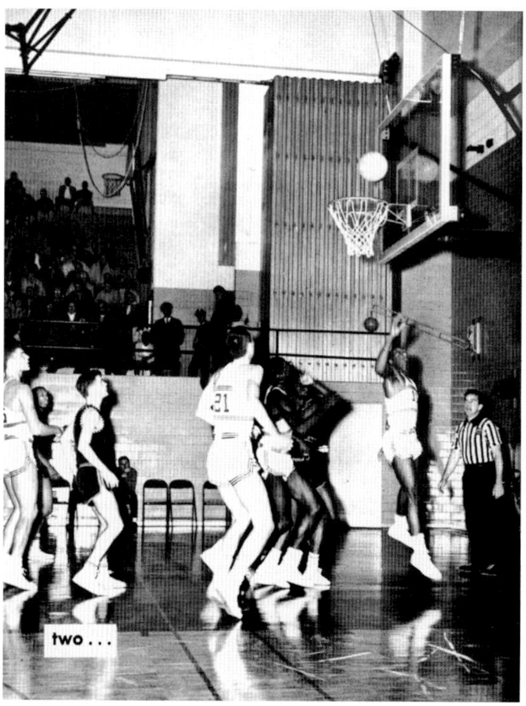

Senior Bill Dunson (airborne) scores two in this 1962–1963 season game at the Buck. Dunson made his mark on River Rouge's outstanding history by earning an All-State appointment and scoring 16 points in that season's Class B final versus No. 2–ranked Hudsonville Unity Christian. After Hudsonville pulled with two, 38-36, Dunson's key jumper, sandwiched by Boice Bowman and Larry Brazon, clinched the 59-49 win for Rouge. (River Rouge *Vigilant*, 1963.)

Panther Fred Hudson (32) scores two in the 1963 Class B state tournament, part of a five-title, 48-game streak of dominance that stretched from the 1961 district opener to the 1966 Class B semifinals. Rouge won the 1963 title with a 59-49 win over No. 2–ranked Hudsonville Unity Christian at Jenison Field House. (River Rouge *Vigilant*, 1963.)

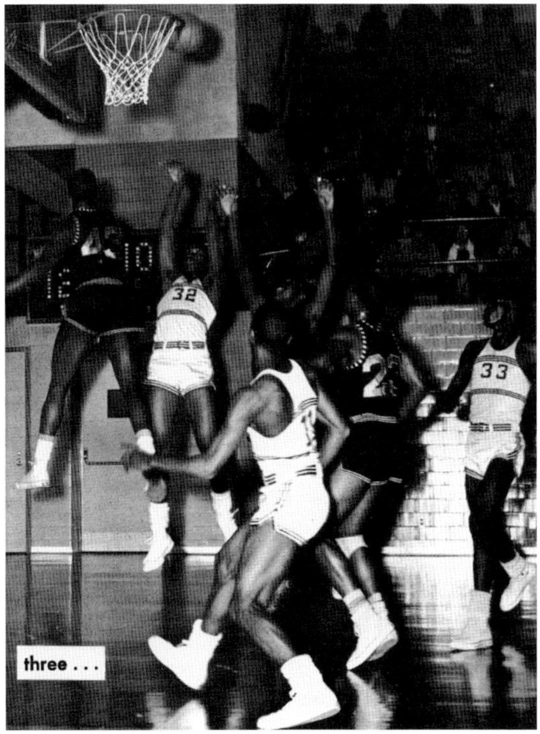

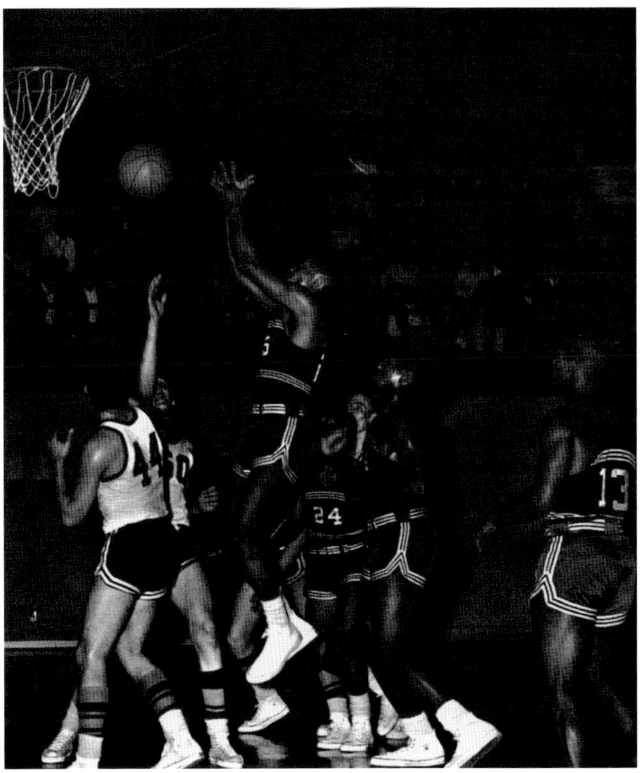

Frank Price attempts to corral a loose ball in the 1964 River Rouge Christmas tournament, an annual tradition until the 2007–2008 season. The Panthers went 6-2 in the Twin-Valley Conference and 24-2 overall in the 1964–1965 season. Price scored 28 points in Rouge's 87-65 Class B finals win over South Haven High that eclipsed the state record for team points in a final, set by Rouge in the finals the year earlier. (River Rouge *Vigilant*, 1965.)

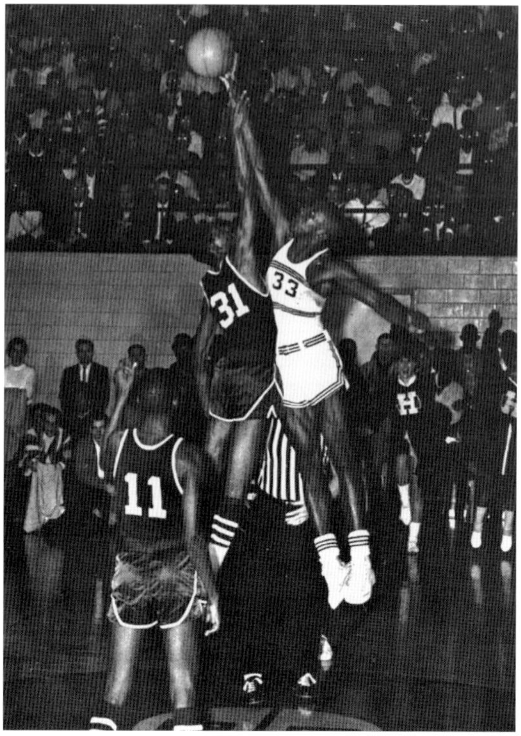

No one had to ask the Panthers to get fired up for Highland Park, as Willie Betts (33) wins the opening tap in front of a sold-out throng at the Buck in the 1963–1964 season. (River Rouge *Vigilant*, 1964.)

Willie Betts remains the only Michigan prep player to start and win four finals. Betts, six feet, five inches in his freshman year of 1961, helped Rouge march to the first of five straight titles by crushing Holland Christian 79-44. In 1962, Rouge blew out East Grand Rapids, 69-36. As a junior, Betts and his No. 1–ranked Panthers defeated No. 2 Hudsonville Unity Christian, 59-49. The 1964 finals victory over Lakeview allowed the All-State Betts to earn his unprecedented place in prep basketball history. (River Rouge Historical Museum.)

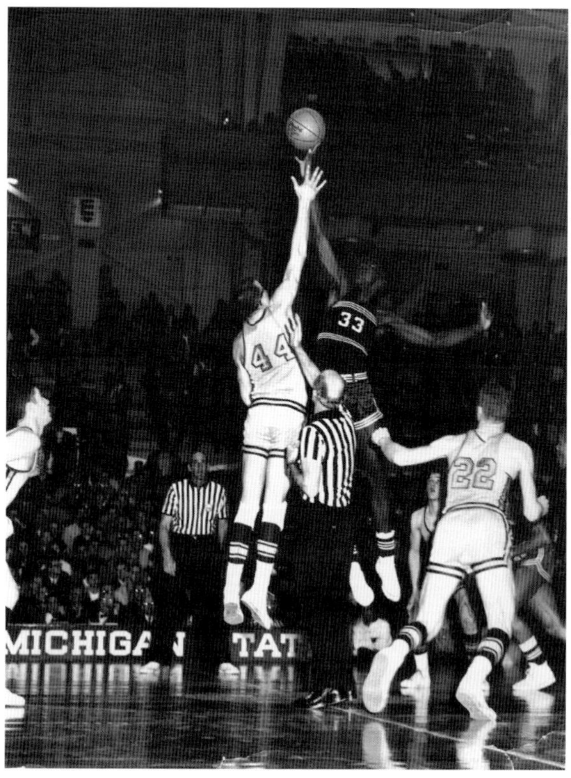

Ben Benford fakes his Ecorse rival skyward before depositing two during the 1965–1966 season. The Panthers defeated their Red Raider rivals three times in the 1965–1966 season, including a district elimination game while extending their amazing 48-game winning streak in MHSAA tournament play. Grand Rapids East Christian, however, led by Bill VanderWoude's 36 points, handed Rouge a stunning 76-66 setback in the Class B finals, denying Lofton Greene's Panthers a sixth consecutive title. (River Rouge *Vigilant*, 1966.)

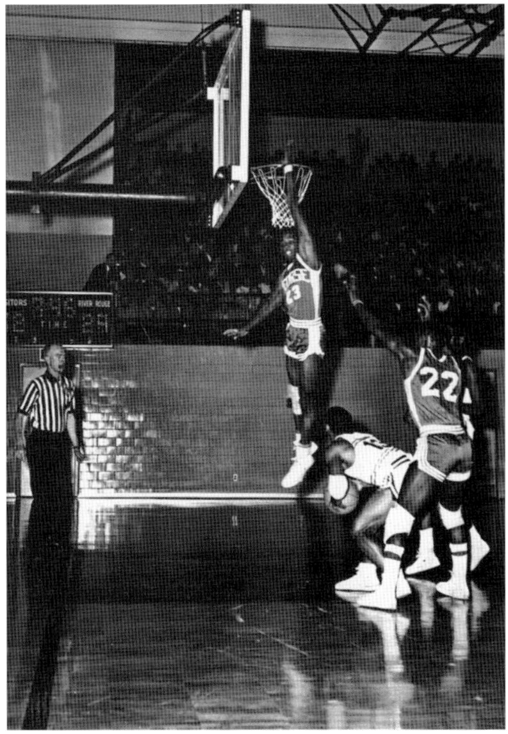

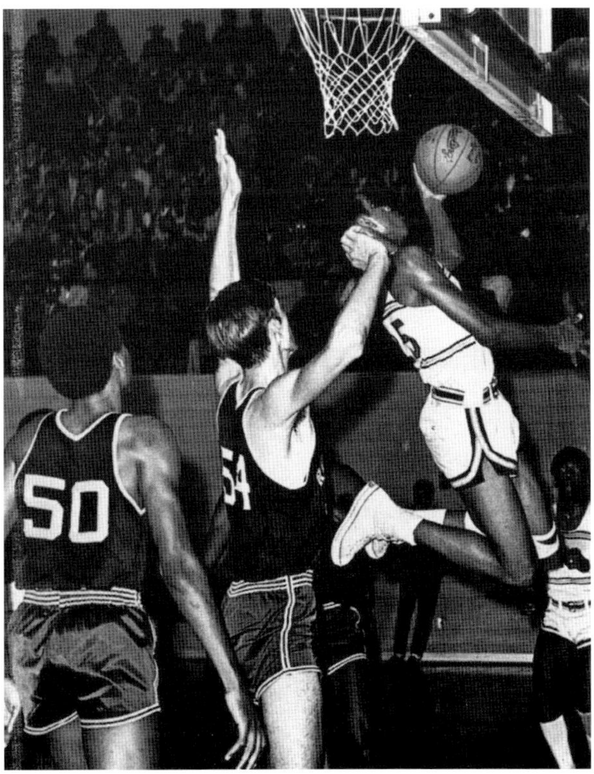

Malcolm Moulton, pictured here scoring in 1970 versus Romulus's John Long (50), joined younger brother Leighton as one of several brother combos to grace the Rouge under coach Lofton Greene. Leighton Moulton starred from 1970 to 1972. (River Rouge *Vigilant*, 1970.)

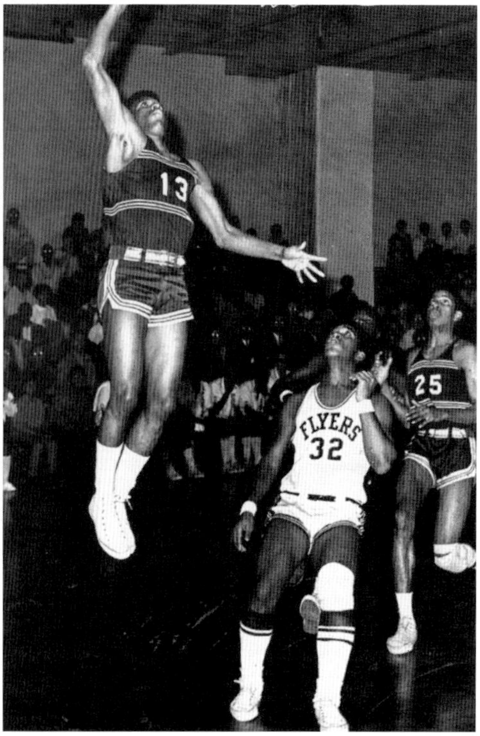

Kenny Russaw scores two in a 1970 game at Ypsilanti's Willow Run High. Malcom Moulton (25) trails the play. Rouge would defeat the Flyers 94-83 in the regional final en route to Rouge's 10th state title. Longtime rivals with Rouge, Willow Run coach Ron Tarrant defeated Greene's Panthers in the quarterfinals of both 1980 and 1981 and hired the retired Greene as a subvarsity coach and later varsity assistant when Tarrant landed at Dearborn Heights Robichaud. (River Rouge *Vigilant*, 1970.)

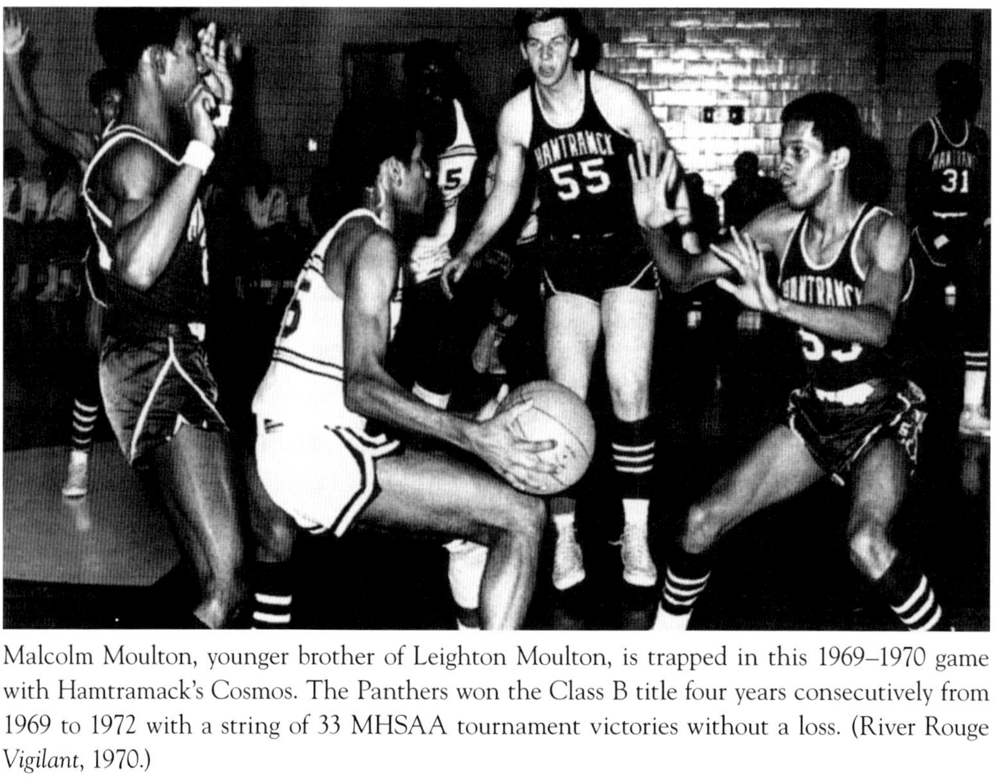

Malcolm Moulton, younger brother of Leighton Moulton, is trapped in this 1969–1970 game with Hamtramack's Cosmos. The Panthers won the Class B title four years consecutively from 1969 to 1972 with a string of 33 MHSAA tournament victories without a loss. (River Rouge *Vigilant*, 1970.)

Malcolm Moulton embodies River Rouge versus rival Ypsilanti's Willow Run High in this 1970 game: talent and effort creates victory. The Panthers were talented, yes, but they also forced their opponents to play a near-perfect game in order to defeat them. Obviously defeats were few and far between during 1970. The Rouge was 22-3 and captured wins 10-17 in the 1970 MHSAA tournament of a 33-game winning streak in tournament play from 1969 to 1972, resulting in four consecutive state titles. (River Rouge *Vigilant*, 1970.)

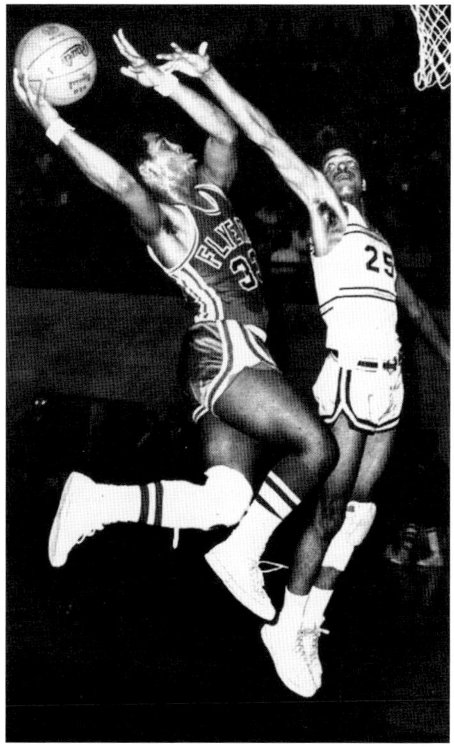

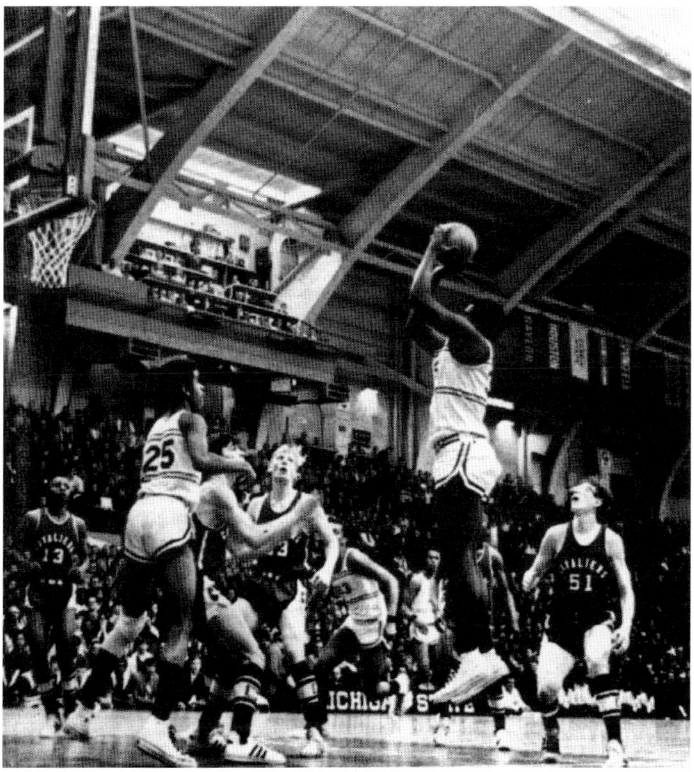

River Rouge always played the big room with a flair and panache that defined the Rouge. This is Dwayne "Big D" Johnson scoring two in a 76-66 win in the 1970 Class B title game with Saginaw Carrollton. Late Detroit sportswriter Joe Falls said the Panthers' annual drive toward the Class B title had "become almost their divine right each March." (River Rouge *Vigilant*, 1970.)

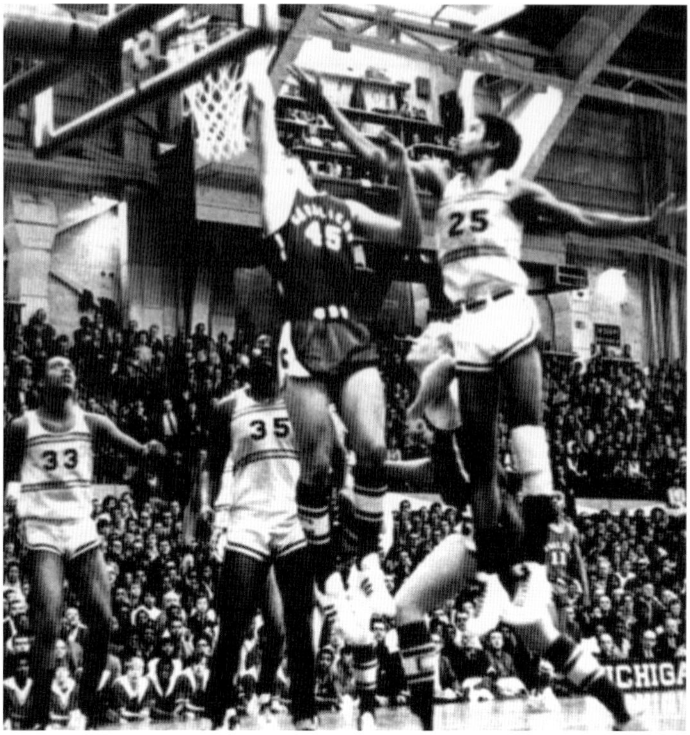

Saginaw Carrollton made the 1970 Class B final a thriller when the Cavaliers stormed back from a 50-33 deficit to take a 64-63 lead. With Rouge ball-handler Marvin Dunson benched with four fouls, Carrollton's Don Kubia (19 points) and Red Jones (15 points) swung the momentum and lead to the Cavaliers; then Rouge took the game and title right back with a 15-2 run. (River Rouge *Vigilant*, 1970.)

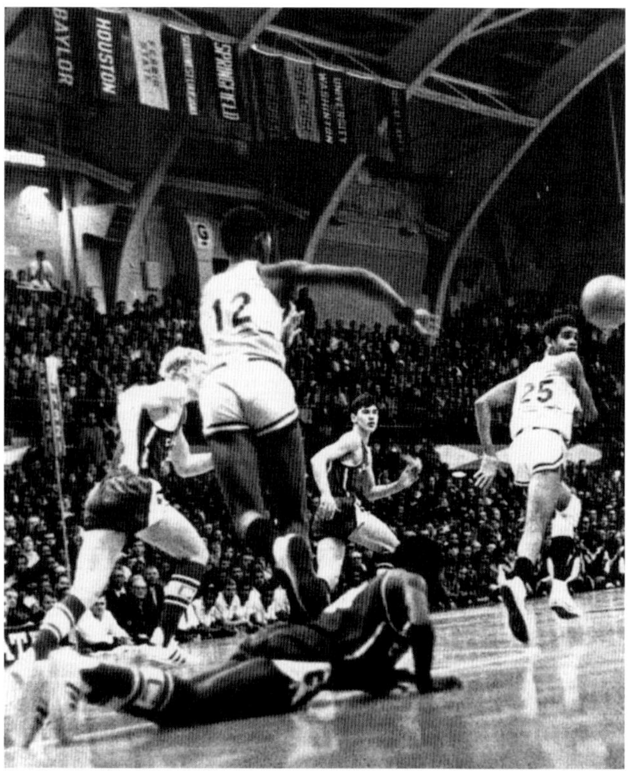

Al Boswell (12), nephew of former Panthers Fred, Lester, and Joe Hudson, passes up court to Malcolm Moulton in the final, desperate moments of the 1970 Class B final. Saginaw Carrollton erased a 17-point deficit to take a 64-63 lead, only to watch Rouge rattle the title from their grasp with a 15-2 run to end the game. In the 38 games played on the state's biggest state, the semifinals and finals, Rouge owns an amazing 33-5 ledger. (River Rouge *Vigilant*, 1970.)

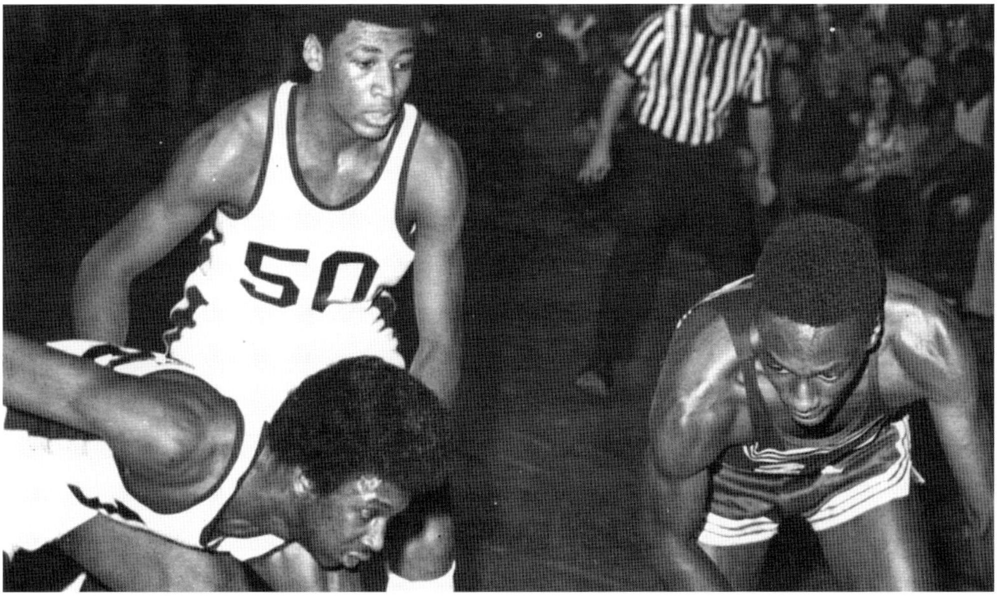

Romulus forward John Long (50) found great success as a collegiate player (University of Detroit-Mercy) and played 15 NBA seasons, including the 1988 Eastern Conference championship season with the Detroit Pistons. River Rouge, however, had prep bragging rights, as it did against many great teams and their greatest players. This game was part of a four-school rivalry with Ecorse, Romulus, River Rouge, and Ypsilanti Willow Run in the Twin-Valley Conference. (River Rouge *Vigilant*.)

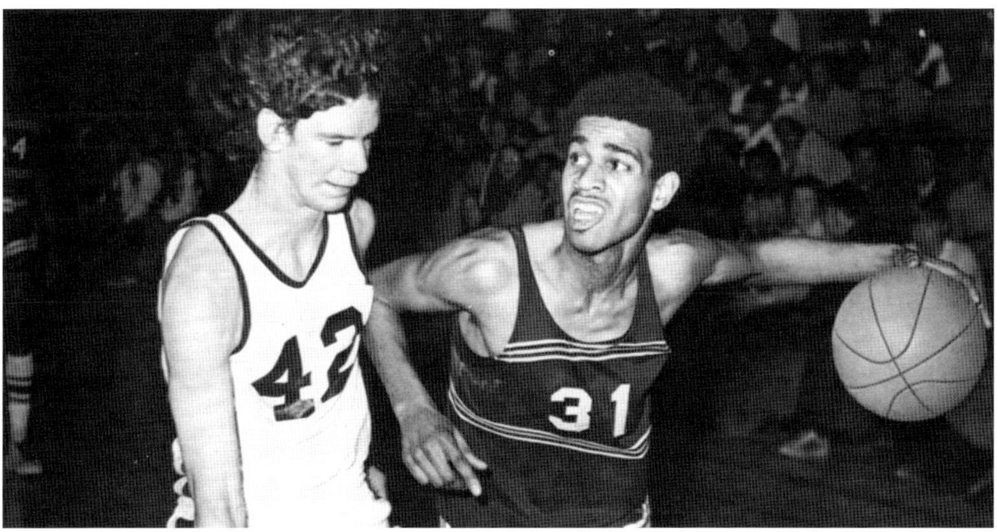

Leighton Moulton (31) is best remembered for leading River Rouge to the 1971 and 1972 Class B titles over Muskegon Heights. The 1971 final, a 71-65 win, was coach Lofton Greene's 500th win at River Rouge. The 1972 title tilt featured Moulton's memorable game-winning foul shots with just two seconds remaining. Not until 1998 would Rouge capture another title. (River Rouge *Vigilant*, 1972.)

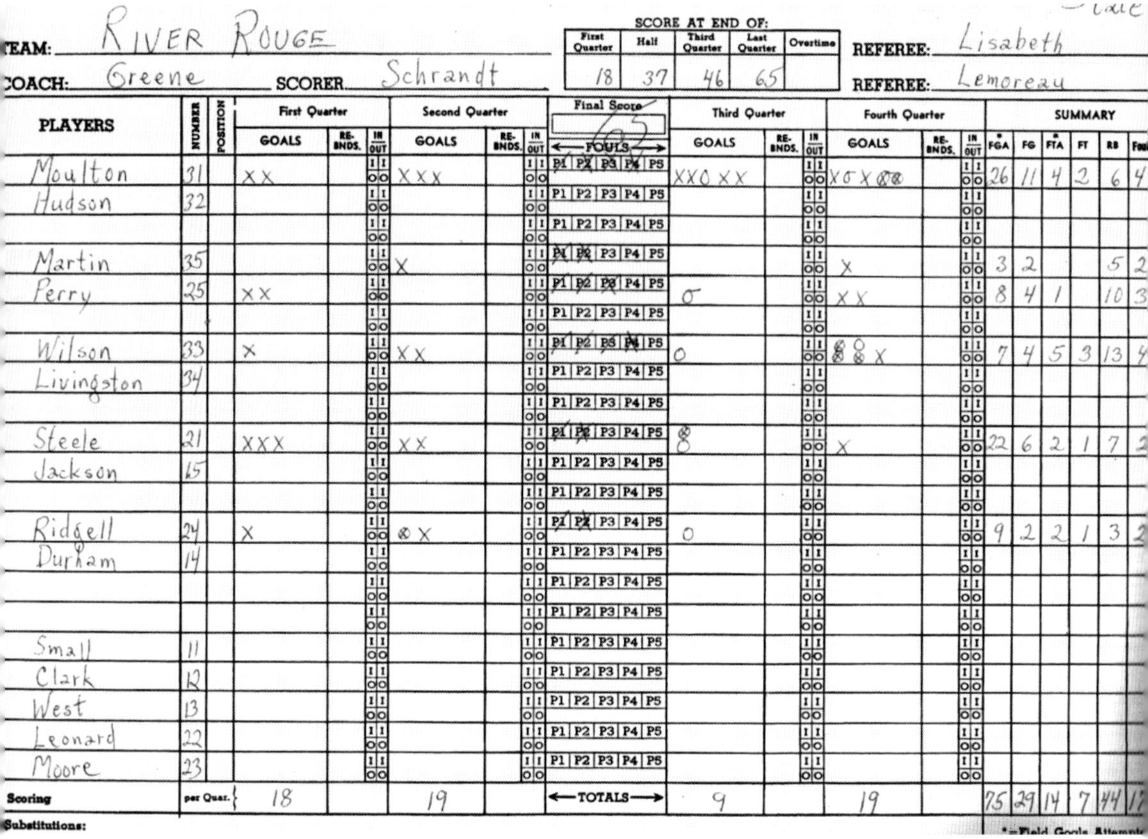

TEAM: RIVER ROUGE
COACH: Greene SCORER Schrandt

SCORE AT END OF: First Quarter	Half	Third Quarter	Last Quarter	Overtime
18	37	46	65	

REFEREE: Lisabeth
REFEREE: Lemoreau

PLAYERS	NUMBER	First Quarter GOALS	Second Quarter GOALS	Third Quarter GOALS	Fourth Quarter GOALS	FGA	FG	FTA	FT	RB	Fouls
Moulton	31	xx	xxx	xxo xx	xox ⊗⊗	26	11	4	2	6	4
Hudson	32										
Martin	35		x		x	3	2			5	2
Perry	25	xx		o	xx	8	4	1		10	3
Wilson	33	x	xx	o	⊗⊗ ⊗ x	7	4	5	3	13	4
Livingston	34										
Steele	21	xxx	xx	⊗	x	22	6	2	1	7	2
Jackson	15										
Ridgell	24	x	⊗x	o		9	2	2	1	3	2
Durham	14										
Small	11										
Clark	12										
West	13										
Leonard	22										
Moore	23										
Scoring per Quar.		18	19	9	19	75	29	14	7	44	17

Final Score 65

Here is the Rouge ledger from Leighton Moulton's Miracle in the 1972 Class B finals. Current Rouge athletic director Willie Johnson remembers sitting next to Leighton Moulton's mother: "We were all crying when we were losing, especially Mrs. Moulton. She was upset we wouldn't pull it out . . . Then the steal, the rebound and score, the turnover and Leighton's jumper, and the foul shots. The crowd was incredible," said Johnson, a member of the 1971 title team. Leighton Moulton's Miracle, the two free throws with two seconds remaining down 64-63 was also remembered by Joe Falls: "He stepped to the line while the crown quieted. The pressure was immense. Moulton looked up, let it go—and swish. Now utter bedlam. Moulton broke towards the center of the court, thrusting his fist into the air . . . but now he had another chance . . . the chance to win it. He made the most of it by dropping the second free throw. That's when the tears started coming out of Lofton Greene's eyes." (River Rouge Historical Museum/Lofton Greene collection.)

Brent Darby (24) earned a spot in River Rouge lore by leading the Panthers to the 1998 Class B title, a 60-54 win over Marshall High. During the school's first championship since 1972 and first title game appearance since 1976, Darby scored 20 points. Rouge survived Marshall's furious fourth-quarter comeback and Ryan Van Dyke's game-high 24 points to earn the 13th state title in school history. (MHSAA archive/Gary Shook.)

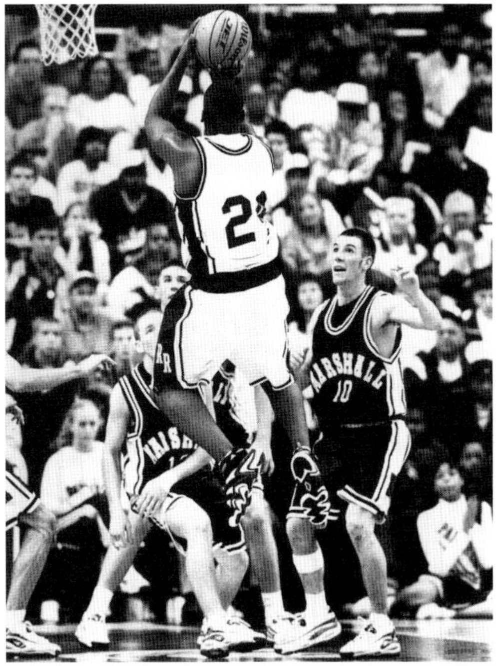

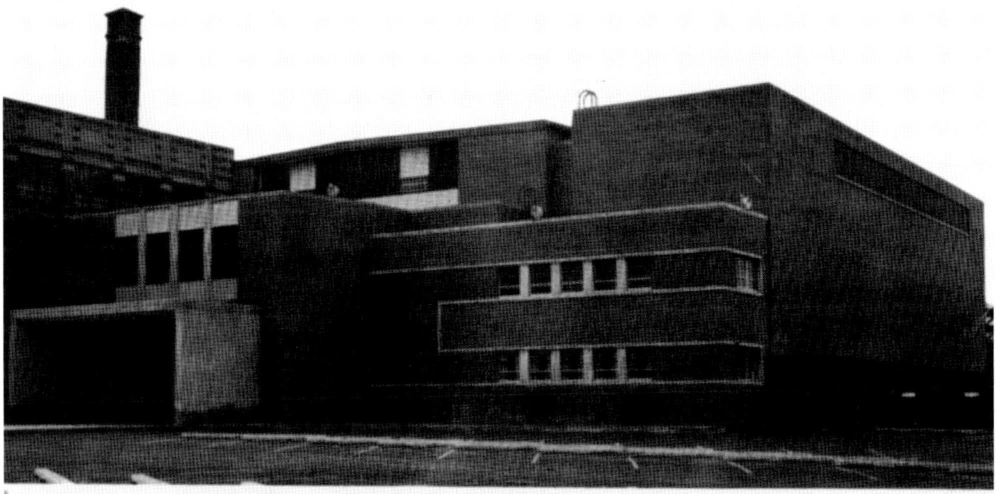

FRANK "BUCK" WEEBER GYMNASIUM

RIVER ROUGE HIGH SCHOOL
RIVER ROUGE, MICHIGAN

The "House that Buck Built" was the home to River Rouge's incredible success, including 12 of the 14 Class B titles River Rouge has won and 14 of the 18 Class B title games Rouge has appeared in. The building used to be attached to the school but now stands opposite the current high school; the former school building was razed five years ago. A leaking roof and failed plumbing have shelved the Buck, but River Rouge is soliciting and enlisting community-wide help to save the Buck. (River Rouge Historical Museum.)

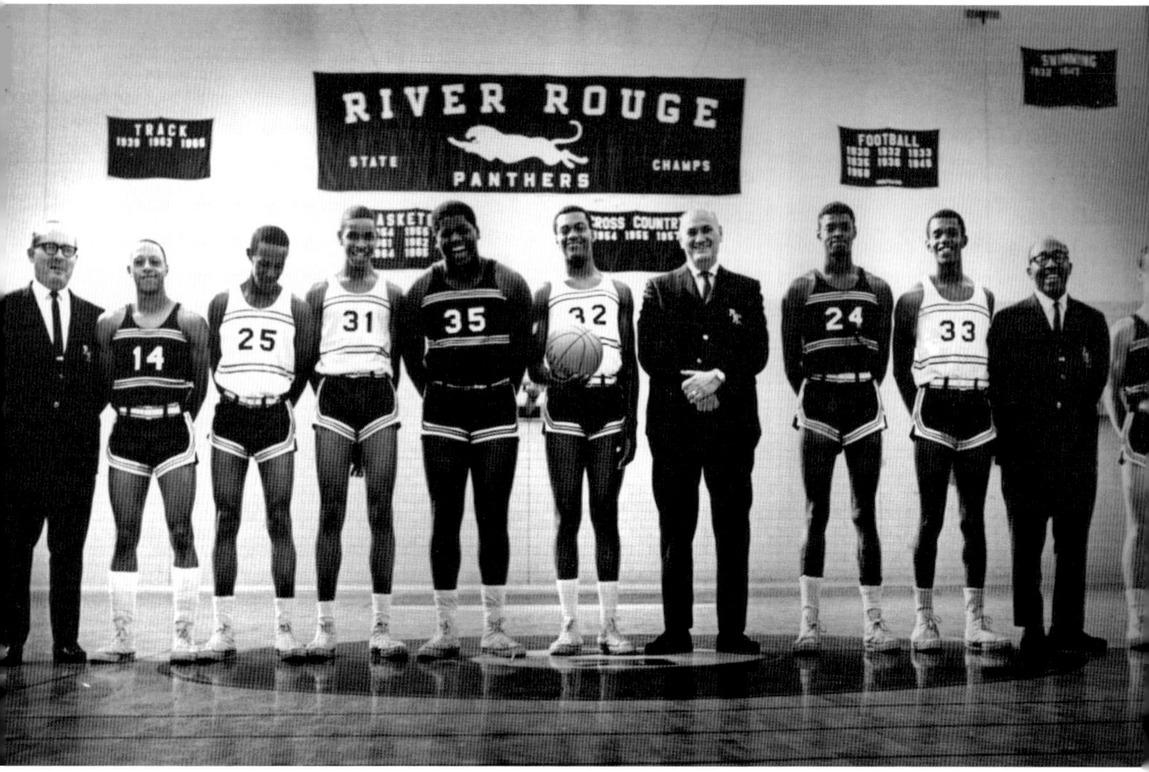

River Rouge's band of championship brothers includes, from left to right, ninth-grade coach James Duffy; Rodney Whimfrey (14), 1969 team member, whose brother Roger played on the 1972 titlist; Marvin Dunson (25), 1970 title, brother of 1963 titlist Bill; Malcolm Moulton (31), 1969 and 1970, brother of Leighton, 1970–1972; DeWayne "the Diesel" Johnson (35), 1970; Richard Clark Jr. (32); coach Lofton Greene; Curtis "Knight" Martin (24), first cousin to Blanch Martin of the 1954 team; Victor Warton (33), 1968 and 1969, drafted by the Buffalo Bills; coach DeWayne "D-D" Smith, member of the 1954 title team and successor to Greene; and Clayton Young (15), 1971 title winner. The dean of all basketball coaches statewide is Rouge's Lofton Greene. Greene won 710 of his amazing 739 wins at the Rouge. He claimed 12 Class B titles in 17 title game appearances. Greene was part of the inaugural Basketball Coaches Association of Michigan (BCAM) Hall of Fame class in 1985. (River Rouge Historical Museum.)

6

Great Coaches

Metro Detroit's greatest prep basketball teams are forever linked to metro Detroit's greatest coaches.

Post–World War II featured Chicago's Will Robinson at Detroit Miller, Chuck Hollosy at Detroit Austin, and Bernie Holowicki at St. Hedwig and later St. Gregory. When Miller closed, Robinson turned Detroit Pershing into champions, Hollosy went to Grosse Pointe South, and Holowicki relocated to Detroit De La Salle.

Detroit's northern suburbs expanded in the 1950s and 1960s. Art VanRyzin established Pontiac High as a powerhouse with a late charge in 1960 that would sustain the Chiefs for two decades. Chuck Jones left Ohio for Royal Oak High, which split into rivals Royal Oak Dondero and Royal Oak Kimball. After more than 40 years of service at Kimball, Jones is practically remembered as Mr. Kimball more than the school's namesake. Roy Burkhart closed Ferndale Lincoln, opened Ferndale High, and won two titles in four years (1963 and 1966). Bill Foley left Catholic Central after winning the 1961 Class A title, and Holowicki filled the void at 6565 West Outer Drive.

Dave Soules gave East Catholic High championship status in the 1970s. Steve Rhoads entrenched himself at Berkley High, and the Bears became a formidable challenge for almost 25 years. University of Detroit High grad Bill Norton was the only coach Birmingham Brother Rice had known, but Michigan soon learned about Norton and his Warriors, who won the 1974 title. Darrell Pursiful guided talent-laden Highland Park to some of metro Detroit's most memorable victories and the 1975 title. Pontiac Central's Ralph Grubb, who succeeded VanRyzin, endeared himself as one of coaching's favorite sons for chasing the title that ultimately eluded the chief of Pontiac.

Perry Watson turned Detroit Southwestern into a powerhouse, and Ben Kelso churned three consecutive championships at Detroit Cooley in the 1980s. William Winfield crusaded Detroit King to five state titles; Mary Lillie-Cicerone led the charge to four state titles for Birmingham Marian. They are both still chasing Regina's Diane Laffey, winner of over 600 games in basketball.

Johnny Goston took Pershing to four straight finals in the 1990s. Greg Esler won Macomb County's only championship at St. Clair Shores Lakeshore. Kurt Keener and Frank Orlando became the statewide legends at Detroit Country Day, and Derrick McDowell resurrected Detroit Redford. Esler took over at De La Salle, and Laffey relocated with her Saddelites to Warren.

Metro Detroit's prep basketball legacy of the past and present and that of future generations are in capable hands.

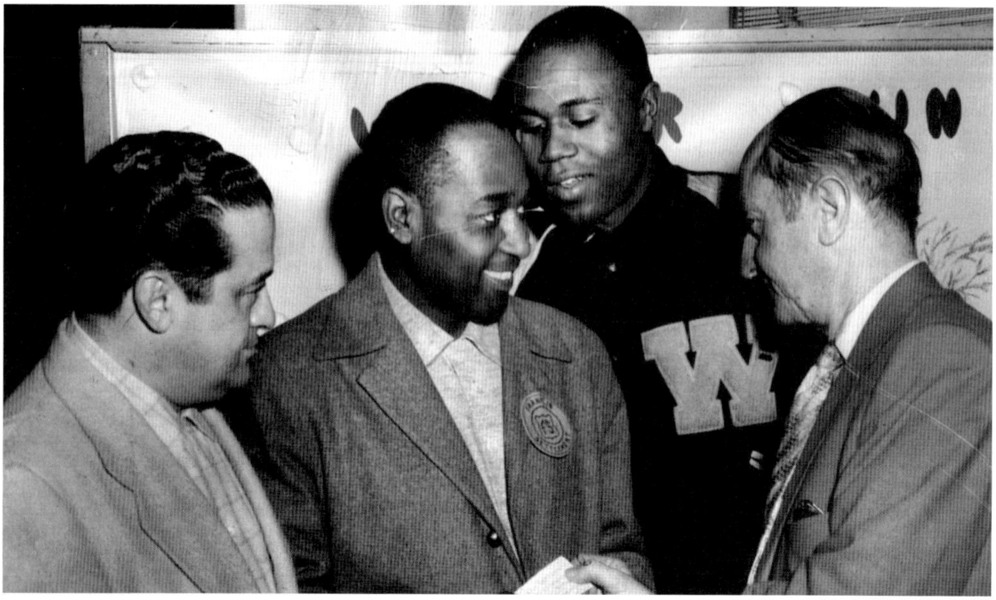

Chicago's Will Robinson relocated to Detroit to calm tensions stemming from the 1943 race riots. After a successful stint at Detroit Miller High, Robinson earned Detroit Pershing two MHSAA titles (1967 and 1970). Robinson is handed an admission card to Franklin Housing Settlement in 1954 from Joseph Beattie as Eddie Deloretto (left) and former Miller player Charlie "Kingsnake" Primas observe. (The Detroit News/Heinze Hoffman.)

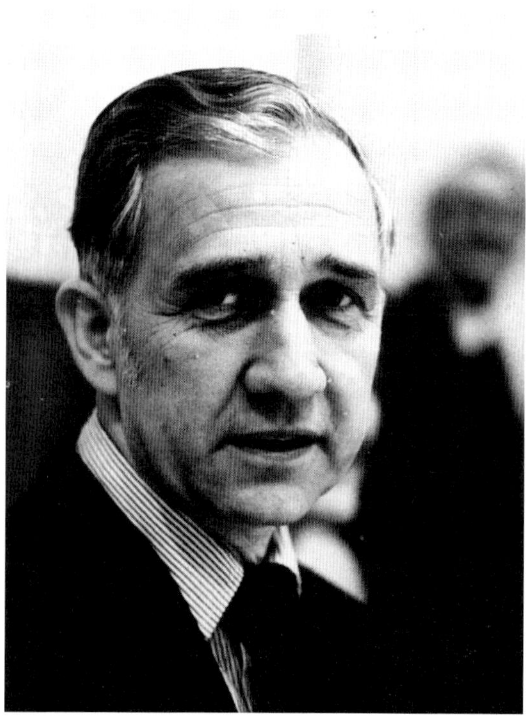

BCAM Hall of Fame member Bernie Holowicki coached four Detroit Catholic League schools to a 612-216 ledger. Holowicki started at St. Hedwig in 1953, moved to St. Gregory, took over at De La Salle, and ended his career at Catholic Central in 1994. He led Catholic Central to the 1976 state championship—the last MHSAA champion in Class A won by a private school. (The Detroit News.)

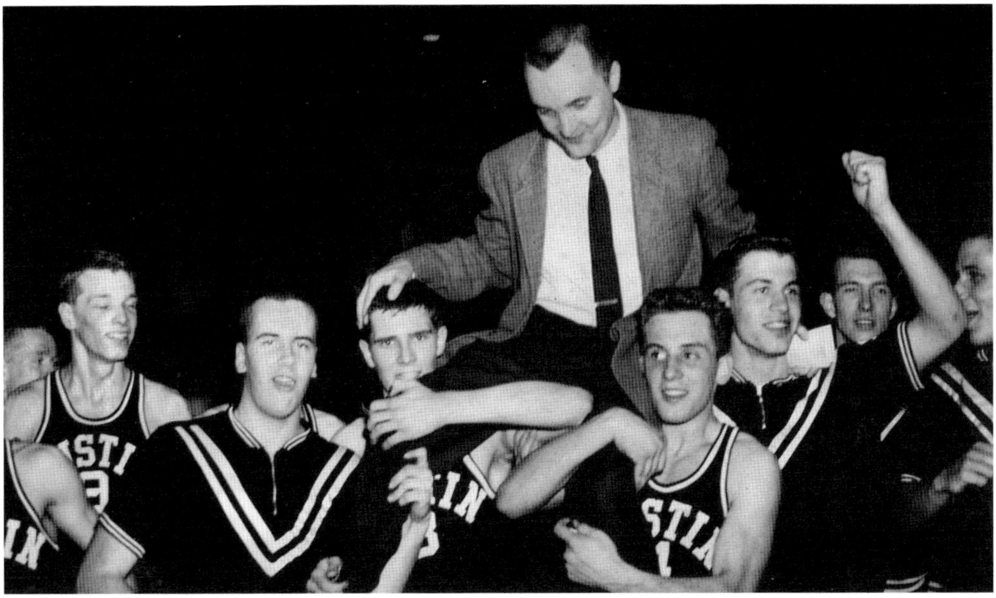

Chuck Hollosy's legacy was already secure when the crew cut, square-jawed coach relocated to Grosse Pointe High in the early 1960s after leading Detroit Austin to back-to-back Class A finals in 1957 and 1958. His 1958 Friars won perhaps the greatest finals game ever, when Benton Harbor's Chet "the Jet" Walker and Austin's Dave "Big D" DeBusschere dueled. Walker scored 25, DeBusschere netted 32, and Austin won, 71-68. (MHSAA archive.)

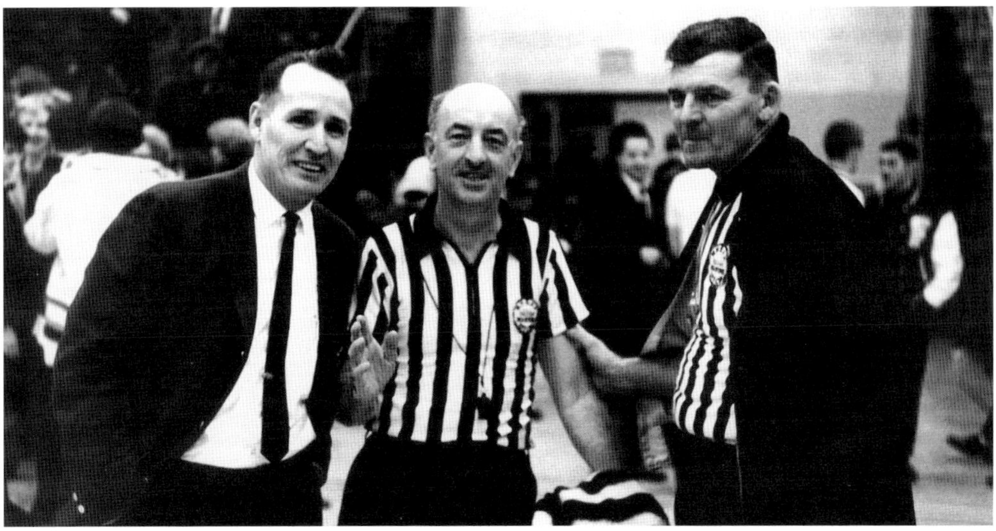

Ferndale's Roy Burkhart (left) and Casey Lopata (right) share this picture with an unidentified official. Burkhart's Eagles captured the 1963 and 1966 Class A state titles. He was named to the state coaches' hall of fame in 1973, the BCAM Hall of Fame in 1986, and earned something even legendary coach Lofton Greene can not boast: an undefeated state championship team. Burkhart's 1963 title team was 22-0 and won three straight one-point games in the regional final, quarter, and semifinals. (Stan Lopata family collection.)

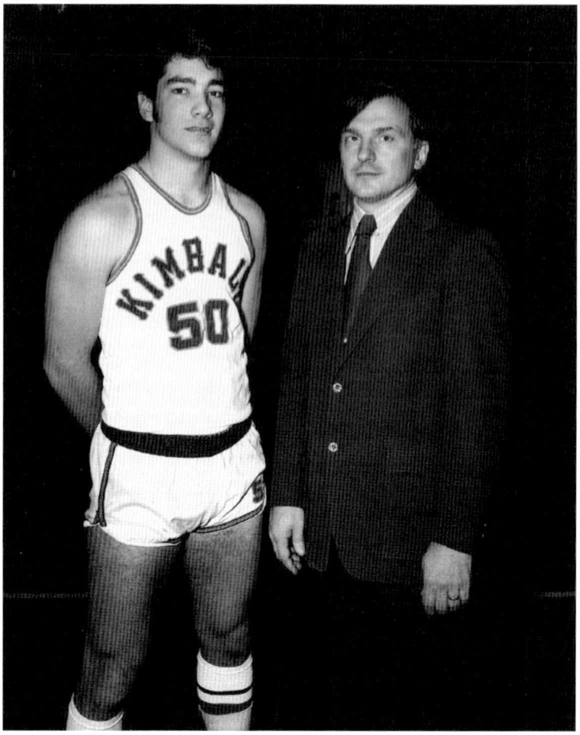

No coach advocated his district and school more than Royal Oak Kimball High's Chuck Jones. Shown with 1972 captain John Sichta, the Ohio native earned a 225-147 record at Kimball—including a 6-2 mark versus Detroit's PSL in MHSAA playoff games—from 1967 to 1984. Jones earned the Bush and Forsyth awards, four different state or national athletic director awards, and enshrinement in the state coaches' hall of fame (1986). (Chuck Jones collection.)

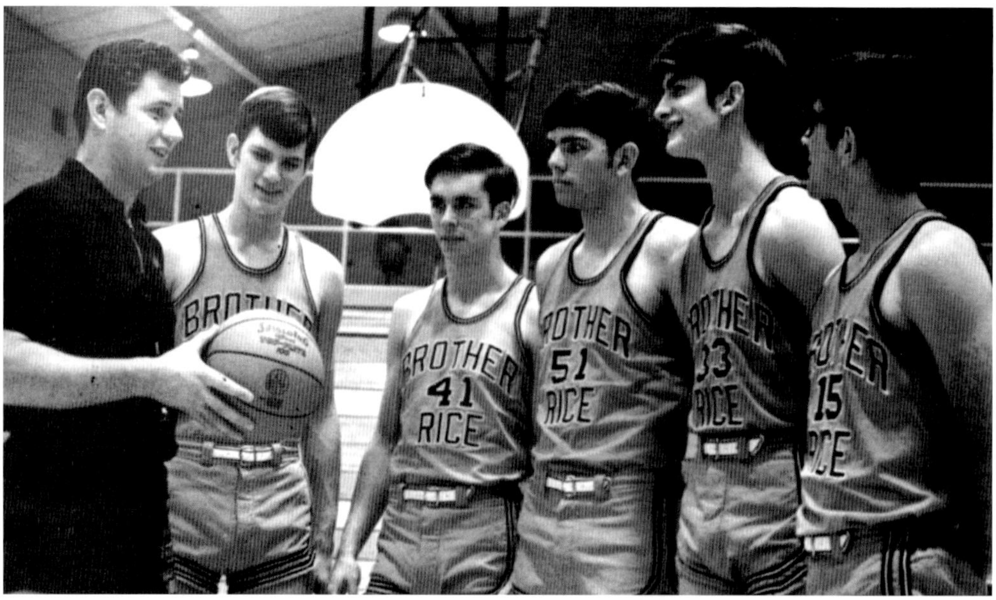

From left to right, Bill Norton shares some face time with Mark Olesnavage, Mark Hafeli, Joe Springer, Paul McGill, and Steve Foster in 1969–1970. Norton's Rice teams were 328-139, captured 12 districts, five CHSL crowns, and the 1974 Class A championship. Norton sandwiched two stints at Rice between a year at Michigan State University before posting 107 wins, three districts, and two league titles at Groves. (Bill Norton collection.)

Dave Soules never wore fancy suits, he worked in a run-down gym, and walked listed from the 111 keys hanging from his neck. However, Detroit East Catholic's 10 appearances in MHSAA championship games and eight state titles say more about Soules than any tailored suit or shiny gym floor. Soules earned a well-deserved BCAM Hall of Fame induction in 1998. After East Catholic closed in 2005, Soules coached at Riverview's Gabriel Richard until he passed in 2009 with an overall record of 589-279. (The Detroit News/ Alan D. Lawrence.)

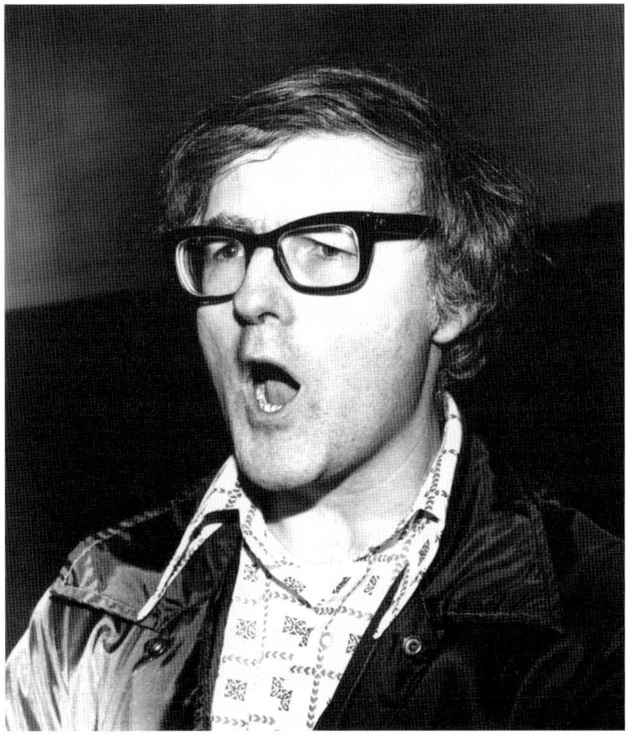

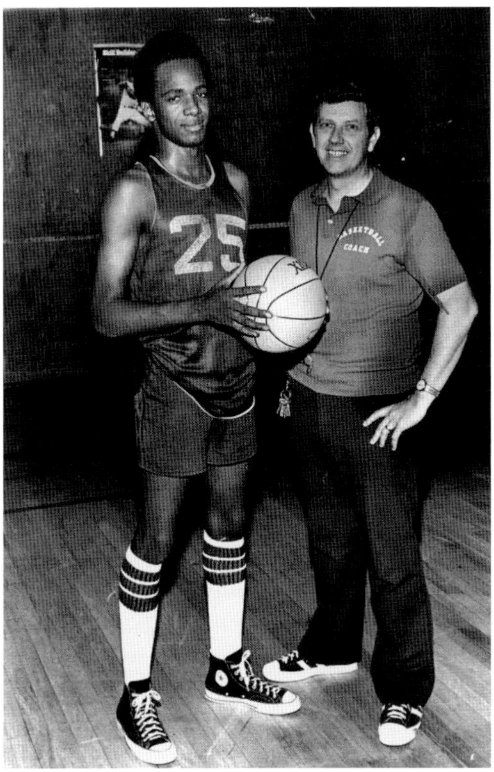

One of Detroit's two incorporated enclaves, Highland Park's bench leader was Darrell Pursiful during the year Terry Duerod led the Polar Bears to a memorable state title, defeating Berkley and Bruce Flowers in a memorable quarterfinal. Pursiful was elected to the BCAM Hall of Fame in 1992 and the state coaches' hall in 1996. (The Detroit News/Duane E. Belanger.)

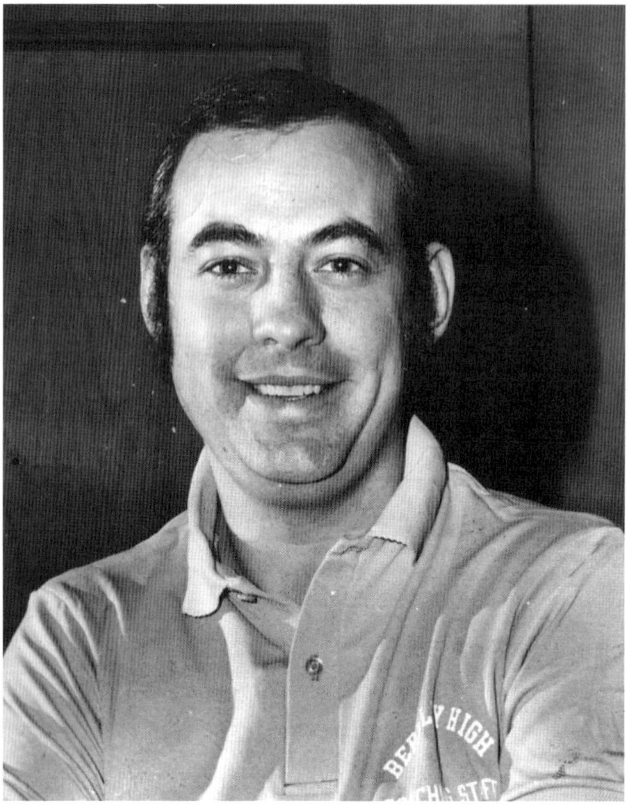

No coach molded the Berkley Bears into annual contenders before or after in any sport as Steve Rhoades did from 1970 to 1995. Under Rhodes, Berkley won a handful of league titles, seven district crowns, and the 1975 regional title with Bruce Flowers. His 1975 Berkley team won 25 consecutive games before losing their only game of the season to Highland Park in the Class A quarterfinal game. Rhoades is a member of both the BCAM Hall of Fame (2005) and the state coaches' hall (1999). (The Detroit News/Steffen.)

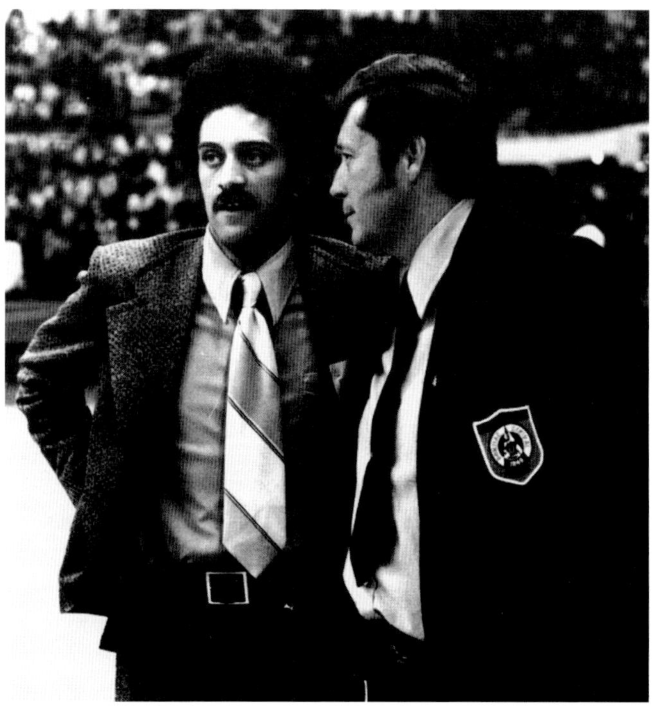

Saginaw High's Charlie Coles (left) and Pontiac Central's Ralph Grubb share some pregame pleasantries before the two longtime rivals from the Valley do battle in the 1976 Class A semifinals. Coles's Trojans nipped Grubb's Chiefs by a 53-52 count. (The Oakland Press/ Rolf Winter.)

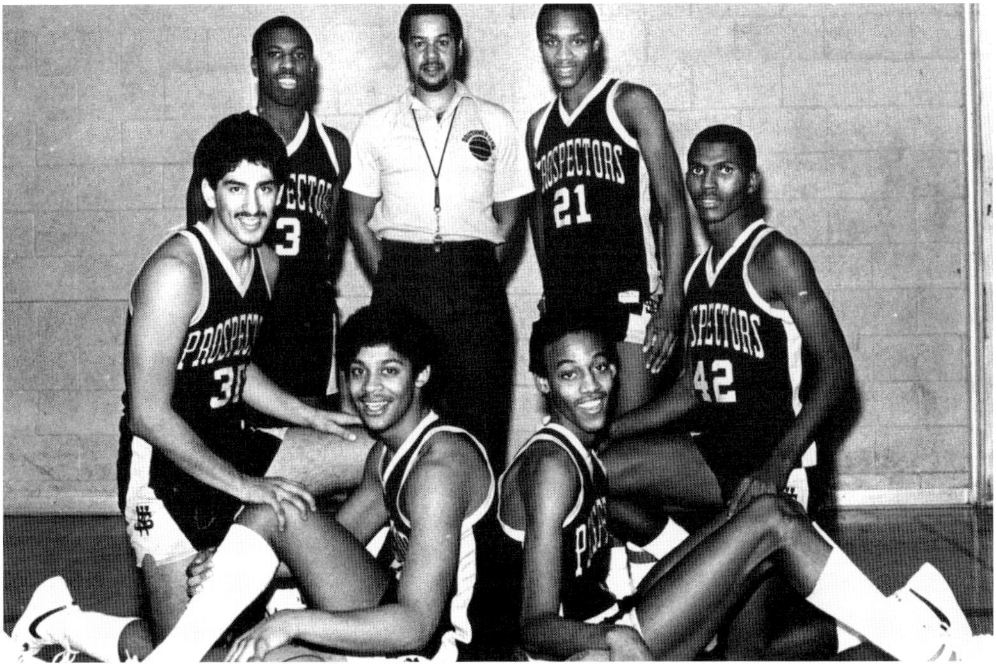

Perry Watson, 302-34 at Detroit Southwestern from 1978 to 1991, earned 10 MHSAA final fours, nine MHSAA finals, nine PSL titles, and two Class A championships. His 1990 team was Detroit's first-ever PSL/MHSAA champion. The 1991 Prospectors earned the No. 1 rank in *USA Today* with Watson as National Coach of the Year. Watson was inducted into the BCAM Hall of Fame in 2002 and became the Horizon League's winningest coach with his 261-198 mark at the University of Detroit-Mercy. (The Detroit News.)

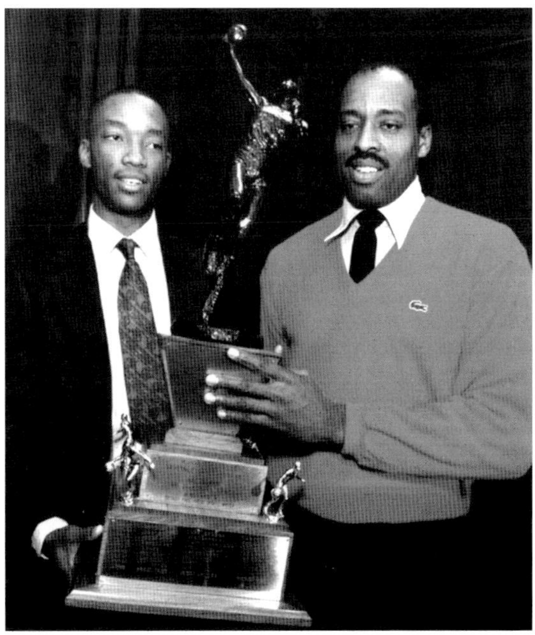

Flint's Ben Kelso coached three metro schools but made his mark from 1984 to 1998 at Detroit's Cooley High. His Cardinals won three consecutive MHSAA Class A titles (1987–1989), 12 district, six regional, and one PSL crown. He has since relocated at Detroit's Central High. (The Detroit News/Koeffler.)

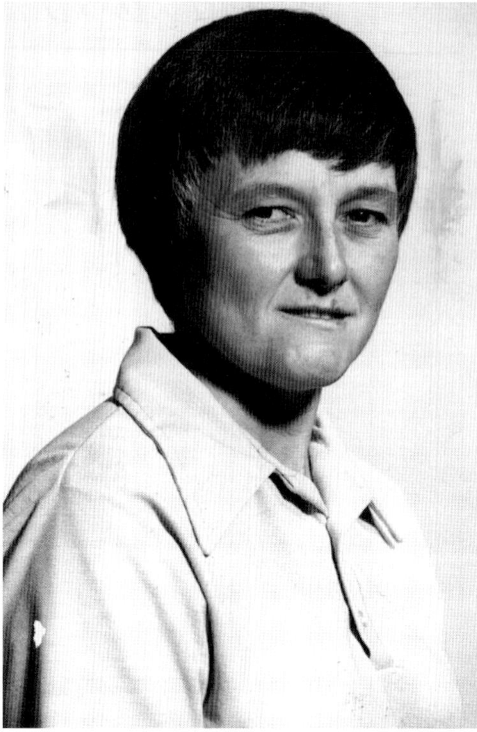

Coach Diane Laffey is a National High School Sports Hall of Famer, adding to her BCAM induction (1994) and state coaches induction (1997). Class A finalists in 1979, 1981, and 1983 and winners of four CHSL titles in basketball, Regina has also won five MHSAA softball crowns and 11 CHSL softball titles under Laffey. Her career ledger of 564-345 in basketball and 967-327-3 in softball leave a legacy even legends dream of. (The Detroit News.)

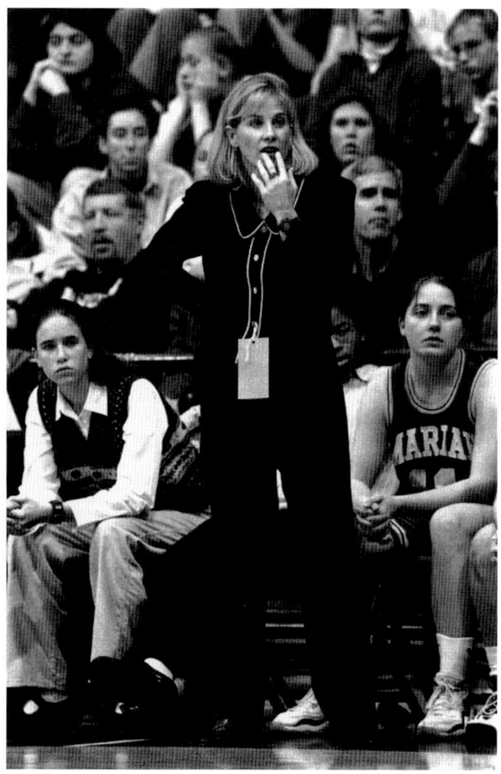

Mary Lillie was an all-state pistol of a player at Coopersville High near Grand Rapids; coach Mary Lillie-Cicerone is no different in 26 years at Birmingham Marian. Her Mustangs have won 11 Catholic League titles, 22 districts, five appearances in the state's title game, and four Class A championships. Lillie-Cicerone's overall record is 467-164. (MHSAA archives/Gary Shook.)

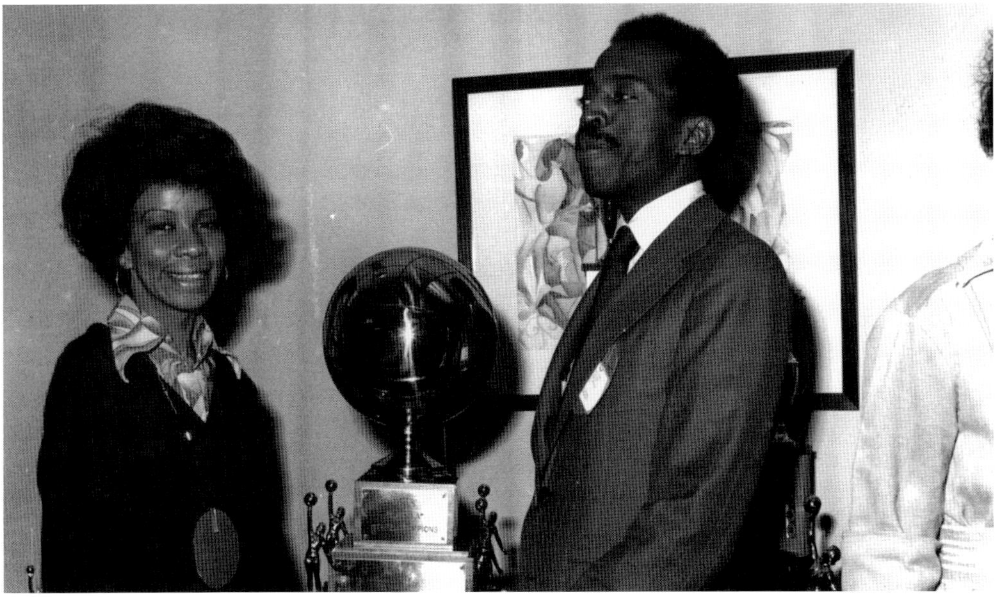

The first girls' state championship in PSL history and just the fourth overall since 1930 was delivered by coach Brenda Gatlin and Detroit Northeastern. The 1975 Falcons won the Class A title by defeating Catholic League power Farmington Hills Mercy. Gatlin has since relocated at Detroit Southeastern, where she serves as school principal. (MHSAA archives.)

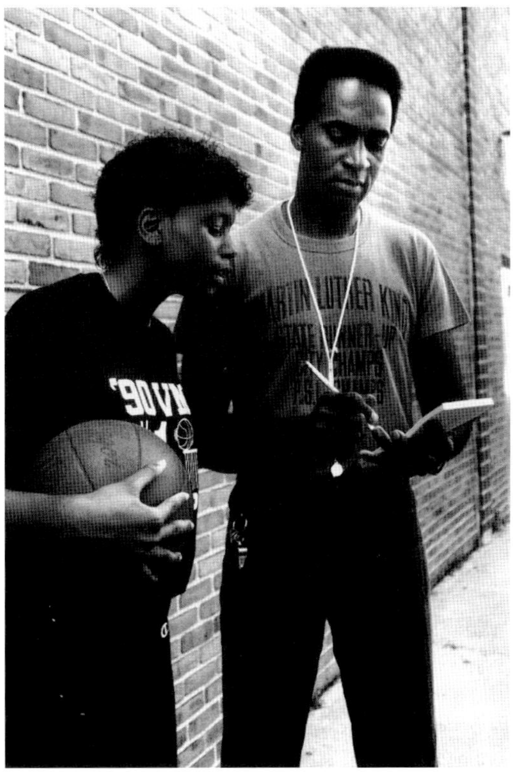

William Winfield began coaching as a fill-in for a sick colleague in 1982 at Detroit Southeastern High. Nearly 30 years later, Winfield is one of Michigan's most successful girls' basketball coaches. Shown here with 1990 Miss Basketball winner, Markita Aldridge, Winfield moved to Detroit King in 1984. Under Winfield, King won five MHSAA titles and advanced to 11 MHSAA finals, making Winfield Michigan's version of Lou Gerhig, one of the greatest replacements of all time. (The Detroit News/Charles Tines.)

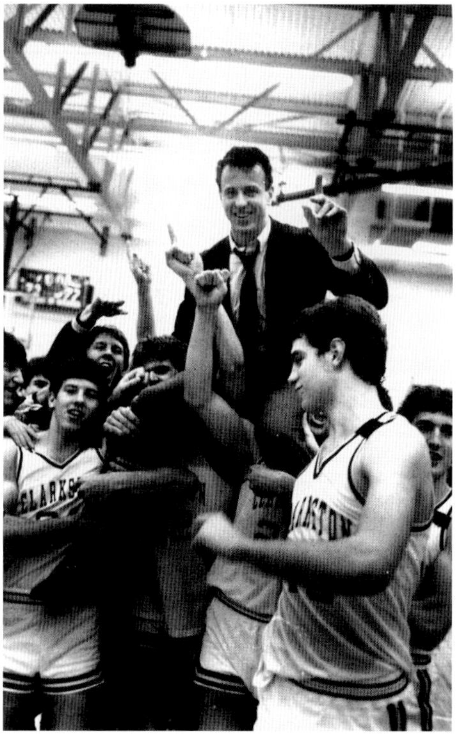

While humility would never allow him to admit it, Dan Fife is Mr. Clarkston. Fife has been the school's boys' varsity coach since 1982, advanced after just two years of coaching the school's freshman. Fife earned his 500th victory on February 17, 2009, over longtime rival Pontiac Central, 70-46. Fife's Wolves have earned 19 conferences titles, 21 district titles, and 9 regional crowns. Fife's 2009 team advanced to the state semifinals, falling to Kalamazoo Central High's Maroon Giants. (The Oakland Press/Rolf Winter.)

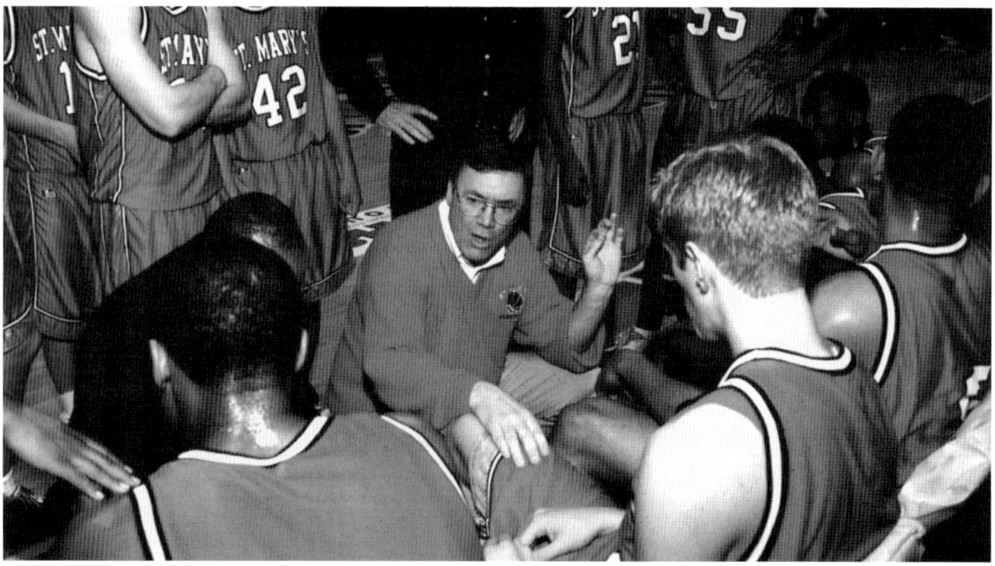

George Porritt's two stints at Orchard Lake St. Mary's have followed some legendary names in Orchard Lake St. Mary's history. Other notables from the lakeside school's considerable history are Rev. John Rakoczy's 275-78 mark from 1954 to 1972 and Bob Shoemaker's 124-24 ledger from 1977 to 1983. Porritt has efficiently continued the tradition of Michigan's second-winningest prep cage program (behind Saginaw High) with a 227-108 record from 1987 to 1992 and 1998 to the present. (MHSAA archive/Gary Shook.)

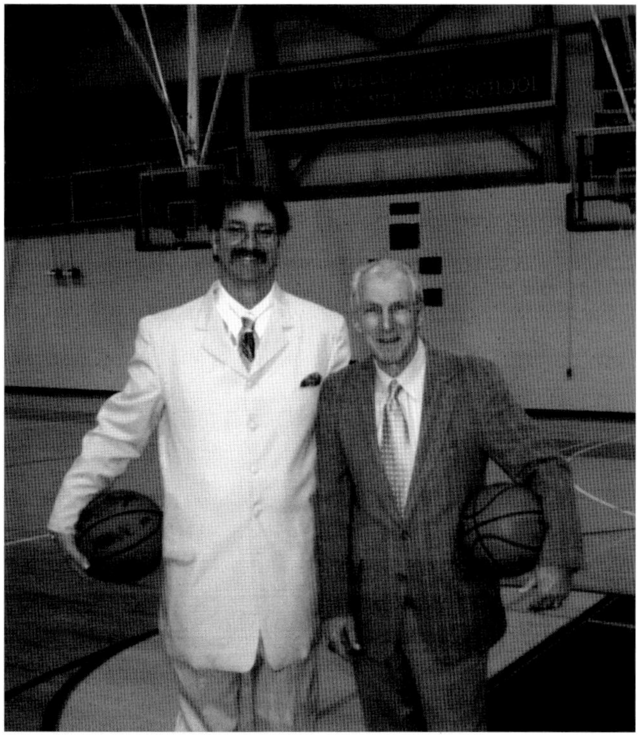

Debate remains as to which basketball coach is best at Detroit Country Day: Kurt Keener (left) or Frank Orlando. Keener, who reported his record as 585-164, is famously associated with Chris Webber and Shane Battier, but seven boys' Class B titles in seven finals appearances speaks for itself. Orlando, who reported a 581-97 ledger, has won 9 titles in 12 girls' basketball title games. (Detroit Country Day.)

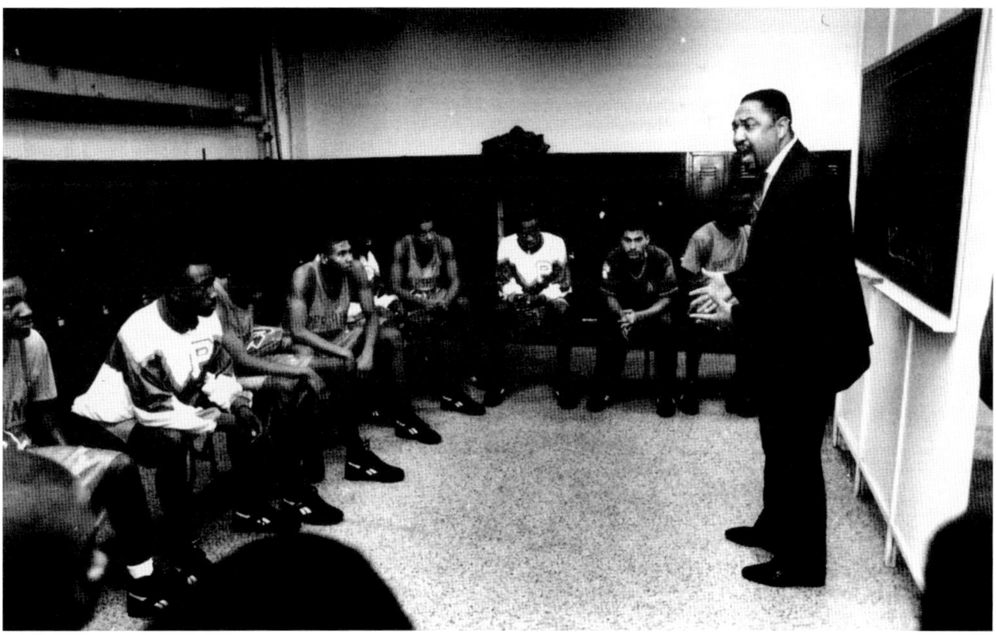

Johnny Goston took Detroit Pershing to back-to-back Class A titles in 1992 and 1993 and four consecutive trips to the Class A finals from 1992 to 1995, before a heart attack ended Goston's life. Speaking at halftime of Pershing's 1993 quarterfinal win over Walled Lake Central, Goston was equally passionate about kids and basketball. (The Detroit News/Joe DeVera.)

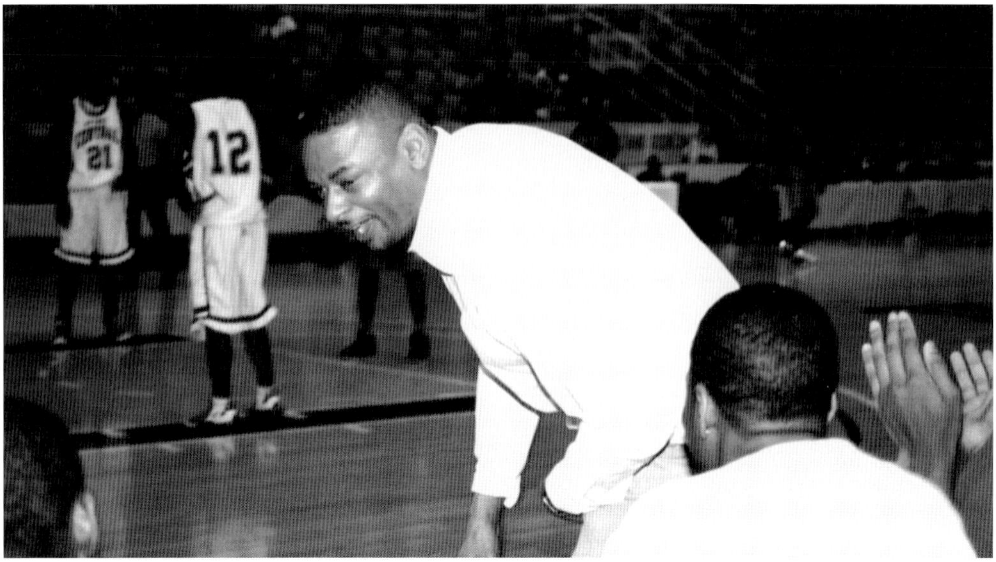

Detroit Northern grad Derrick McDowell turned dormant Detroit Redford into champions in 12 short years as Huskies' head coach. McDowell's 194-70 record reveals seven district titles, three regionals, three MHSAA semifinals, and two MHSAA championship game appearances (1997 and 2002). His Redford teams played five PSL title games, winning the 2001 and 2005 city crown. He assumed the associate head coach's position at Eastern Michigan University in 2005. (Nancy Jewitt archive.)

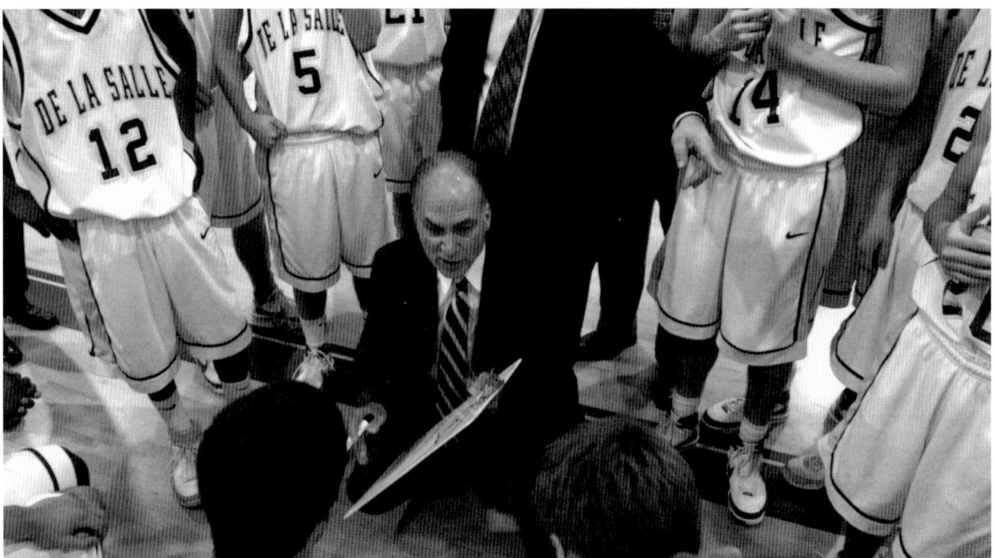

Winning Macomb County's sole championship in any class of boys' basketball, Greg Esler remains an east side staple. Esler guided St. Clair Shores Lakeshore to the 1994 Class B title. Since relocated to Warren's De La Salle High, Esler won Catholic League titles in 2001, 2002, and 2009 and advanced to the 2007 Class A semifinals. (The Detroit News.)

7

Playoffs, All-Stars, and Championships

In nearly 100 years of hosting the annual championship basketball tournament, some of the MHSAA's greatest moments have been the first-person elation and heartbreak for some of metro Detroit's most famous teams.

The 1958 marquee matchup of Benton Harbor's Chet "the Jet" Walker versus Detroit Austin's Dave "Big D" DeBusschere is perhaps the headliner to all MHSAA title tilts. MHSAA historian Dick Kishpaugh called Hamtramck's 80-79 overtime loss to Lansing Sexton in 1959 the greatest MHSAA finals game ever. Calvin High's last-second layup versus Orchard Lake St. Mary's in 1994 was a picture-perfect moment, as was Detroit East Catholic's buzzer-beater in the 1997 Class D finals.

River Rouge High's mark of 12 state titles and 144-13 tournament record from 1951 to 1976 merited their own chapter in this book. And many a potential state champion from Detroit's proper or the outlying suburbs have survived a rugged road to the MHSAA's finals only to meet defeat at the hands of a school from Flint or Saginaw, just as many of the best teams from those two cities were bested by Detroit's champions.

The PSL's absence from the MHSAA tournament from 1931 to 1961 represents metro Detroit's deplorable history of race relations over several generations rather than an acute representation of the MHSAA.

Detroit Pershing led the charge back to the tournament in 1962 with five straight wins before a loss in the Class A semifinals to Saginaw. The Doughboys earned Class A titles in 1967 and 1970. Perry Watson's Detroit Southwestern teams of 1982–1991 embarked on a run of nine appearances in the Class A finals in 11 seasons, winning Class A titles in 1990–1991. Ben Kelso and Detroit Cooley won three straight Class A titles from 1987 to 1989 without winning the PSL, proving the fierce city game's merits. Pershing also earned four straight appearances in the Class A finals.

Smaller Catholic League stalwarts like East Catholic, Holy Redeemer, and Southgate Aquinas are among a handful of Detroit parochial schools to be crowned champions. Detroit Country Day, where Chris Webber and Shane Battier prepped, became an elite proving ground for championship players among tony homes and fancy cars.

These are some of metro Detroit's proudest champions on Michigan's biggest high school basketball stage.

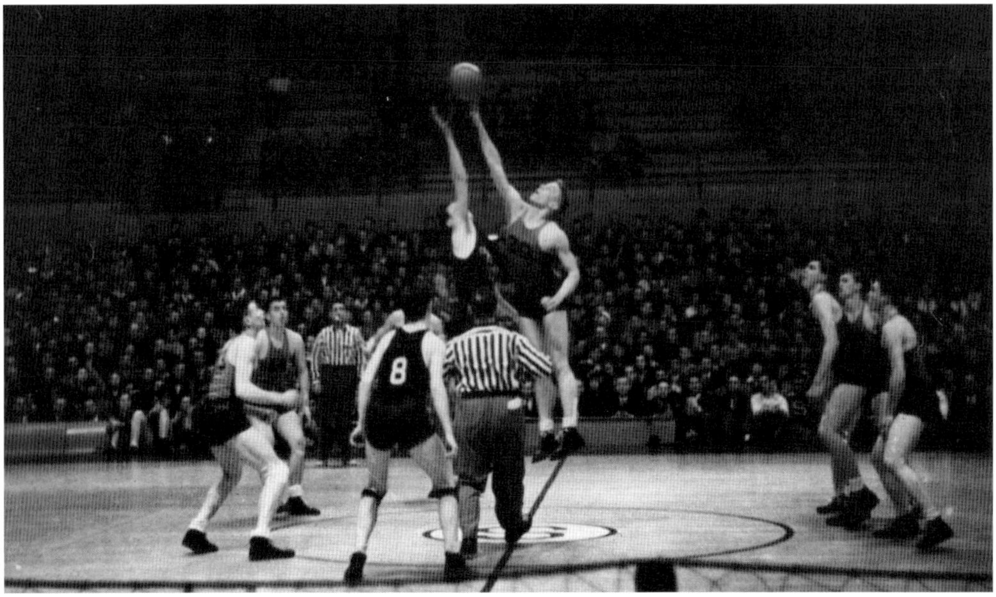

The first Detroit-proper school to compete for a state title in the post–World War II era was Detroit Country Day, who played in the 1946 Class D finals at Jenison Field House. The Yellowjackets dropped a 42-27 decision to coach Walt Briney's Bridgeman Bees, who played all 11 players and were led by John Camp's 19 points. (Detroit Country Day archive.)

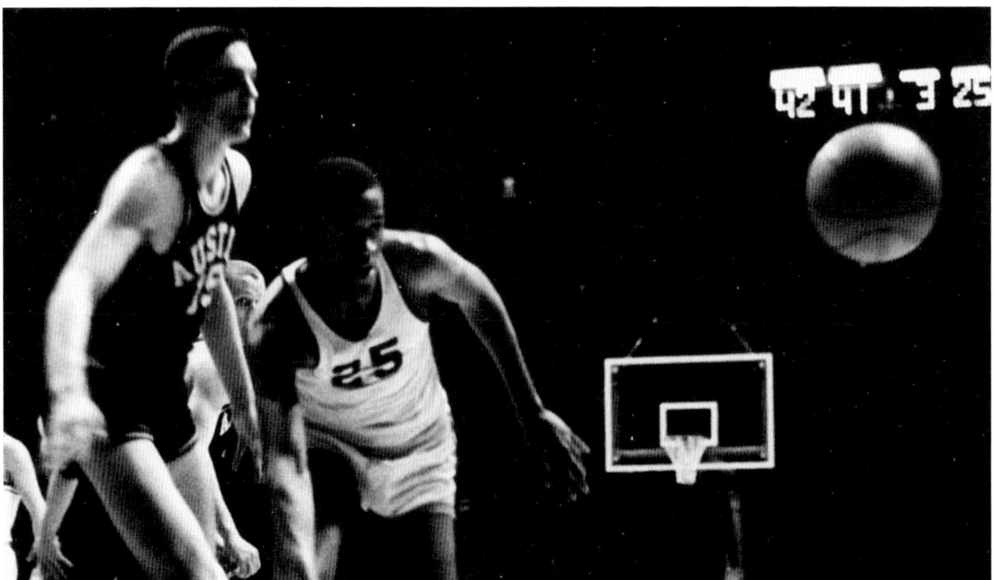

Detroit Austin's Dave "Big D" DeBusschere (19) and Benton Harbor's Chet "the Jet" Walker (25) battle during the famous 1958 Class A title game. Walker netted 25, DeBusschere scored 32, and Austin took home a 71-68 triumph. Both players played major collegiate and professional basketball, extending their duals a number of years. (MHSAA archives.)

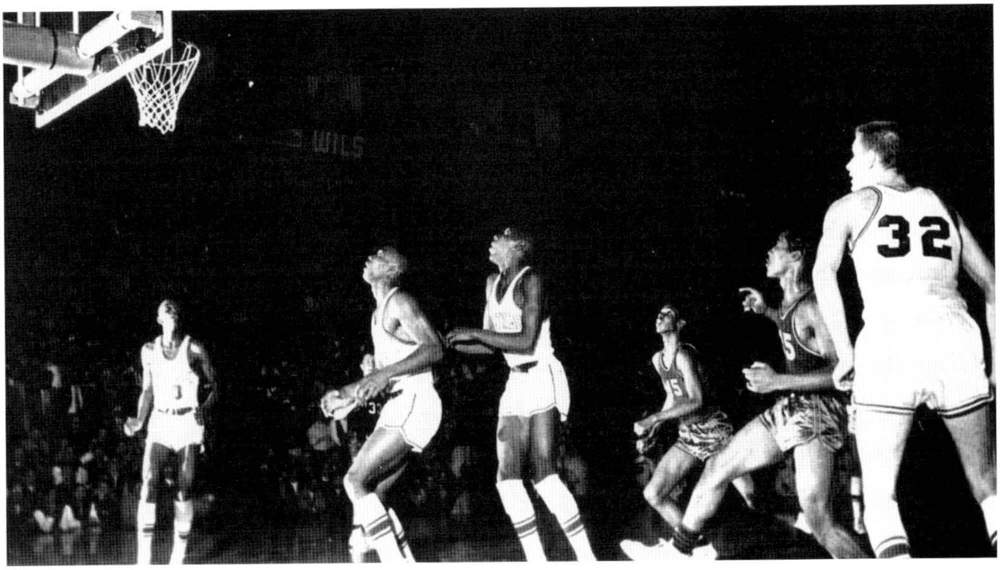

MHSAA historian Dick Kishpaugh called Lansing Sexton's 80-79 overtime win in the 1959 Class A final over Hamtramck's Cosmos the best championship game ever. Hamtramck led 43-26 at half and 60-45 after three quarters. Sexton's Bob Davis hit two free throws to force overtime at 72. Hamtramck's Art Reid hit a free throw to give the Cosmos a 79-78 lead with 17 seconds left, but Davis (35), shown here taking the game-winning try, lifted a shot that eclipsed the game's final gun. Pandemonium enveloped Jenison Field House. (MHSAA archives.)

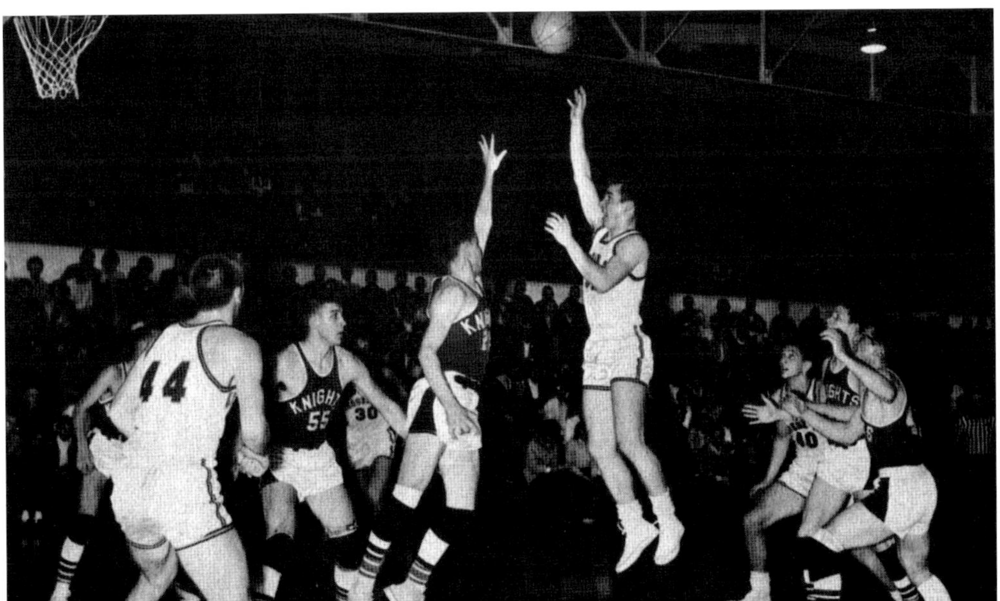

Grosse Pointe High's Rick Bridges shoots for two over a Detroit Osborn defender in the 1962 MHSAA district opener. Grosse Pointe, which borders Detroit and annually battles Detroit's east side public schools, took this game 65-26. (*Grosse Pointer*, 1962.)

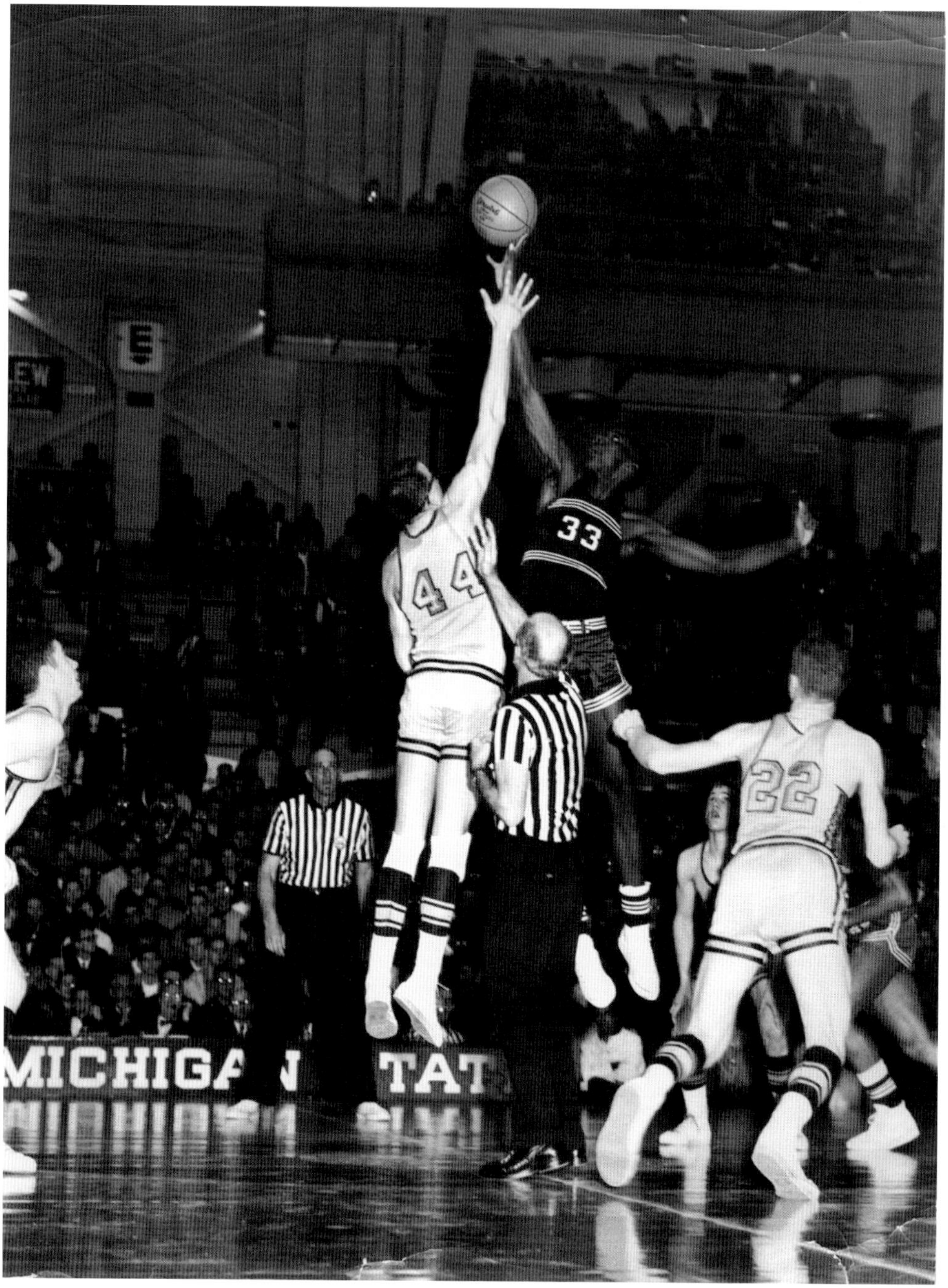

Perhaps fittingly, the only player to start four consecutive MHSAA championship games in any class or division hails from Michigan's incomparable prep dynasty, River Rouge High. Willie Betts was an All-State performer who won all four title games he started. This game, an 86-67 win in the 1964 Class B title tilt versus Lakeview High, was also significant to legendary Rouge coach Lofton Greene—it was the 100th MHSAA tournament win for the "Old Kentuckian." (MHSAA archives.)

James Pitts (25), an All-City, All-PSL, All-West Side selection on the *Detroit News*'s 1964 Metro teams, cheers his Detroit Northwestern teammates in the waning moments of a thrilling victory over Detroit Pershing. The Colts downed Detroit Northern in the PSL 1964 final 61-45, topped Grosse Pointe St. Paul in Operation Friendship 49-42, and advanced to the regional final before bowing to Monroe High. (The Detroit News/James R. Kilpatrick.)

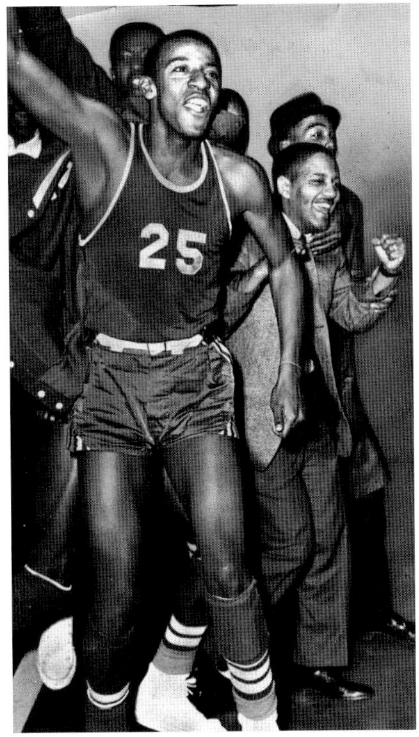

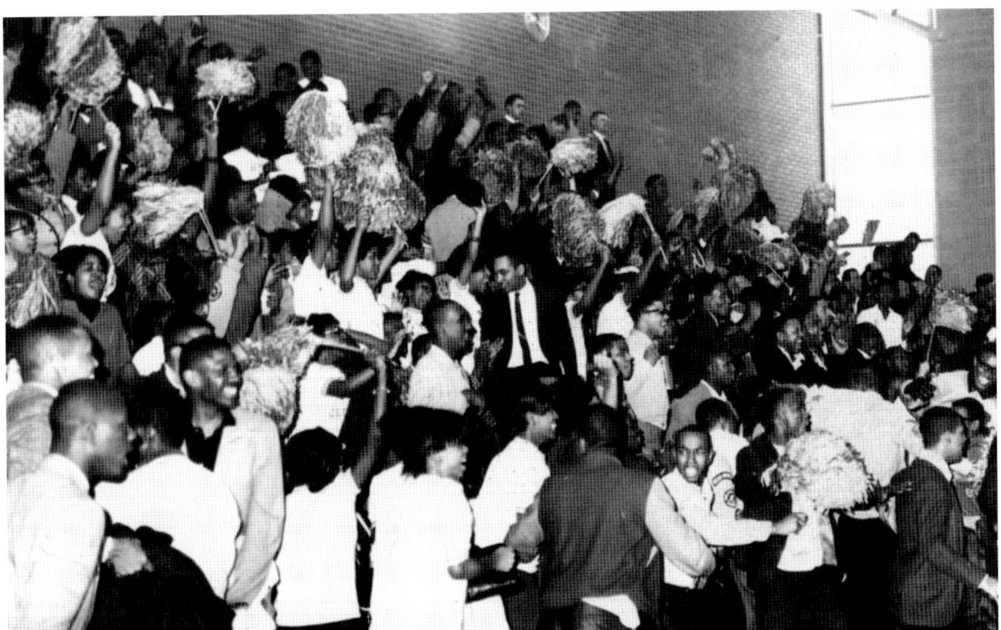

Detroit Northwestern's improbable victory on February 22 in the 1967 PSL playoffs over longtime city rival Detroit Pershing brought Northwestern's cheering masses onto the floor after the Colts' victory. (The Detroit News/Drayton "Doc" Holcomb.)

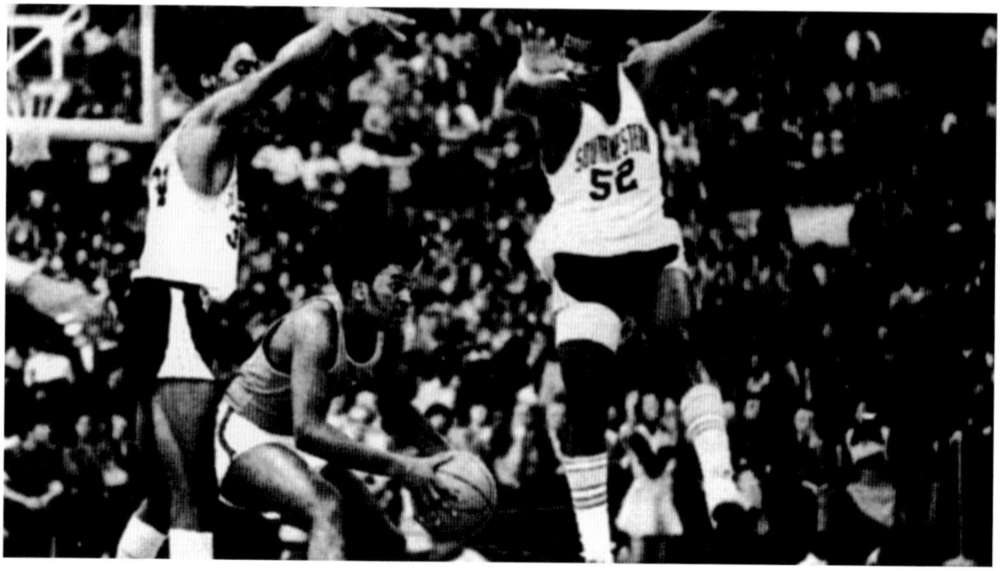

Two schools well versed in the hard hat approach and hard-luck results met in the 1973 Class A semifinals at Michigan State's Jenison Field House. Detroit Southwestern, coached by Bob Whitehouse, would win this game over Pontiac Central's Chiefs 75-68. The next day, Southwestern topped Saginaw 66-60 to earn the school's first Class A title. (MHSAA archives.)

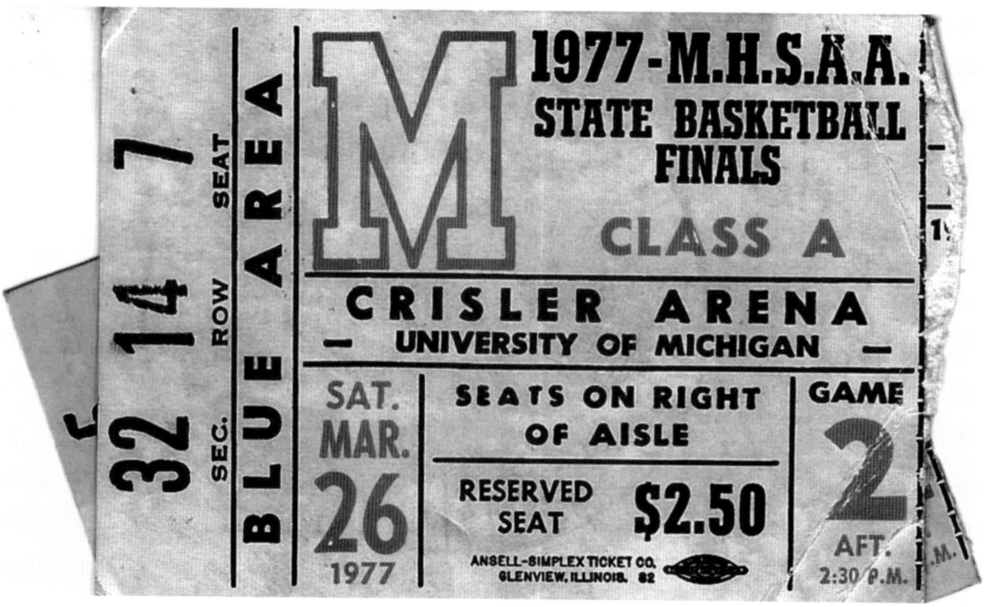

Ticket stubs from the 1977 Class A finals in Birmingham Brother Rice coach Bill Norton's scrapbook evoke memories of one of Michigan's incredible championship games. Rice held a seven-point lead in the fourth but Earvin "Magic" Johnson pulled his Lansing Everett Vikings back into the lead 49-47 with three seconds to play. Rice's Kevin Smith got to half-court and let go with a heave that banked in to tie the game at the buzzer. Everett won in overtime, 62-56. (Bill Norton collection.)

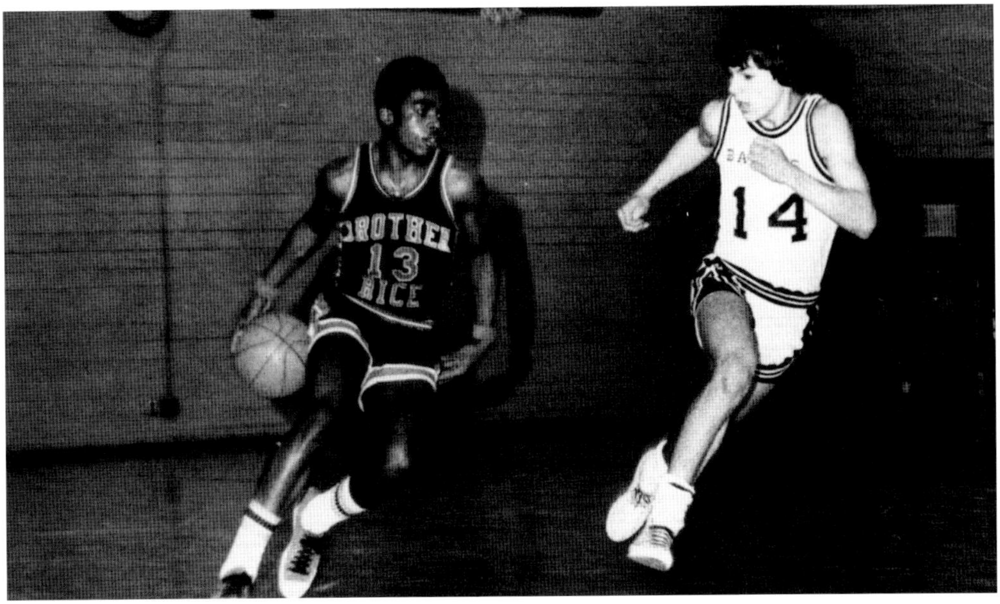

John Maloney was a first-year assistant coach to Bill Norton at Birmingham Brother Rice when the Warriors issued this 72-50 defeat in the 1974 district finals to Bloomfield Hills Andover (above). Four years after being an assistant for Rice's Class A title winners, Maloney was tabbed as the Baron coach, and Maloney's Barons shocked Norton's No. 10 ranked Warriors, 58-53 in the first round of the 1978 state tournament. (Bill Norton collection.)

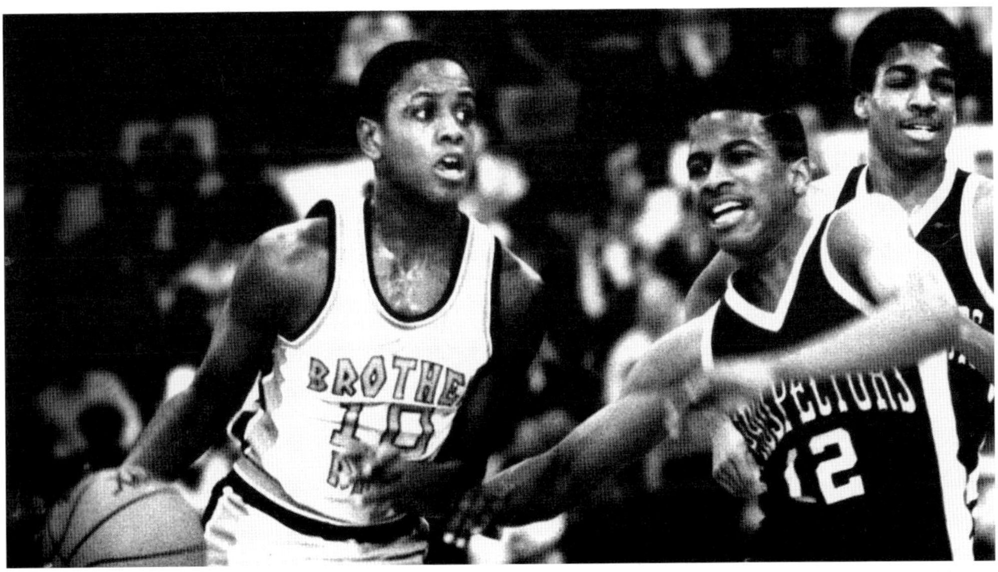

B. J. Armstrong and Birmingham Brother Rice had plenty of drive but the Warriors could not down Perry Watson's Detroit Southwestern Prospectors, 60-57 winners of this Class A semifinal played on March 23, 1984. The Prospectors would drop the Class A final the next day by a 64-43 count to Flint Northwestern. Armstrong attended the University of Iowa before being drafted by the Chicago Bulls. (Oakland Press/Doug Bauman.)

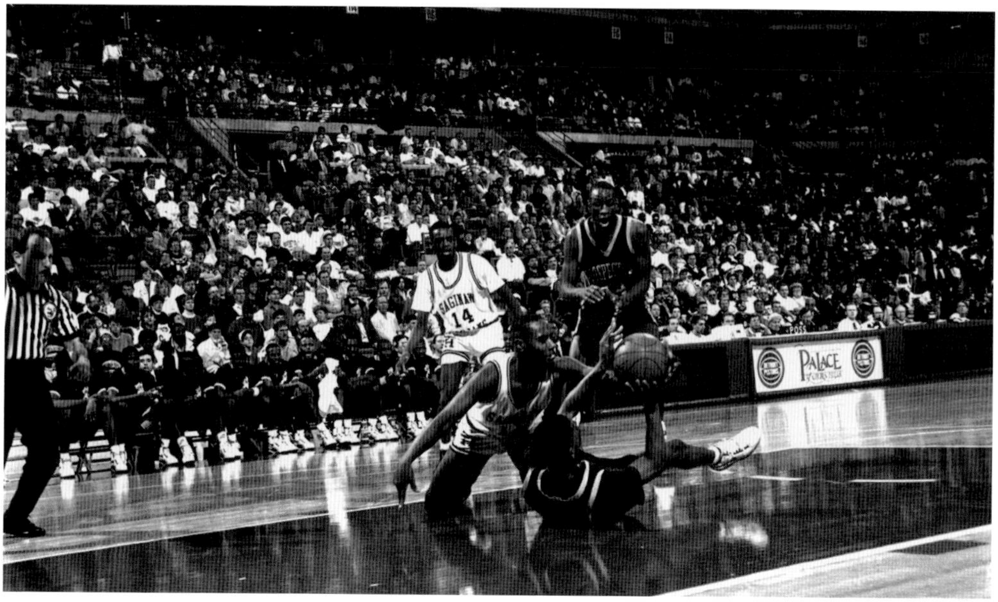

Detroit Southwestern's Howard Eisley (on floor) is called for traveling by referee Don Vogt as Voshon Leonard calls for the pass and Saginaw's Daniel West (10) and Julian Taylor (14) contend. After seven losses in the title game of the previous eight seasons, Eisley, Leonard, and Jalen Rose delivered coach Perry Watson's first championship in a 67-54 victory. (MHSAA archives/Gary Shook.)

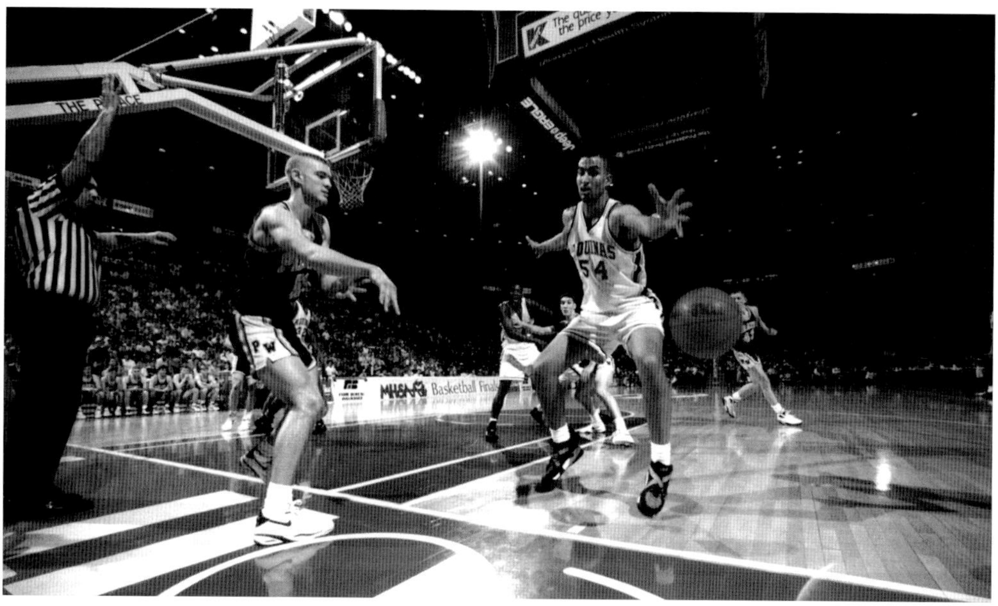

Southgate Aquinas's Jon Garavaglia (54) led his Raiders to the school's first MHSAA title in the 1993 Class C finals at the Palace of Auburn Hills with a 50-44 win over Ryan Wohlfert (51) and Pewamo-Westphalia High. Aquinas won the 1993 Catholic League championship and defeated Detroit Cass Tech in the Operation Friendship Game by a 56-53 count; Garavaglia won the Mr. Basketball award for 1993. (MHSAA archives/Gary Shook.)

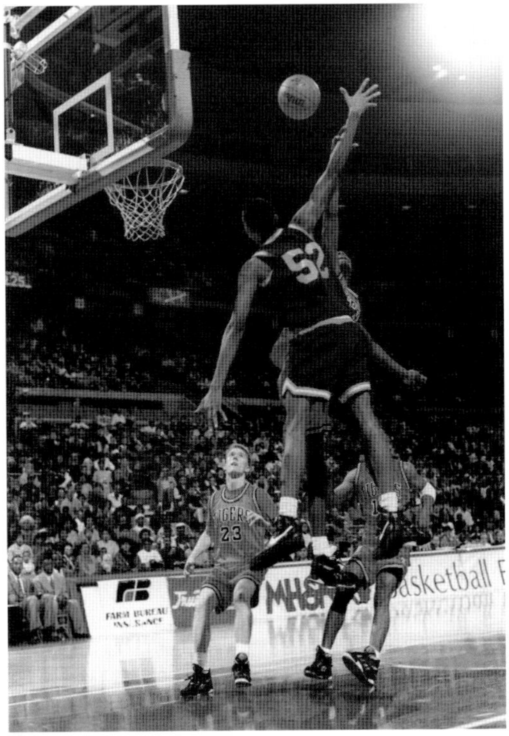

Detroit Pershing's Shawn Hill easily rose above his competition and the same can be said of his Doughboy teammates, who stifled Benton Harbor into a meager 42-point effort in Pershing's runaway 74-42 triumph in the 1992 Class A finals. Only Detroit Southwestern has made more consecutive trips as a PSL representative in the post–World War II era. (MHSAA archives/Gary Shook.)

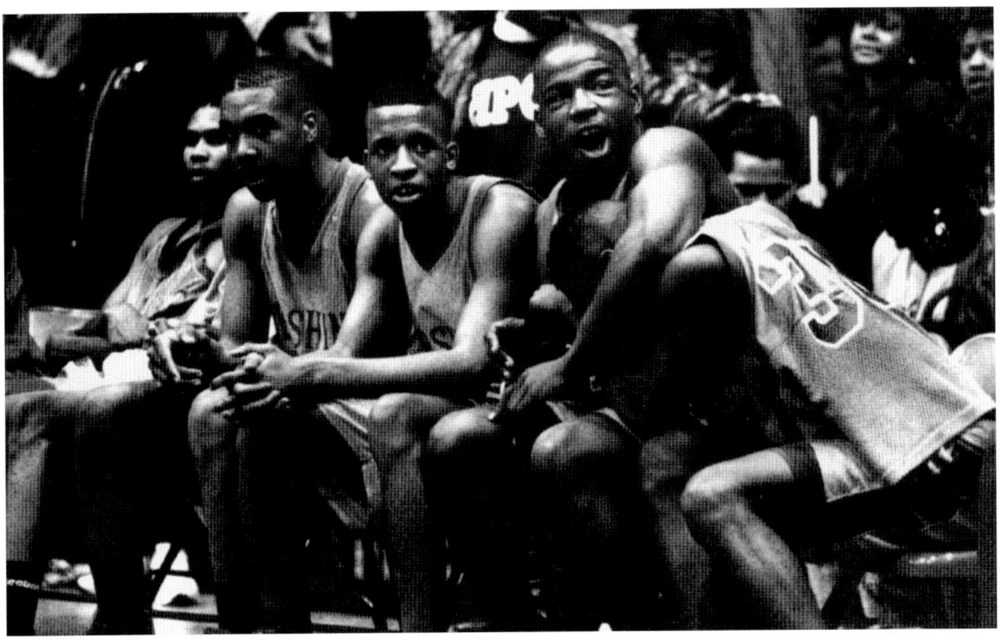

The Pershing Doughboys of 1992–1995 went to four consecutive Class A state finals, winning the first two over a Michigan basketball powerhouse bordering Lake Michigan, Benton Harbor. Pershing dropped the 1995 final to Flint Northern but returned to the title game in 2000, 2008, and 2009, winning the 2009 class crown over Kalamazoo Central High. (The Detroit News archives.)

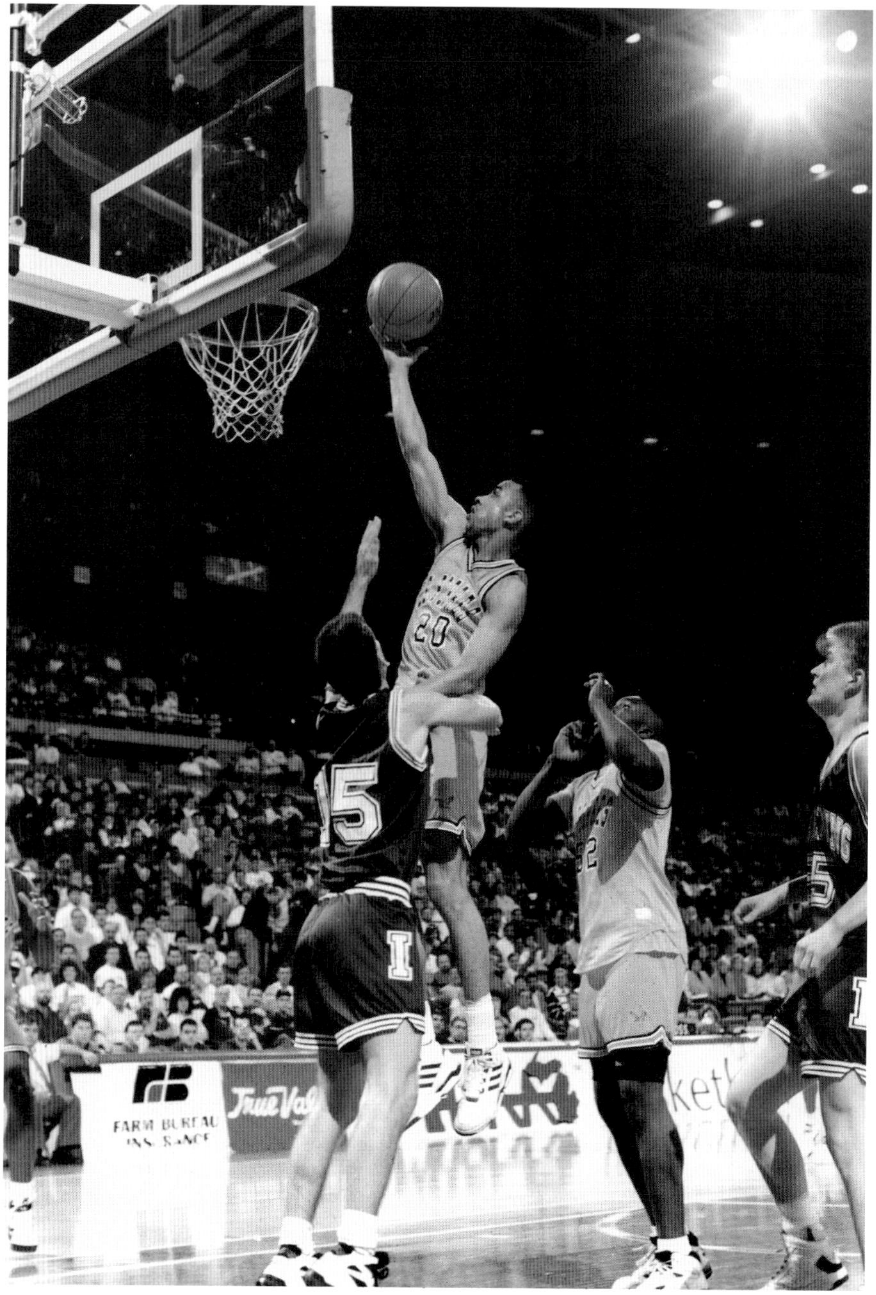

Detroit St. Martin DePorres' Brian Tolbert soars for two in the 1992 Class C championship. The Eagles earned 145 MHSAA tournament wins in 175 tries, winning 26 districts, 15 regionals, and 8 state titles. DePorres closed in 2005 with longtime rival Detroit Benedictine. DePorres played 12 CHSL title games, winning 7. Benedictine played in seven CHSL title games, winning six. Tolbert attended Eastern Michigan University, leading the 1996 Eagles to the first victory by any school over Duke in the first round of the NCAA tournament in 55 seasons. (MHSAA archives/ Gary Shook.)

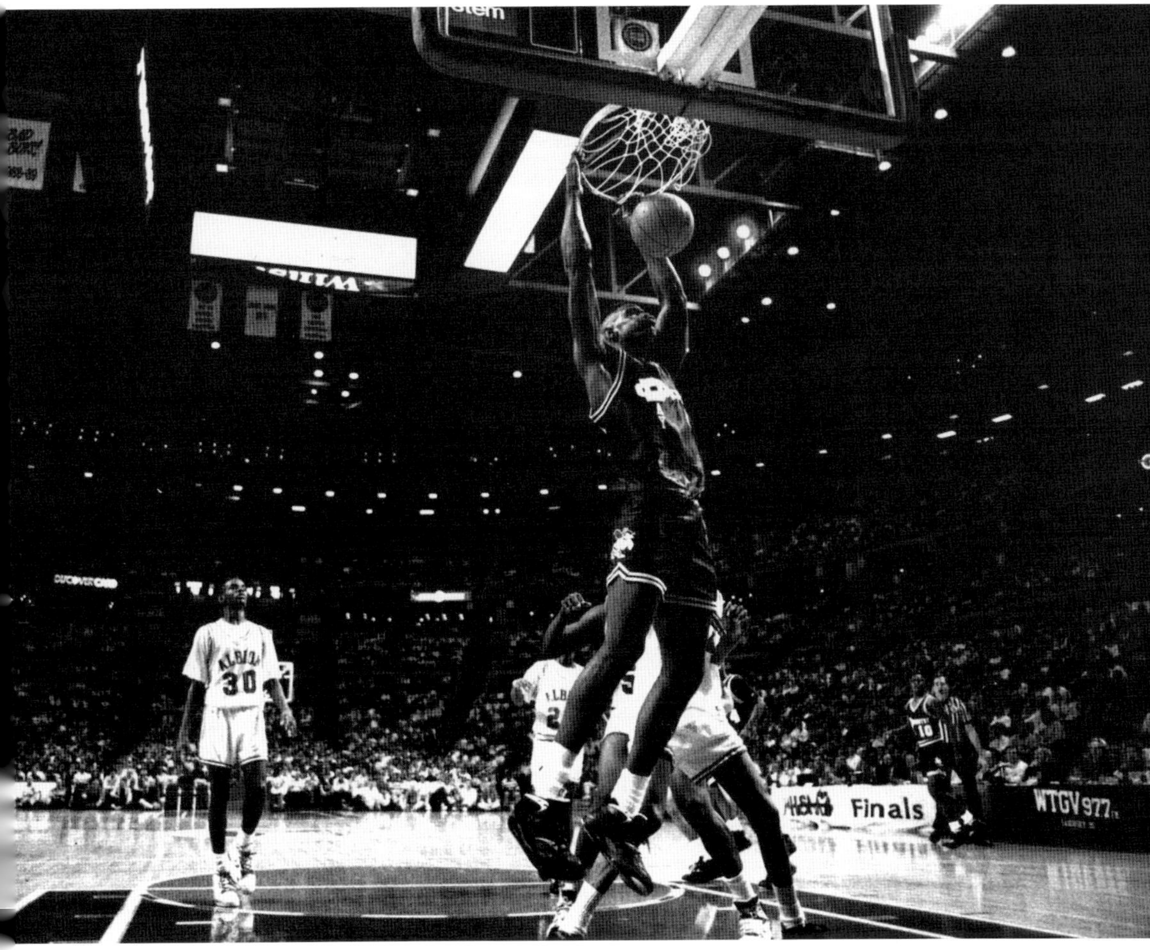

Chris Webber's talent was a sight to behold but more than a few Detroit prep basketball fans wonder aloud still today what Detroit Southwestern's 1990 and 1991 teams with Voshon Leonard, Howard Eisley, and Jalen Rose, among others, would have looked like with Webber, shown here dunking on Albion High in the 1991 Class B finals, a 68-57 Detroit Country Day win. When Webber's mother, Delores, enrolled him at Country Day, all talk of what might have been began in earnest. Webber led Detroit Country Day to three consecutive titles from 1989 to 1991, the 1989 title coming in the Class C title game and the 1990 and 1991 titles in Class B after Detroit Country Day moved up in classification. (Detroit Country Day.)

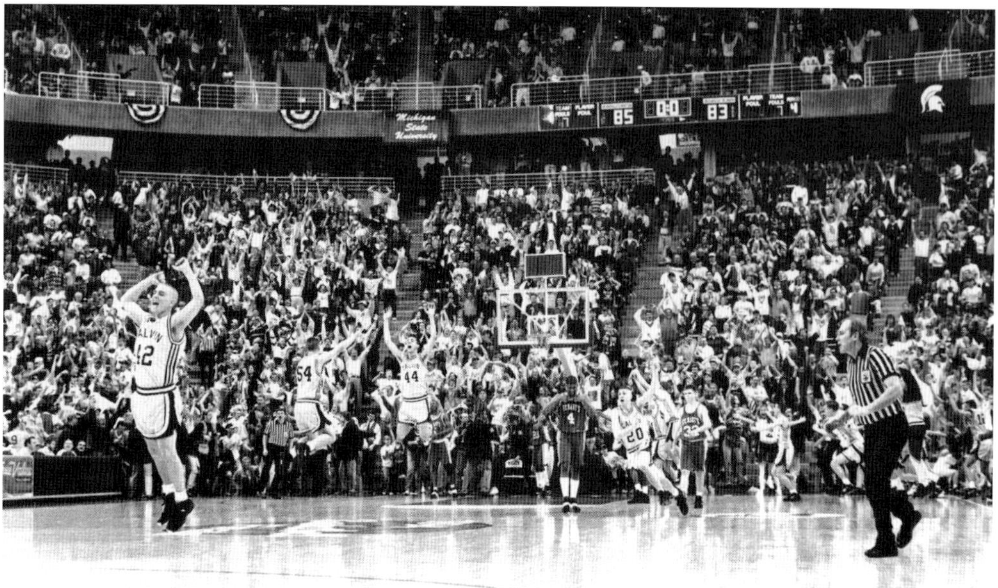

Calvin High executed a perfect end-to-end scoring play that culminated in a game-winning layin to defeat Catholic League power Orchard Lake St. Mary's and this picture-perfect moment on the floor of the Breslin Center. The Quakers 85-83 victory over George Porritt's Eaglets in the 1994 Class C finals was a great MHSAA moment. (MHSAA archives/Gary Shook.)

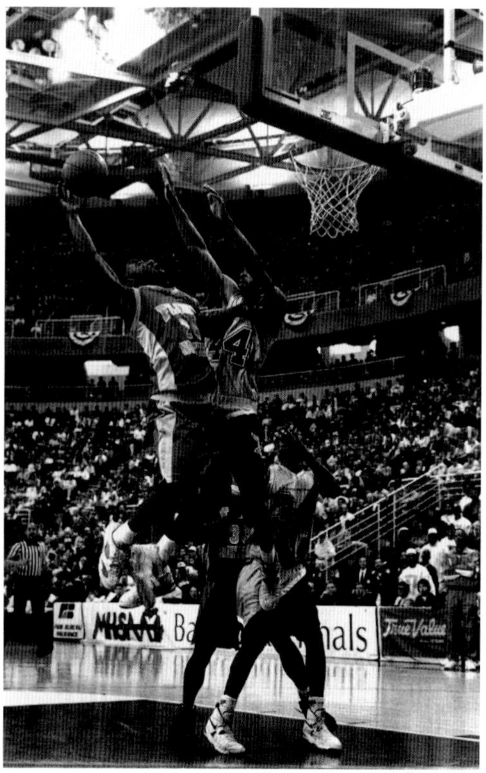

Flint Northern's 86-64 win over Detroit Pershing in the 1995 Class A finals at the Breslin Center was a precursor to Michigan State University's "Flintstones." Several Spartans from the 1998–2000 Michigan State University team hailed from Flint, including Northern guard Mateen Cleaves, who soars and scores versus Pershing. (MHSAA archives/Gary Shook.)

Detroit's East Catholic enjoyed a few final moments in the sun before it shuttered in 2004, but nothing brightened the Shamrocks more than Andrew Mitchell's buzzer-beating three-pointer to defeat Wyoming Tri-Unity in the 1997 Class D finals at Michigan State University. (MHSAA archives/Gary Shook.)

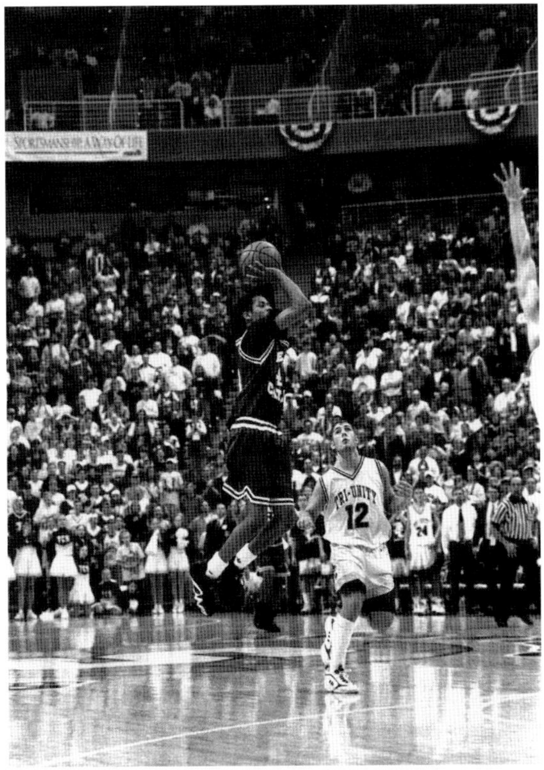

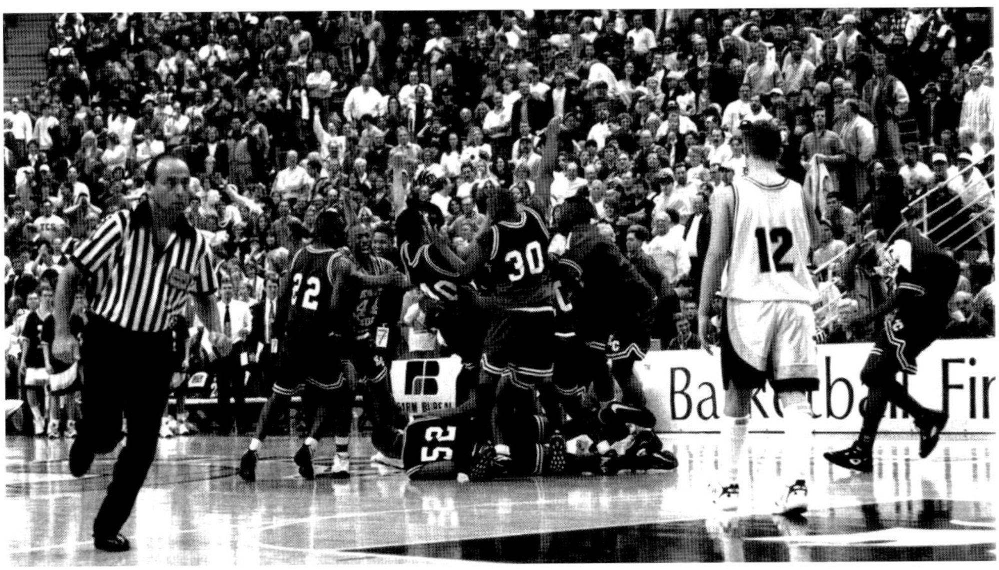

Bedlam and unbridled joy befit East Catholic High on the floor of Michigan State University's Jack Breslin center. This is the championship celebration after the referee counted Andrew Mitchell's three-point field goal to lift the Shamrocks to a 63-60 win in the 1997 Class C title tilt. The Shamrocks earned a Class C state title in 1973 and Class D titles in 1990, 1986, 1983, and three consecutive titles from 1979 to 1981. (MHSAA archives/Gary Shook.)

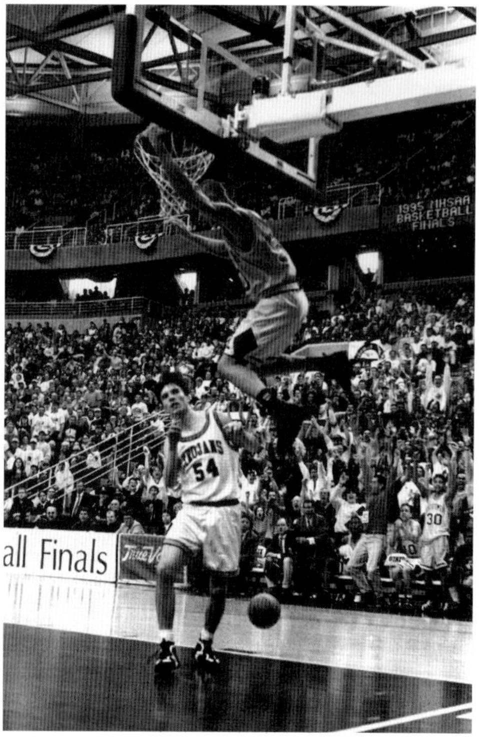

The Lions played outside its famous Holy Redeemer High gymnasium for the 1995 Class D finals but one could not take the energy and enthusiasm out of the Redeemer's Lions, shown here in the emphatic, final moments of their 55-46 win over Crystal Falls Forest Park. Located beneath the shadow of the abandoned Michigan Central Depot in southwest Detroit, Redeemer's 2005 closing signaled the end of an era for Catholic League schools in Detroit. (MHSAA archives/Gary Shook.)

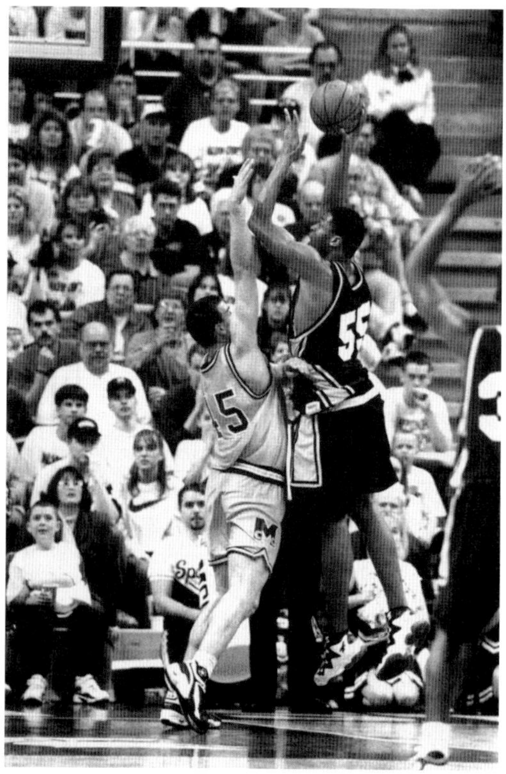

Aloysius Anagonye and the Detroit's St. Martin DePorres Eagles had their way with Mason County Central High in the 1998 Class C title game. DePorres opened in 1968, closed in 2005, and won 145 MHSAA tournament games in 175 starts. The Eagle boys won eight state titles with three coaches, Durand Shepherd (2003), Derrick Owens (1998, 1999, and 1986) and Ed Rachel (1985, 1986, and 1992). (MHSAA archives/Gary Shook.)

Detroit Country Day's Shane Battier rises to meet Kris Vydareny's shot with rim-high defiance in the 1995 Class B final at Michigan State University's Breslin Center. Country Day earned its fourth state title by defeating East Grand Rapids 53-43. Battier, who went on to play at Duke and has remained an NBA staple since, had his No. 55 retired by the Beverly Hills school. (MHSAA archives/Gary Shook.)

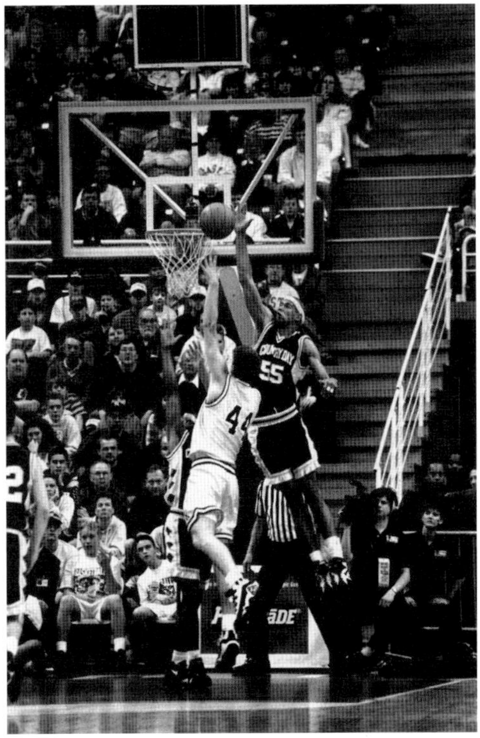

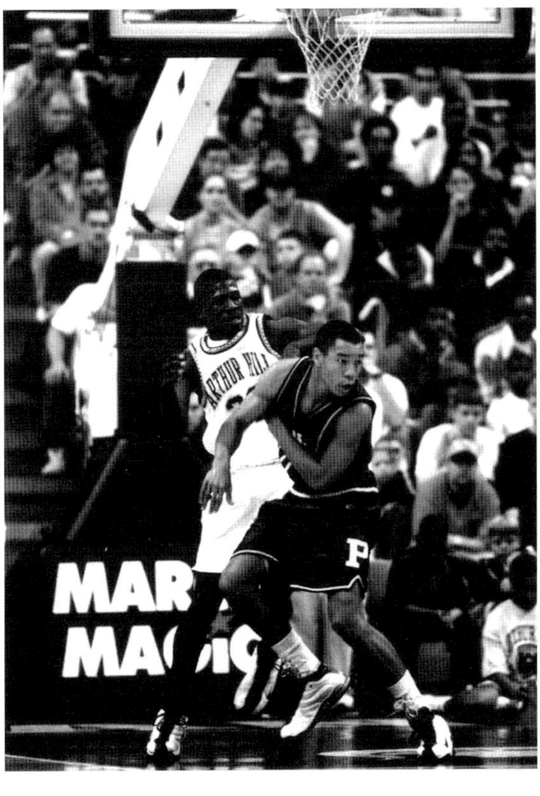

Two future Big Ten rivals met in the 1999 MHSAA Class A finals as LaVell Blanchard of Ann Arbor Pioneer and Jason Richardson from Saginaw's Arthur Hill put each to the test at Michigan State University's Breslin Center. Ann Arbor Pioneer triumphed over Arthur Hill 54-47 and Blanchard traded the purple and white for Michigan's maize and blue. Richardson called Breslin home as a Michigan State University Spartans and won the 2000 NCAA title with Michigan State University. Richardson plays for the NBA's Phoenix Suns. (MHSAA archives/Gary Shook.)

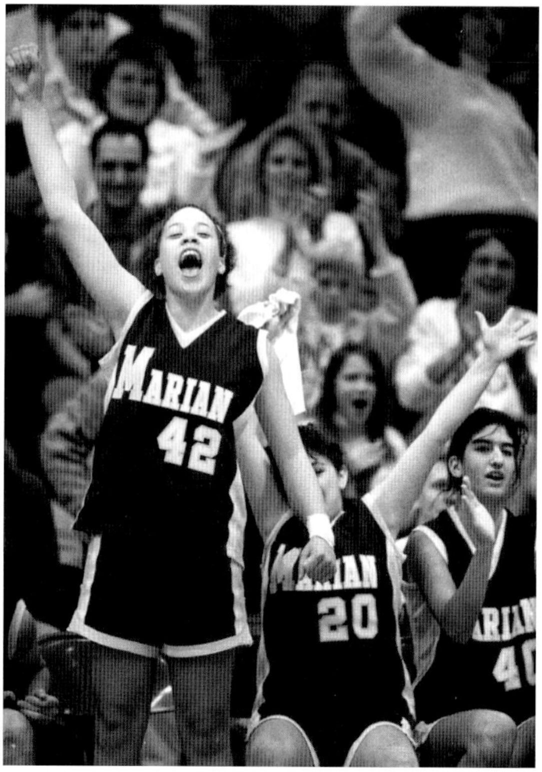

Birmingham Marian's passion and enthusiasm cannot be corralled any longer in the waning moments of the Mustangs' 1988 Class A title game victory over Flint Powers and their legendary coach Kathy McGee. Mustangs Trina Govan (42), Jamie Racine (20), and Carmela Garofalo (40) and the throng of Marian fans behind them celebrate the first of four Class A championships. The 71-49 win was the commencement of five title game appearances in 11 seasons from 1988 to 1998 for Marian and coach Mary Lillie-Cicerone. (MHSAA archive/ Gary Shook.)

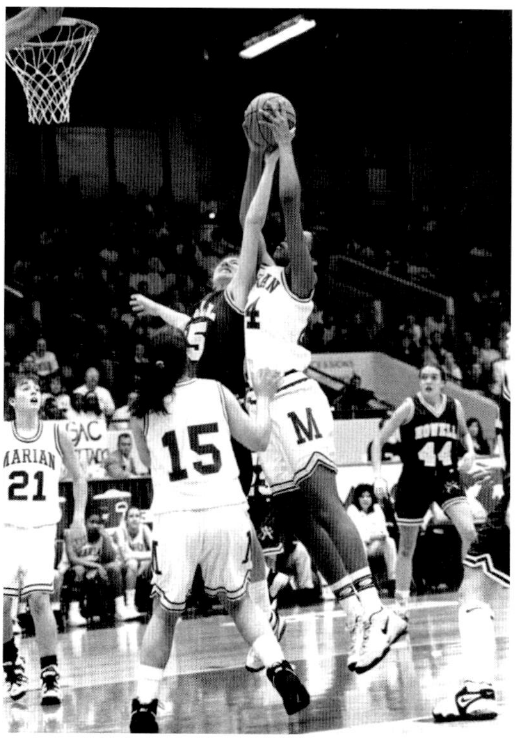

Howell's Highlanders faced Birmingham Marian in the 1996 Class A championship. Although Marian's Nicole Anaejionu's 12 points and 15 caroms halted the Highlanders and Cary Musko by a 54-40 score, Howell's girls' basketball program was one of the better programs in metro Detroit circles for most of the 1980s and 1990s. (MHSAA archive/Gary Shook.)

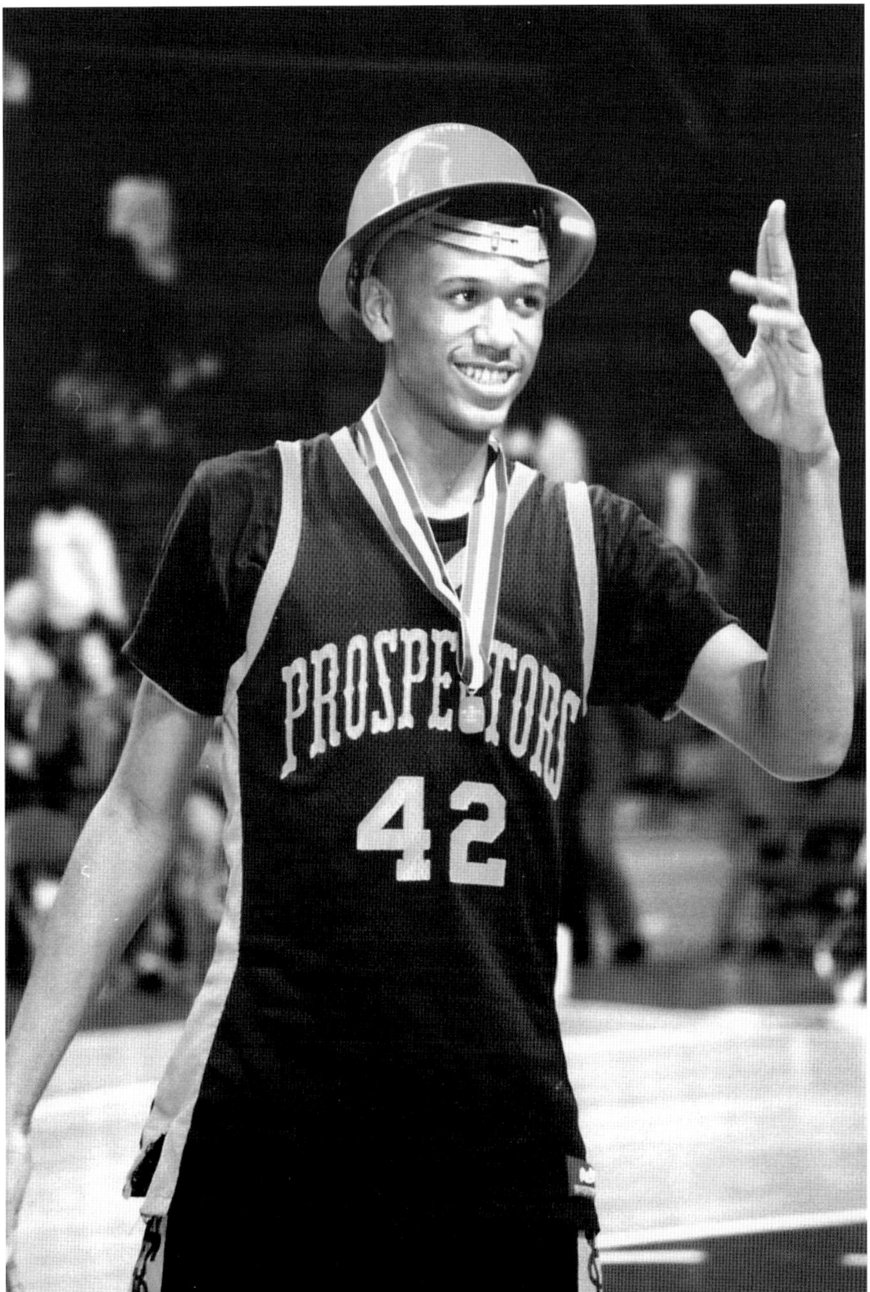

Detroit Southwestern Prospector Jalen Rose celebrates the 1990 Class A championship. Rose, named to the McDonald's and Dapper Dan All-America teams in 1991, led Southwestern to three PSL titles, two state titles, attended the University of Michigan as part of the "Fab Five" and earned All-Big Ten and All-America honors in two of three seasons at the University of Michigan before 13 NBA seasons. Rose's maize and blue No. 5 was retired by the University of Michigan in the winter of 2006. (Gary Shook/MHSAA archive.)

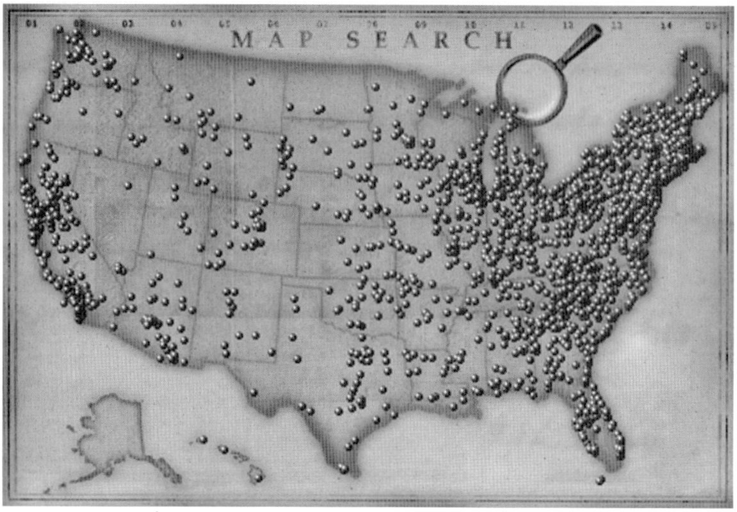
MAP SEARCH